Another Stage

Another Stage

Kanze Nobumitsu and the Late Muromachi Noh Theater

LIM BENG CHOO

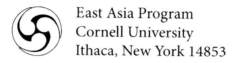

East Asia Program
Cornell University
Ithaca, New York 14853

The Cornell East Asia Series is published by the Cornell University East Asia Program (distinct from Cornell University Press). We publish books on a variety of scholarly topics relating to East Asia as a service to the academic community and the general public. Address submission inquiries to CEAS Editorial Board, East Asia Program, Cornell University, 140 Uris Hall, Ithaca, New York 14853-7601.

Cover Image: One of the main halls of Shōkokuji, the temple believed to be Nobumitsu's final resting place. Photograph courtesy Lim Beng Choo, September 2010.

Illustrations on pages xxx, 52, and 156:
Details of the opening, middle, and final sections of the Nobumitsu Portrait Inscription post-scripted by Hayashi Dōshun, Kan'ei 18th. Used with permission from the Nogami Memorial Noh Theatre Research Institute of Hosei University.

Number 163 in the Cornell East Asia Series
Copyright ©2012 Lim Beng Choo. All rights reserved.
ISSN: 1050-2955
ISBN: 978-1-933947-83-9 hardcover
ISBN: 978-1-933947-63-1 paperback
Library of Congress Control Number: 2012949522
Printed in the United States of America

∞ The paper in this book meets the requirements for permanence of ISO 9706:1994.

This volume is dedicated to Karen Brazell
(1938–2012)
sensei and friend
you are forever missed

CONTENTS

Acknowledgments ix
Introduction xi

ACKNOWLEDGMENTS

In the long process of working on this book, I have received much valuable advice, assistance and support from many people.

To start with, I want to say a big thank you to the first people who read the initial version of the book, my thesis committee at Cornell University. Professors Karen Brazell, Bret de Bary, and Tsu-lin Mei asked questions and gave suggestions that strengthened the book and helped shape its direction. Michael Bourdaghs and Lingzhen Wang critiqued the chapters and were the best possible dissertation-writing comrades. Special thanks also go to Ayako Kano, Susan Klein, Paula Long, Kyoko Selden, Susan Specter, Huazhi Wang, Tomoko Yoshida, Joshua Young.

Professor Monica Bethe commented on the first draft of the thesis. Professors Omote Akira, Richard Emmert, Nishino Hauro, Oda Sachiko, Yamanaka Reiko and Kurushima Noriko provided generous assistance with advice on sources and ideas, together with warm friendship. I appreciate greatly the kindness and encouragement these professors showed to a young scholar.

During my short stint at University of California, Berkeley, I have learned greatly from Professors Susan Matisoff, Marc Holton, and John Wallace. Thanks also to colleagues, friends, and students at the Department of Japanese Studies and the Faculty of Arts and Social Sciences, National University of Singapore, who listened to my presentations and offered valuable feedback.

Funding from the Hitachi Foundation, the Sumitomo Foundation, the Freeman Foundation, and the National University of Singapore allowed me to make trips to Japan and the United States for research and time to write. I am very grateful for all their support.

This book has benefited greatly from the anonymous readers and my editors. I would like to thank all three of the readers for their insightful comments and valuable suggestions. Thanks also to Mai Shaikhanuar-Cota for her technical expertise and patience.

Last but not least, I want to thank my close friends Okada Keisuke and Okada Hina, my family Tan Hak Yee, Madge Hislop, Alison Hislop and Scot Hislop, for the many inspiring exchanges, unwavering support and encouragement throughout this long journey. Thank you for being there for me.

This book is dedicated to Karen Brazell, my sensei, for everything she has taught me.

INTRODUCTION

Kanze Kojirō Nobumitsu 観世小次郎信光 (1435–1516), the late Muromachi noh practitioner, has left behind many noh plays that remain popular in the contemporary noh repertoire. Some examples include *Funabenkei*, which presents first a romantic tale and then a ferocious battle; *Chōryō*, which is based on the story of a famous Chinese warrior; and *Yugyō Yanagi*, whose protagonist, the aged willow tree spirit, is identified as one of Nobumitsu's most successful creations.

Present-day Japanese scholars identify Nobumitsu's noh plays as demonstrating the *furyū* style, which is also often associated with the general aesthetic features in plays composed by Nobumitsu's peers. There are some Japanese scholarly works that attempt to explain this feature, although nothing to date has been done in English. A review of existing Japanese material on either furyū, Nobumitsu, or the late Muromachi period only brings up more questions: who is Nobumitsu and what else has he written? What is a furyū play? Why are the late Muromachi noh plays associated with the furyū style? How do these plays relate to the historical and cultural specificities of the time? Do we see this kind of style in other time periods? And, perhaps most important, what significance does late Muromachi noh (including both the practitioners and their works) have in contemporary noh discourse?

One of the best ways to answer these questions is through a detailed examination of the representative noh practitioner of the time—Kanze Kojirō Nobumitsu. Nobumitsu's life and long career as a prominent troupe leader, prolific noh composer and expert performer is an integral part of the noh scene of his time, while the specific political, cultural and social elements interacted and engaged with the development of the genre and its practitioners. In other words, Nobumitsu is not only an important individual practitioner who created important plays that left a strong legacy on the noh theater, his life and work also inform the discursive construct of noh during the late Muromachi period. Learning about Nobumitsu will provide the modern audience and readers with more knowledge of the late Muromachi noh theater and the modern noh discourse.

Historical Development of Noh

At the outset, it will be useful to review the general history of noh before setting out on a discussion of the late Muromachi period. This review will not only provide the broad historical background of noh in general but also fill in the gaps that exist in historical accounts of noh.

Noh scholars Omote Akira and Amano Fumio, in *Nōgaku no Rekishi* (能楽の歴史 History of the Noh theater), consolidated earlier works with their own research and formulated eight historical periods of noh development from the Heian period to the present.[1]

The first half of this historical trajectory comprises the periods of formation (形成期 *keiseiki*), accomplishment (大成期 *taiseiki*), and development (展開期 *tenkaiki*), and ends at the

---

1. See Omote and Amino (*I*) 1987, 6–191. This book is not the only scholarly work that situates noh in its historical framework, although many other historical accounts tend to include discussions of other genres, e.g., Suwa and Sugai, 1998. Ortolani 1990, chronologically introduces the major genre of each period, although not in as much depth as Omote and Amino's study.

beginning of the Tokugawa period, which historians call the transition (転換期 *tenkanki*) period. This first half is followed by two major periods, each divided into two parts: the first and second parts of the "official ritual of state" period (式楽前期 *shikigaku zenki*, 式楽後期 *shikigaku kōki*),[2] and the two parts of "Noh Studies" (能学前期 *Nōgakuzenki*, 能学後期 *Nōgakukōki*).

The formative period is identified as the time from the Heian through the Kamakura periods, when noh was still known as *sarugaku*, and when elements of comical entertainment were very common.[3] Then Kan'ami Kiyotsugu (観阿弥清次 1333–1384) and his son Zeami Motokiyo (世阿弥元清 1363?–1443?) came on the scene in the Muromachi period, which officially began when the Ashikaga warrior General Ashikaga Takauji (1305–1358) established his military headquarters in the Muromachi area of Kyoto in 1336.[4] The following two centuries saw the development of what later generations termed the *Kitayama* (北山 Northern Mountain) and *Higashiyama* (東山 Eastern Mountain) cultures, warrior cultures that manifested the personal ambitions and characters of their advocates, Ashikaga Yoshimitsu (1358–1408) and Ashikaga Yoshimasa (1435–1490), respectively. Throughout this period an incessant, and at times irrational, power struggle raged between factions of the court and various powerful military families. In 1467, the decade-long Ōnin War (1467–1477) broke out, plunging the country into a century of civil warfare. The Muromachi period officially ended in 1573, when the fifteenth

2. Looser 2008, translated *shikigaku* (式楽) as "official ritual of state." I have decided to use his translation, as his rendering best conveys the meaning of *shikigaku*.

3. The Heian period lasted for about four hundred years, from around the late eighth century to the early 1180s, followed by the Kamakura period, which ended in 1333 when the Kamakura Bakufu was demolished. Yokomichi et al. (*I*) 1992, 8–29.

4. Like all historical periodization, there is more than one definition of these early Japanese historical divisions. According to Asao et al. 1996, the Heian period is commonly identified as starting in 794 (Enreki 13) and ending in 1192 (Kenkyū 3). See Appendix 7 for a list of successive Ashikaga shogunates.

Ashikaga shogun Yoshiaki was ousted from his military head-quarters by Oda Nobunaga (1534–1582).[5]

The next thirty years or so is often referred to as the Azuchi-Momoyama period by Japanese historians. In 1603, after victory in the Sekigahara War in 1600, Tokugawa Ieyasu was conferred with the title of shogun, thus starting the Edo Bakufu. The Tokugawa period, also known as the Edo period, lasted until 1867. In this book, I define the late Muromachi period as lasting from the onset of the Ōnin War until 1573.

In Omote and Amano's schema, the most critical stage to the development of noh is the Muromachi period. The second stage, the period of accomplishment, refers to the time when Kan'ami and Zeami defined and constructed noh discourse through the former's superb performance skills and the latter's prolific writings. The third stage, the development period, begins with Zeami's immediate successors Konparu Zenchiku (1405–1470?) and On'ami Motoshige (1398–1467). It ends in the mid-sixteenth century, before Oda Nobunaga and Toyotomi Hide-yoshi (1537–1598) came to power. According to Omote and Amano, this period saw the active participation of pseudo-amateur groups in performance, while the major Yamato troupes, the Konparu and Kanze, were facing a crisis of waning support.

The last stage—the "transitional" period—started when noh theater was rejuvenated by the renewed ardent support of the powerful military generals Oda Nobunaga and later Toyotomi Hideyoshi. Oda commissioned a noh performance as a celebration for the Ashikaga general Yoshiaki (1537–1597) in 1568 (Eiroku 11), and was a devoted patron of the four major noh troupes, just as his predecessors, the Muromachi shoguns, had been.[6] The four major noh troupes continued to receive positive

---

5. See Berry 1994 for a critical analysis of the civil warfare in Kyoto during this period. Also see Keene 2003 on Yoshimasa and Imatani and Yamamura 1992, 45–78, on Yoshimitsu. For a comprehensive description of the various aspects of Muromachi society, see Hall and Toyoda 1977.

6. Omoto and Amino (*I*) 1987, 80–81.

attention from the military leaders, which reached a peak in 1597. In that year Hideyoshi began offering stable stipends to the four major noh troupes, marking a new historical stage in noh history. With the enthusiastic patronage of the military generals, the reward system and performance format stabilized, resulting in a very different noh theater in the Edo period and subsequently, the present day.

In the first half of the Muromachi period—when Kan'ami and his peers were performing—the noh theater began its gradual evolution from a semireligious ritual performance on temple and shrine grounds to a highly aesthetized theater employing poetry, music, song, and dance, albeit often still imbued with religious significance. The precise origin of *sarugaku* noh cannot be identified, and therefore it is very difficult to determine the exact point in time when noh theater started to evolve from a plebian semireligious performance into a more refined theater. According to Zeami, his father Kan'ami and Kan'ami's contemporaries, such as Itchū and Inuō, were great performers who had inspired him in his own artistic endeavor. Kan'ami had also established new singing and dancing techniques, which became the structural foundation of noh plays as we know them today. Some of Kan'ami's plays, such as *Matsukaze*, were edited by Zeami and have become representative examples of noh.

Today's students of noh by and large are familiar with what happened during the time of Zeami and his immediate successors, thanks to the voluminous work done by researchers both in and outside of Japan. Studies have also been done on the noh theater of the Edo period, especially on the military institution's roles and on the *Iemoto* system.[7] Nevertheless, what happened during the second half of the "development" stage (the late-Muromachi period) has not attracted much attention. It was a time when the four major noh troupes engaged in fierce competitions of all kinds: performing and composing new plays, securing top

---

7. Also see Looser 2008 and Rath 2004, Yokota-Murakami 1997, Fumio 1997, and Nishino and Hata 1999 for discussions of various aspects of Tokugawa period noh theater.

or sole performance priority with religious institutions, fighting for patronage from the powerful military generals, etc. At the same time, we see the appearance of different kinds of "amateur" participants. There were the *"shirōto,"* performers who were paid but did not belong to any major troupes; and there were also enthusiastic fans who learned to chant and compose.[8] During this period, the noh theater engaged with the late Muromachi period in ways unique to its time—these ways will be examined by a close reading of Nobumitsu's plays in this book.

To summarize, I believe that it is during Zeami's time that sarugaku noh started to develop toward the status of an officially "sanctioned" art form with Zeami's assiduous writing of treatises and composition of plays. And two generations later, during Nobumitsu's time, noh finally achieved the position of a form of cultural capital. The Edo period saw the last major development of the noh theater, and plays edited and refined during this period have the closest affinity with what we see today.

Three Generations of Noh Practitioners

One important feature of the noh landscape is the relationship among the various noh troupes and practitioners within each troupe—be it genealogical or artistic. It is, however, complex and not as well documented as present-day readers would like. What people of the present know of the performance repertoire of that time relies mainly on performance records, scattered mention in journals and other historical documents, as well as Zeami's treatises. The impression that present-day popular plays were equally important during the late Muromachi period is probably

---

8. Shirōto (素人) is a term used to describe people who practiced noh but did not belong to any troupes. Nishino and Hata 1999, 266, classifies this group of performers under "tesarugaku" (手猿楽). Noh performers who do not belong to the major noh troupes have always existed, and they include a wide group of people ranging from court elites to females. See Rath 2004 for a discussion of the female group. For general discussion see Nose, 1972, chapter 8; Yokomichi et al. (III) 1987, 289–295.

a result of the inaccessibility of information. The emergence of new historical documents therefore brings surprising information about the noh scene. The discovery of the earliest performance record in 1999 by Yashima Sachiko illustrates this point clearly.[9] Yashima's discovery is the record of a performance at Kōfukuji (Kōfuku Temple) in 1427 (Ōei 34). The program and the list of performers involved indicate a more amicable relationship among the branches of the Kanze family, as well as a repertoire that challenges contemporary perceptions of noh repertoire of that time. Quinn most succinctly summarizes the implication of this discovery:

> [S]ome of the titles mentioned are quite surprising because they seem to correspond to extant plays whose primary attractions are spectacular staging or technical virtuosity rather than poetic lyricism such as Zeami advocated. Until the discovery of this program, many scholars had assumed that plays that draw heavily on spectacle were more characteristic of late Muromachi styles that postdated Zeami.[10]

It is clear, from this earliest program, that the style of noh plays was not as clearly defined as thought; nor was the relationship among the different Kanze family branches as alienated as believed. The artistic influences and social affiliations among the practitioners were intricate, implying that any attempt to discuss late Muromachi noh practitioners will need to be prefaced with an introduction to the other noh practitioners for a more informed background. In this section, I will divide the noh practitioners into three generations and elaborate on the characteristics of the third generation, to which Nobumitsu and his peers belong.[11]

---

9. Yashima 2000, 50–56. Also see Omote 2000, 27–32, and Mikio 2003, 123–127, for comments on the implications of this earliest performance record.

10. Quinn 2005, 32.

11. Another way of dividing noh practitioners into historical periods can be

The first generation includes Kan'ami and Inuō, together with a few others—all of whom we have limited knowledge.[12] This first generation of practitioners is known more for their performance skill than their compositions, with the exception of Kan'ami. Not only did Kan'ami devise new musical rhythm and dance styles, he also composed several noh plays such as *Jinen Koji* (Priest Koji), *Matsukaze* (Matsukaze) and *Eguchi* (Eguchi)—many of which his son Zeami later revised.[13] There are also noh plays from this period that are not attributed to any specific composer; they are given the general name "*kosakunō*" (古作能 early noh).

Zeami, On'ami, Motomasa (?–1432) and Konparu Zenchiku are the major members in the second-generation. Zeami was On'ami's uncle, although the two practitioners ended up treading very different paths in their performance careers. Zeami left behind a large number of treatises and noh plays, while On'ami left only the reputation of a great actor. Motomasa, Zeami's son, and Zenchiku, Zeami's son-in-law, both composed noh plays that reflected Zeami's influence. Motomasa was the Kanze troupe leader for about ten years, succeeding his father Zeami. He died in his thirties, and only a handful of plays, such as *Morihisa* (Morihisa) and *Sumidagawa* (Sumida River) are attributed to him.[14] Zenchiku was popular as a performer, and together with On'ami he enjoyed great fame as one of the two best performers of his time. He was also a prolific writer whose religious and poetic knowledge can be seen in both his treatises, such as *Rokurin Ichirō*, and noh plays, such as *Bashō*. [15]

---

found in Yokomichi et al. (III), 1987, 121–136. This book divides noh compositions (from the earliest time to the present) into three stages, paying most attention to the intermediate stage, which includes practitioners from Zeami to Nagatoshi and the amateur composers.

12. Other than the occasional mention of their names and activities in historical documents, much of what we know of these performers is from Zeami's treatises.

13. See Yokomichi et al. (III), 121–147 for a detailed account of these achievements. Also see, Omote and Amino (I) 1987, 35–37.

14. These noh plays are identified in Go on (五音) one of Zeami's treatises. See Yokomichi et al. (III), 1987, 222–242, for a general introduction to Motomasa's life and work.

15. See ibid., 203–221, for a general introduction to Zenchiku. Also see Thornhill 1993, Atkins 2006, and Pinnington 2006. 2, for book-length studies of Zenchiku.

The third and final generation of professional noh practitioners who left behind a substantial number of noh plays are Nobumitsu, Kanze Nagatoshi (1488–1541) and Konparu Zenchiku's
grandson Konparu Zenpō (1454–?). According to *Nōhonsakusha
Chūmon* (An index of noh composers), thirty-one noh plays are
attributed to Nobumitsu, out of which fourteen are still performed
today. The number of plays created by Zenpō and Nagatoshi is es-
timated to be more than twenty, although only about five of each
are still performed.

Plays by the Third Generation Practitioners

Plays by the third generation practitioners exhibit characteristics that differ from the majority of noh plays performed today.
In *Funabenkei* (Benkei on board) by Nobumitsu, for example, we
see a play that adeptly weaves together the bravery and wit of the
loyal retainer Benkei with the tale of a sad romance, followed by a
ferocious battle. Another example, *Momijigari*, also by Nobumitsu,
tells the story of the Taira general Koremochi. This dramatic play
with its mesmerizing characters has continued to charm audiences
since the Muromachi period.[16]
Nobumitsu's contemporary Konparu Zenpō also produced
plays that emphasize visual elements and drama. One of the several
existing plays attributed to Zenpō is *Hatsuyuki* (Hatsuyuki, the pet
bird), a short two-part *mugen* (dream) play in which a pet chicken
attains enlightenment after her owner offers a seven-day prayer
session for her.[17] This play is unusual in that there is no waki role.
In Act One, the shite plays Hatsuyuki's owner; in Act Two, the shite
takes up the role of the pet chicken and performs a thanksgiving
dance, while Hatsuyuki's owner is played by the tsure.[18]

---

16. Translations of both plays can be found in Tyler 1992. Also see Chapter 2
for an in-depth discussion of the plays.

17. Mugen noh (夢幻能), or dream play, is an important category identified in
present-day noh discourse. See Chapter Five for more details. Also see Nishisei
1986 and Lim 2005, 35–37, for a discussion of Hatsuyuki.

18. One characteristic of the noh theater is that each individual character

Kanze Nagatoshi, Nobumitsu's eldest son, also has several noh plays attributed to him, such as *Rinzō*, which is characterized by the large number of performers appearing on stage.[19] The *rinzō*, a huge circular stupa-like stand where temples place their holy scriptures, is often situated in the middle of the temple hall. In this play the waki, a holy monk, visits a temple in Kitano where five thousand volumes of holy Buddhist scriptures are stored in a *rinzō*. While the priest is admiring the scriptures an old man, performed by the tsure, suddenly appears. He is the protecting deity of the *rinzō*. Together they hail the transmission of Buddhism from China to Japan and sing praises to Buddhism. In Act Two, another deity, Fudaishi, performed by the shite, appears with his two attendants (kokata, child performers). The deity Fudaishi brings a case-full of scriptures as a present for the monk, and the play ends with the attendants and the two deities each performing a celebratory dance.

One characteristic of the noh theater in this period can be seen in the role-character relationship. The waki might be absent, as in *Hatsuyuki*, or the shite performer might play two different characters, as in *Funabenkei*. Note that although we do occasionally see two different shite characters in some of the earlier plays, this practice was less common during that time, and the results less dramatic. For instance in *Fujito*, the shite plays the mother of a murdered fisherman in Act One and the anguished ghost of the fisherman in Act Two. This play, probably by Zeami's son Motomasa (1394?–1432), focuses on the sense of suffering and

---

is performed by specific role-type, e.g., "shite" or "waki." In this book I call the relationship between the role type and the character the "role-character relationship." The basic role types in a noh play are the shite and the waki. Shite, literally the "doer," is sometimes translated as the protagonist. Characters are often identified by the role types that perform them. Usually a role will perform the same character throughout a play (one act or two acts). For example, a shite performer takes up the character of a warrior in act one, and continues to play the same character in act two. Other times, however, the character each role takes may differ in the two acts. For instance, in *Funabenkei* the shite plays a beautiful woman and later a ferocious ghost.

19. Sanari 1982, 3373–3385.

injustice shared by the mother and son.[20] This is very different in nature from the late-Muromachi plays, in which the shite plays two vastly different characters in order to heighten the dramatic impact and demonstrate the range of the acting.

Another distinctive feature of many of the plays created during this period is the deployment of elaborate stage props. Nagatoshi's *Rinzō* uses two of these: the *rinzō* that opens on eight sides and a platform on which the deity Fudaishi sits. Zenpō's *Ikkaku Sennin* (The wizard Ikkaku) has a hut and a rock cave, represented by two simple stage constructions. Almost every play produced by Nobumitsu requires some kind of stage prop. For example, the boat in *Funabenkei*, the platform used for Yōkihi's bed in *Kōtei* (The emperor), the stand of blooming plum blossoms in *Kochō* (The butterfly), and a prop to represent the ancient willow tree in *Yugyō Yanagi* (The priest and the willow).[21]

In terms of musical instruments, many plays from this period employ the stick drum (*taiko*) as well as the two hand drums (*ōtsuzumi* and *kotsuzumi*) and the flute. The stick drum, which is often used to create a lively and boisterous effect, is an important component in many plays that end with a quick tempo *maibataraki* dance. Compared to plays produced by Zeami and Zenpō, a much larger number of plays by Nobumitsu and his contemporaries end with a dance performed with the accompaniment of a stick drum. One example is *Kōtei*, which concludes with a battle between the illness demon and the exorcist. In short, in view of the examples provided, one can argue that in general plays created in Nobumitsu's time have different emphases from those of the second generation. The former are more dramatic and lively, the latter more introspective and elegant.

In many of Nobumitsu's other plays, the primary focus is neither solely on the main character nor on their internal experiences. Instead we see a stronger emphasis on the external dramatic events, and the responsibility for the presentation of

---

20. Nishino 1998, 39.
21. See Sachiko 1985: 20–49. Also see Yokomichi 1992 for a list of props used on noh stage.

these events is distributed among the various role types. As the noh historian Nōgami Toyoichirō (1883–1950) has pointed out, shite-focus performance (*shite-ichinin-shūgi*) is an important characteristic in many noh plays, especially those created before the Ōnin War attributed to Zeami and Zenchiku.[22] Later plays, like those that I have just mentioned, often ascribed a more important dramatic significance to the waki character, and sometimes even the tsure and kyōgen characters. We no longer see the shite monopolizing the entire stage. Closely related to this role-character feature is the number of characters actually appearing on the stage. The plays composed by Nagatoshi, the youngest of the three major noh composers and practitioners of the late Muromachi period, often had many characters and props on the stage. One example is *Rinzō*, described above. Another is *Kasui* (The river), which has more than ten different characters.[23]

After the Muromachi Period

Starting with Ashikaga Yoshimitsu's patronage of Zeami, the formerly marginalized sarugaku performers and the genre they

---

22. See Nogami 1948, 1–42. Nogami comments that noh is the kind of play that focuses on the shite and the shite alone (シテ一人主義 shite ichinin shūgi), when he refers to mainly mugen noh plays that are composed by Zeami and his contemporaries. Tracing the historical development of dengaku and sarugaku, Nogami argues that the noh theater is a theatrical form that emphasizes only the shite. All other role types, including the waki, resemble the audience in that they are observers most of the time, and that they do not enage in any form of dramatic confrontation with the shite. Nogami also argues that noh is not meant to be "realistic" but is a genre that emphasizes "showing" (miseru) and "hearing" (kikaseru), or more accurately, "to make the audience listen by means of style" (shikata ni yotte, kikaseru mono). If we contrast this style with the plays produced by Nobumitsu and his peers, we will be able to see that there is a changing trend in these later noh plays to expand beyond the practice of focusing on the shite when presenting the play. There are, of course, advantages and disadvantages to this new trend. The obvious advantage is the possibility of enacting the events as they unfold, although at times this is done at the expense of the poetic aesthetics which is especially essential when the shite performs "solo."

23. Yokomichi and Omote (II) 1960–1963, 195.

represented rose steadily in the social and cultural hierarchy.[24] This change in the social and cultural definition of the genre is part of an intricate trajectory of political and economic development that helped shape, among other things, the audience-performer relationship. The incessant civil wars that occurred after the Ōnin War greatly weakened the financial power of the military and religious institutions—the sources of traditional patronage and income for noh troupes. The Kanze troupe, like others, ventured beyond the capital and performed in the provinces as far away as the Kyushu area[25]. This expanded geographical scope was another important feature in the changing social scene.

The noh theater developed within this new social context was understandably different from that developed during the earlier two generations of noh practitioners. The relatively smaller number of plays created during the late Muromachi focused more on the active and external, in contrast to plays that are meditative. A much wider scope of themes also became the norm rather than the exception.

And what happened in noh theater after Nobumitsu's time? To answer this question, it is important to discuss briefly another military patron, Toyotomi Hideyoshi, who unified Japan in 1590 and started a new political era. According to noh historian Steven Brown, "Hideyoshi's patronage and involvement with noh helped create a cultural space within which noh drama would eventually be designated the official ceremonial music and entertainment (*shikigaku*) of the Tokugawa shogunate."[26] It is clear that Hideyoshi and some of his successors had a tremendous impact on noh. They selected, categorized, and refined the repertoire. The

---

24. See Lim 2004: 111–133, for more details on the interactions between performers and the social and cultural elite.

25. In medieval diary records such as *Inryōken Nichiroku* (The Inryōken Journal, 1435–1466, 1484–1493) and *Sanetaka Kōki* (Diary of Sanetaka, 1474–1536) we see mention of Nobumitsu's activities at the temple and at Sanetaka's home. Elsewhere I have discussed Nobumitsu's involvement in the cultural circles of the late Muromachi period court officials and Zen prelates. See Chapter One for a more detailed discussion of these journeys. Also see Lim 2004.

26. Brown 2001, 119.

gradual selection process resulted in fewer than three hundred plays remaining in the modern repertoire.[27] Among those that have survived is a group of plays that were labeled *ikyoku* (exotic pieces) during the time of the fifth Tokugawa shogun Tsunayoshi (1646–1709). Many of these plays, revived thanks to Tsunayoshi's preference for unconventional plays, were later termed furyū noh in modern noh scholarship, and many of these were produced by late Muromachi noh practitioners, best represented by Nobumitsu.

In 1960, the visual-oriented style of noh plays composed by practitioners such as Nobumitsu, Zenpō, and Nagatoshi was labeled "furyū noh" by Yokomichi Mario in his two volume *Yōkyokushū* (Collection of noh plays) in the "Classical Japanese literature series" (*Nihon Koten Bungaku Taikei*) published by Iwanami Shoten.[28] Yokomichi addressed the nature of plays by late Muromachi noh practitioners and proposed that in order to differentiate these plays from earlier ones a specialized name should be given to them. He suggested "furyū" because the term "always has had a lively and spectacular connotation since the ancient period."[29]

Yokomichi's commentary is very important, as it succinctly describes the nature of plays by Nobumitsu and his peers. The name furyū noh not only highlights their distinctive emphasis on

27. Looser 2008, 3, n7 elaborates on the implication of the legislation of noh as the official ritual of state and aptly summarizes it as "… these [institutional] divides have helped the noh to become a repository of a more transcendently essentialized Japanese identity." To a certain extent this Japanese identity plays a part in the formation of contemporary noh discourse which deems furyū style plays inferior. But to further pursue this issue in the present book would distract attention from the main subject, Nobumitsu.

28. Classical literature anthologies often include performance genres such as noh and kabuki. We see here a conscientious participation of consumers (readers) and producers (publishers, scholars) in the construction of a body of "classics" that theoretically represents the highbrow culture of premodern times. In the case of noh, this inclusion seems to reaffirm the literary value of the genre, contributing to the more literature-oriented emphasis of the noh paradigm. I discuss this in more detail in Chapter Six.

29. Yōkyokushū 1960–1963, 11. See Chapter Six for a more in-depth discussion of furyū.

dramatic elements and visual presentation, it also (probably unintentionally) implies that possibly a different perspective can be adopted to examine late Muromachi noh plays. This new perspective is particularly clear when furyū plays are compared with those by Zeami and his followers. At the end of Yokomichi's commentary, he hints at the "inappropriate" popularity of the furyū style plays while affirming the higher aesthetic values of plays produced by Zeami. Yokimichi's definition also echoes the position of many noh scholars of his generation and earlier.[30] It is no exaggeration to say that Zeami is the main architect in constructing the noh paradigm that we all know today. But the overwhelming emphasis on and romanticization of Zeami and his noh aesthetics in modern noh discourse has become at times an insurmountable obstacle to a better and more comprehensive understanding of noh and also limits our understanding of medieval cultural history.[31] Fortunately, in recent years Japanese scholars have started to drift away from concentrating solely on Zeami and have begun to work on other areas. Two recent works on the late Muromachi noh theater have been written by Yamanaka Reiko (1998) and Ishii Tomoko (1998), and Omote Akira presented his latest findings on the birth date of Nobumitsu in 1999. In English-language noh scholarship, however, there are still relatively few studies on the late Muromachi period, although many excellent scholarly works on Zeami and Zenchiku continue to be produced.[32]

---

30. A few scholars have published papers on topics pertinent to the late Muromachi noh scene, such as Haruo 1973; Nishisei Hideki 1986, 15–30, on Konparu Zenpō; and Oda 1985, on the development of stage props.

31. It was an illuminating moment for me when I heard the living national cultural treasure, shite performer Kanze Hideo, discuss his childhood training. In a public talk in Singapore on April 4, 2002, the renowned shite performer repeatedly cited Zeami's treatises on the importance of early training for performers, as if there had been no change in any of the performance elements between Zeami's time and now. (Again, Looser's 2008 work illustrates the perception of time, which is beyond the scope of this book.) Aside from the problem with ignoring the six hundred years between Zeami's treatises and the present, Kanze Hideo's numerous references to Zeami also demonstrates the canonical position of Zeami's theories.

32. There are plenty of examples: Zeami's treatises have been translated by

About This Book

The goal of this book is to fill the gap in English-language scholarship on late Muromachi noh. I examine the specific cultural and societal framework in which Nobumitsu functioned as a noh practitioner—ranging from troupe management to composition and performance. In the process of discussing Nobumitsu's career, life and peers, I would like to find answers to the questions I posed at the beginning of this book. My ultimate intention is to propose an alternative way to discuss and debate noh theater in present-day noh discourse.[33]

I start with the proposition that even though it is often regarded as being less important in contemporary noh scholarship, late Muromachi noh theater was really quite eventful, especially as practiced by Nobumitsu and his contemporaries. Nobumitsu, whose extant plays are second only to Zeami in number, has not received enough scholarly attention. A detailed study of his contribution and significance in the late Muromachi period will not only introduce an important noh practitioner to English-language noh scholarship, but, equally important, it will illustrate the significance of his work and times within noh history.

In order to coordinate what seems to be a fairly ambitious argument situated in two different time periods—the late Muromachi and present—I have divided this book into four parts. This introduction provides an overview of the book: its aims and

Rimer and Yamazaki 1984; Hare 1986 and 2008 discusses Zeami's biography and gives annotated commentary on his plays and treatises; de Poorter 1986 presents a detailed translation and analysis of Zeami and his treatises; Nearman published a series of translations and commentaries of Zeami's Kakyō and Kyakuraisho in the 1980s and another series on Zenchiku's Rokurin Ichirō in the 1990s; Quinn 2005 examines in detail Zeami's treatises; Looser 2008 and Yokota 1997 discuss Tokugawa period noh; Thornhill 1993, Atkins 1999, and Pinnington 2006 have all done studies on Zenchiku.

33. Even though this may seem to imply that my intended audience are readers who are more knowledgeable of the noh theater, I do intend this book to be read also by those who are interested but who have not had encountered the genre before. I believe that the noh theater can, and probably should, be introduced to beginners from different perspectives.

approach, structure, and rationale. A general historical account of the noh theater, critical as background information for the ensuing discussion, is also presented here.

Part One continues with the sociohistorical specifics of the late Muromachi period. Referencing various historical documents and contemporary scholarly works, I present a narrative of Nobumitsu's life and time. The most important of these sources is the Kanze Kojirō Nobumitsu Gazōsan (観世小次郎信光画像賛), which was written by Keijō Shūrin (景徐周林 1429–1518), a Zen monk who was Nobumitsu's contemporary. This historical document provides reliable information on Nobumitsu's life, not least because Nobumitsu himself contributed to its writing. Equally important is the nature of the writing and how it sheds light on the perception and reception of noh in the late Muromachi period. Nobumitsu's biography highlights his significance as a noh practitioner during the late Muromachi period; this second chapter also provides a general introduction to some of the common features seen in Nobumitsu's plays.

By presenting a historical overview of the noh theater and Nobumitsu's biography, starting with contemporary scholars' presentation of a noh timeline and ending with an introduction of Nobumitsu's plays, I want to emphasize the importance of relating historical accounts to contemporary discourse—I believe that this approach will yield more interesting discoveries and livelier discussion. I also believe that an understanding of the historical and cultural specifics, including that from recent times, will be critical in providing a more comprehensive picture of noh discourse.

Part Two highlights Nobumitsu's talent as a noh composer who created a wide variety of noh plays that are still enjoyed by contemporary audiences, as well as the general tendency of noh composition in his time. These plays, presented under three different categories—the furyū plays, the *karamono* (Chinese) plays, and the mugen dream plays—are divided according to their most representative characteristics. They are well known as Nobumitsu's plays, and in a wider sense as plays of the late Muromachi period. I try to include the discussion of as many

Nobumitsu plays as possible. When I need to make a choice, decisions are made in accordance with my intention to situate this book as part of a wider debate in the contemporary scholarly discourse on noh—I focus more on plays that are better-known and are still performed. In other words, plays that are easier to access. I discuss the individual merits of each play, calling attention to features that make them good theater. Close reading and discussions are not restricted only to these plays—comparisons with other plays help to substantiate my arguments.

Part Three switches the focus from Nobumitsu and late Muromachi noh plays to modern noh discourse, examining the concept of "furyū noh"—a term that is often used simultaneously with late Muromachi period noh plays. An understanding of this modern construct, which is partially premised on Zeami's aesthetic paradigm, is very useful in illuminating the reception of late Muromachi plays in comtemporary noh scholarship. In this final part of the book, I construct the likely trajectory of the term and try to answer the question Why, despite its refined features as a theatrical genre, the noh plays of Nobumitsu and his peers have been treated as somewhat inferior. It is important to examine this aspect of contemporary noh discourse because it will provide alternative ways to think about noh theater.

Between Zeami's time and the Tokugawa period, noh theater ventured in various directions, with different participants attempting innovative trajectories—perhaps more as a means of survival than a conscious effort in the development of the genre. Among these participants of noh, Nobumitsu and his peers' works occupy a special position in that they not only represent the potential of a new noh theater, but they are also witnesses to the history of noh. I argue in this book that Nobumitsu and the late Muromachi period should be accorded a more important position in noh history and suggest another perspective from which the noh theater can be examined.

Part One

○観世小次郎畫像

本朝に優鳴者観世小次郎信

光故童阿の第七子也童阿者

輩於華康蓮應而相公尤見衆

輩者也俊宄其敬羊俟之芽嘉

賓之戀登歌畫る當劇舞發擎神

頭ヲ呈鬼面或作武夫桓ノ之

息或以為歸人呻嘆之姿於須史

頃千態万状冷觀者喜怒哀樂

之情勤蕩于其肉天下奇觀也

偕光克傳父俊然而推讓於為

父之後者而不屬髯但以擊鼓

Chapter One
THE *NOBUMITSU PORTRAIT INSCRIPTION*

The *Kanze Kojirō Nobumitsu Gazōsan* (観世小次郎信光画像賛 *Kanze Kojirō Nobumitsu Portrait Inscription*, hereafter *Nobumitsu Portrait Inscription*), an inscription appended to a portrait of Nobumitsu, was completed around 1488 by the Gozan (五山 Five Mountains) Zen prelate Keijō Shūrin (1429–1518). Unlike most portrait inscriptions that provide merely eulogized "factual" information, we are able to learn much more than Nobumitsu's life in this relatively lengthy narrative. What started as an ordinary tribute in praise of one man's career achievements quickly developed into a lively yet rare discussion between the writer Keijō and the subject Nobumitsu. Some similarities between this inscription and earlier writings related to Nobumitsu's predecessors can be traced, although upon close scrutiny we see that the *Nobumitsu Portrait Inscription* illustrates a stronger sense of identity of the performer and his theater. The writer Keijō's active participation in the discourse on performance is yet another indication of the social status and cultural value of noh during the time.

This chapter starts with a general historical account of portraiture in Japan, highlighting the fact that only people from certain social backgrounds were able to make portraits of themselves. That both Nobumitsu and his father On'ami had their portraiture made indicates the gradual change of social status

1

of the noh theater from what it had been in earlier generations. Even though one finds traces of stylistic similarities between Kisei's On'ami portrait inscription and Keijō's Nobumitsu portrait inscription, it is clear that Keijō's inscription is a much more complicated text that provides significant insights into late Muromachi noh theater. What is recorded in the *Nobumitsu Portrait Inscription* provides important information pertaining to Nobumitsu's life and work, and equally important is the very existence of the document itself—both aspects of the inscription combine to further substantiate our understanding of the noh practitioner and his time.

Portrait-making and Inscription

Portrait-making and the composition of accompanying inscriptions, usually in the form of parallel verse, started in Japan as early as Prince Shōtoku's (574–622) time.[1] Apparently influenced by the Chinese, portraits initially were used mainly for religious purposes. In the Japanese medieval period, inscribed portraits acquired new popularity with the rise of Zen Buddhism, and it became increasingly common for religious as well as secular figures from a certain class background, both living and dead, to have their portraits made. The main function of having one's portrait made is either commemorative or memorial. Political figures such as the emperor Gotsuchimikado (1442–1500, reigned 1464–1500) and shogun Ashikaga Yoshimasa (1436–1490, reigned 1449–1473), zen monks such as Ikkyū Sōjun (1394–1481), and even historical figures such as the *Manyōshū* poet Kakinomoto no Hitomarō (?–?) had their portraits made for purposes ranging from ritual rites to commemorating their presence at poetry competitions.[2]

---

1. See Hickman et al. 1996 for a general history of portraiture in premodern Japan.
2. Phillips 2000, 150–152.

It also became common practice to append a short verse or piece of prose to laud the achievements of the person in the portrait. Very little is known of the history of these portrait inscriptions, although one source argues that the earliest form was known as "*san*," which also means "in praise of." A word originally related to Buddhist religious practice in China, it referred to the chants sung to hail the Buddha.[3] Elsewhere, "san" is explained as "a poem that praises the (generally human) subject of the painting ... a poetic complement."[4]

Many portraits done in the Kamakura and Muromachi periods have not survived, nor is there any information about the painters who made these portraits. This is the case with the Nobumitsu portrait: it is not extant, and its painter is unknown. The only historical source that indicates its existence is the appended inscription, by Keijō Shūrin, anthologized and recorded in various historical texts.

Portrait inscriptions were often written in an intricate combination of prose and verse, classical Chinese–style writing (*kanbun*) and Japanese. There are no apparent rules regarding the length of the inscriptions: some of them are as short as a few lines, while others amount to several paragraphs. Sometimes a preface or even a postscript that offers background information will be appended. The content of a portrait inscription, however, is generally predictable. Since they were often only meant as an ornamental congratulatory gesture, portraiture inscription is often impersonal and formulaic. Several rhetorical devices are commonly used: for instance, the practice of comparing the subject to ancient Chinese sages, the use of each character of the subject's name to start new lines, and the use of parallel lines. Because of these rather standardized, albeit informal, approaches to portrait inscriptions, they are usually only gestures of recognition without much personal information. The names and titles found in the anthology *Gozan*

---

3. See Fontein and Hickman 1970, xl–xlii, for a discussion of the history of Japanese Chinsō, or Portrait Inscription.
4. Phillips, 47–48.

Bungaku Zenshū show that the portraits were mainly of people with some kind of official rank. There is no mention of commoners or people without a title—it is obvious that only people of a certain social status had their portraits made.[5] The implications for the social status of noh performers when they have their portraits made is therefore significant when we consider the much inferior treatment they faced two generations earlier.

On'ami and His Portrait—the *Kanze Tayū Gazōsan* (観世太夫画像賛)

There are at least three portraits of noh practitioners in the historical records, as well as one of the *dengaku* performer Zōami (増阿弥 ?–?), who lived, it is assumed, between Zeami and On'ami's time.[6] Only one of the portraits among these, that of the drummer Miyamasu Yasaemon (1483?–1556), painter unknown, is still extant. The four-line verse that praises his drumming skill is placed on the top part of the picture scroll above the figure who is supposed to be Miyamasu.[7] The other two portraits, both earlier than this one, belong to father and son On'ami and Nobumitsu. The actual paintings are lost, but the inscriptions are documented in various places, providing a reliable source for examination of these two portraits.

On'ami's portrait inscription was written by the Zen monk Son'an Kisei Reigen (1404–1489).[8] In this inscription, On'ami's

---

5. Tamamura 1967.

6. *Dengaku*, together with *sarugaku*, is another popular performance genre during the medieval period. It was a keen competitor of sarugaku and there was influence from dengaku in the sarugaku performance. Dengaku, however, did not survive and very little is known about it today.

7. See Kokuritsu 1999 for a picture (on the front cover) and an explanation (p. 39) of the portrait. An image of this portrait can also be found on the home page of the Nogami Memorial Noh Theatre Research Institute of Hosei University: http://www9.i.hosei.ac.jp/~nohken/index.html.

8. Kisei Reigen had an unusual career path in the Gozan order. He was best known for his literary pursuits, especially *kanshi* ("Chinese"-style poetry). Keijō

excellent performance style is recorded in a vivid manner:

> The art of noh can be either significant or
> trivial. Whoever acquires its essence will startle
> the world. Indeed, the wonders of the performer
> lie in his art. He [On'ami] touched one's heart and
> dazzled one's eyes. Sometimes he moved rapidly
> in a phantom mask, and sometimes he chanted
> pleasantly, in a manner formal and proper. When
> he was solemn he appeared to be a warrior, and
> when he cried, he was a woman. He danced
> gracefully with his sleeves swaying as if in the
> wind, and sang with his fan flashing as quick as
> lighting. He was able to present a million forms,
> all different from each other. Crowds formed into
> human walls, eager to see him. So enchanted
> were they that reality and illusion could no longer
> be distinguished. His tears saddened me and
> his anger startled me. What more can be said
> about such wonderful art? Who could this be?
> What kind of creature is this? One asked these
> questions at the end of the performance, when
> the actor unmasked himself. It is he whom Lord
> Fukō called the most excellent performer and
> who enjoyed Lord Fukō's patronage. It is Master
> Kanze Saburō On'ami, he, whose beard today is
> silver and hair gray.[9]

Kisei hailed On'ami as an actor whose extraordinary
performance deeply moved the audience. In the eyes of Kisei, and
probably many others who witnessed his performances, On'ami
excelled in conveying the essence of any character or emotion that

---

Shūrin, the author of *Nobumitsu Gazōsan*, studied with him. His anthology can
be found in Uemura 1992.
  9. Lim 2000, 569–570.

he chose to portray. This particular style of performance is known as *monomane*, variously translated as "mimicry," "imitation," or "role playing."[10] On'ami's monomane skill was what brought him and his line of the family to the pinnacle of shogunate patronage—especially after the death of Ashikaga Yoshimitsu—and On'ami's eventual succession to the leadership of the Kanze troupe. Although the first Ashikaga patron of noh, Yoshimitsu might have preferred Zeami's performance and later development of the music and dance-oriented *kabu* (歌舞 song and dance) style noh, On'ami's monomane had its own supporters. In the inscription, for example, Lord Fukō is the posthumous name of the sixth Ashikaga shogun Yoshinori, who became shogun after his brother Yoshimochi's death in 1428.[11] Yoshinori seemed to have favored On'ami greatly over Zeami—in one instance he deprived Motomasa, Zeami's son, of the position of musical director at the Kiyotaki shrine and reassigned it to On'ami. Later, he sent the aging Zeami into exile to Sadō Island.[12]

This favoritism contributed further to the row between the two branches of the Kanze family. Some scholars contend that the relationship between uncle and nephew was also strained by their very different approaches to noh theater.[13] It has long been rumored that because of this rivalry, after his son Motomasa's

---

10. *Monomane* is a difficult concept to translate, like many aesthetic terms used in noh. Literally, the word means "to imitate someone or something," although the subjects of imitation are extremely diversified—from deities and spirits to emotions and movements. Scholars have emphasized the more abstract use of the term by Zeami (see Hare 2008, 31; Brown 2001, 21–30; Quinn 1990, 43–49; Rimer and Yamasaki 1984, xxxix–xli), although from Kisei's description of On'ami's performances, I believe that the term was also used to describe a more direct performance technique—impersonation or imitation—which On'ami was most famous for.

11. Yoshinori was the son of Yoshimitsu and a tyrant whose temper engendered much fear and hatred. He was a patron of On'ami and ironically was assassinated at one of On'ami's noh performances by members of the Akamatsu military family.

12. See Hare 1986, 32, for other details of Yoshinori's harsh treatment of Zeami and his branch of the Kanze family.

13. Ibid., 35.

death Zeami passed his treatises on to his son-in-law Zenchiku from the Konparu family, rather than to his own nephew, On'ami. It is hard to ascertain or evaluate the impact of Zeami's decision, but the last noh practitioner from the medieval period, Konparu Zenpō, who produced numerous noh treatises, did come from the Konparu rather than the Kanze lineage.

With or without access to Zeami's treatises, On'ami enjoyed a successful career, as Kisei has described in the inscription to his portrait. Ultimately, however, Kisei simply commemorated On'ami's achievement following the conventional practices in portraiture and inscription. When the On'ami inscription is compared with Nobumitsu's, some similarities in terms of diction and syntax, especially in the beginning, can be found. But beyond the early sections it is clear that Kisei's inscription for On'ami and Keijō's inscription for Nobumitsu are very different. The *On'ami Portrait Inscription* follows a fixed formula by merely presenting what is conceived to be his successful career and life, thereby abiding by the general function of a portrait inscription. The writer of this portrait inscription, Kisei Reigen, was closely related to the Akamatsu family, who were ardent fans of On'ami. It could have been based on their suggestion that the inscription was written. The straightforward manner of this inscription succinctly highlights the lifetime achievement of On'ami, providing concrete descriptions of his performance skills for later generations to remember him by. In other words, there was probably not a strong personal tie between Kisei and On'ami such as there was between Keijō and Nobumitsu. Keijō's *Nobumitsu Portrait Inscription*, on the other hand, demonstrates many features that are different from the usual business-like nature of inscriptions. It starts with what is commonly found in many other inscriptions—factual accounts of the person in the portrait. This is followed by the unusual insertion of the Kanze family lineage and a pseudo-debate on the meaning of a certain Buddhist sutra. This section, written in a lively free-style prose, is a rare record of a conversational exchange between the inscription writer and the subject of the portrait.

Nobumitsu Portrait Inscription: The Text

As we will see, the *Nobumitsu Portrait Inscription* is of considerable length. The unusual length and format reveal more about
Keijō and Nobumitsu than the actual content of the inscription.
It demonstrates a close personal tie between the Zen prelate and
the noh practitioner, and suggests a more complex relationship between the cultural elites represented by Keijō and the performance
genre represented by Nobumitsu. Not only did Nobumitsu deserve
to have his portrait done, like his father and others in official ca-
pacities, but Nobumitsu's personal input was also duly recorded.[14]
Together with the lengthy explanations and prefatory notes from
Keijō, this very informative inscription provides later generations
with a glimpse of the attitude and perception of both the Zen
prelate and the practitioner toward the noh theater. The first part
of the *Nobumitsu Inscription* presents a systematic exploration
of Nobumitsu's identity starting with his family ancestry. It then
progresses beyond personal history and examines the institutional
history of the sarugaku theater. The last section returns to the
conventions of inscriptions, following the standard format with a
short verse lauding Nobumitsu's life and career.[15] (With reference
to the full text, several features that contribute to the unique nature
of the inscription are discussed in the following section.)

> Kanze Kojirō Nobumitsu—the seventh child
> of the late On'ami—is acclaimed throughout
> this land as a performer. On'ami served the two
> ministers Fukō and Jishō and was much favored
> by them. The wonders of On'ami's art were seen
> in his performances at the mansions of lords and

---

14. Keijō indicates that the inscription was done at Nobumitsu's request to be
a record of the "origins of his art and the beginnings of his family." There is also
in one part of the inscription where he records a disagreement with Nobumitsu.

15. I would like to thank *Monumenta Nipponica* for permission to reproduce
the translation. This material appeared originally in a somewhat different form in
Monumenta Nipponica 55:4 (Winter 2000), pp. 567–577.

nobles and at banquets for the important and famous. He sang and danced, sometimes holding the *jintō* arrow, sometimes wearing the phantom mask. He showed the bravery of a soldier and enacted the pathos of a woman. Within a blink of an eye, he demonstrated a thousand emotions and ten thousand forms. With such performances he aroused the emotions of happiness and joy, anger and sadness in the depth of the audience's heart. The entire realm regarded his art with wonder.

Although Nobumitsu has inherited the true essence of his father's art, he humbly declined to be his successor and did not learn the role of shite. Instead, he chose drumming as his specialty. When the flute sounds, his hand drum and shoulder drum complement its flowing melody. Nobumitsu's hands are as swift as lightning. The continuous beat of his drums silences every other sound and dazzles one and all. In addition, he is intelligent and talented. He investigates the customs and practices that have existed in this land from the times of the gods, and he studies waka poetry. He delves into tales of prosperity and destruction from the Han and Tang dynasties and uses them in his composition of noh lyrics and music. Numerous new plays have been created, but among playwrights, no one surpasses him. At the young age of fifteen, before he attained official adulthood, he was summoned by the retired emperor Go-Hanazono [to perform at the imperial palace]. His Majesty rewarded him with a fan. At that time Lord Jishō was in attendance on the emperor and commanded Nobumitsu to respectfully receive the reward. What greater honor can there be?

Nobumitsu is a descendent of the Hattori, a distinguished house from the province of Iga. The Hattori had three fine sons. The Daimyōjin deity of Kasuga sent a revelation to the eldest son that he should serve the deities by taking charge of music [at the shrine]. His father refused and this resulted in the son's immediate death. The same thing happened to the second son. The parents therefore took the third son to the province of Yamato to pay homage to the Kannon of Hasedera temple. On the way, they met a monk from whom they requested a name for the third child. The name given was Kanze. They then proceeded on their pilgrimage to the Kasuga shrine where they presented the third son to the Daimyōjin in fulfillment of the divine command. Remaining in the province of Yamato, they changed their family name to Yūzaki and took charge of the music for the deities.

The Yūzaki had a fine son who is known as Zeami and who was the favorite of Lord Rokuon. Zeami died at the age of eighty-one during the time of Lord Fukō; his art was celebrated both within and without the court. Zeami's younger brother was called Shirō Tayū; he was the father of On'ami. Zeami's art prospered in the hands of On'ami. He is therefore said to be Zeami's true successor.

Listen! The performers' art started with Hada no Kōkatsu. Those performing now are all descended from him. As for the Kanze family that originated from the Hattori lineage, having received the command of the deities, they are different from the ordinary performer.

This Hada no Kōkatsu was a supernatural being who manifested (keshō) himself during the reign of the thirtieth emperor, Kinmei. One night the emperor dreamed of a child deity. The child deity declared himself to be the reincarnation of the first emperor of Qin. Because of a karmic connection, he was to be born in the Land of the Sun, and he requested to be made an official to the emperor. At that time, there was a flood in the province of Yamato. The Hatsuse River rose rapidly. A huge earthern urn rode the raging torrent and stopped in front of the Miwa Myōjin shrine. Opening up the urn, the people of the area found a gemlike boy. They reported this to the emperor, who declared that it was the child of whom he had dreamed. He raised the child and bestowed upon him the family name Hada. As the years passed the boy's talent and intelligence grew, and at the age of fifteen he was given the position of minister. He served five sovereigns, until the reign of Empress Suiko, when Prince Hōsō oversaw the governance of the land. Prince Hōsō offered rites to the deities of heaven and earth, seeking to pacify the land and benefit the people. For this purpose he made sixty-six masks and commanded Kōkatsu to perform with them. Kōkatsu was ordered to perform both in the Tachibana palace and the Shishinden hall. As a result, all within the four seas was calm and the people of the land were healthy and happy.

The prince took the music of the deities (*kagura*), and splitting the character "deity" (*kami*), named this type of performance sarugaku. According to the *Shuowen*, the character *shen* 申 is equivalent to the character *shen* 神. When Jupiter is in the *shen* direction, it comes under the influence of the zodiac monkey. Later generations thus spoke of sarugaku as "monkey music," relating it to the likes of monkeys. This is quite mistaken.

Kōkatsu eventually entered the province of Settsu and traveled along the shores of Naniwa bay. Riding in a little boat, he let the wind carry him where it would. The boat drifted toward the western sea and reached the shore of Harima. The people of the area gathered to look at him. Seeing that this was no ordinary man and that he had an awesome aura about him, they decided to set up an altar to pay homage to him and called him the Ōara no Myōjin.

In later times, the sixty-second emperor, Emperor Murakami, in the midst of his numerous commitments found time to read *Sarugaku ennenki* (Chronicle of Sarugaku as a source of long life), compiled by Prince Hōsō. The emperor told his ministers that there was nothing better than sarugaku to delight the deities in heaven and pacify the populace on earth. He immediately ordered Hada no Ujiyasu, a descendent of Kōkatsu, to restore this art. There was also a certain Mr. Ki (*Ki no soregashi*), who was married to Ujiyasu's younger sister. The two of them together revived the art and performed dances daily before the great palace hall. The Emperor thought that sixty-six items were too many to be completed in a day, so he selected and organized them into three pieces: *Inatsumi no okina, Yotsumi no okina,* and *Chichi no jō.* After that, these three items were passed down in the Hada family to Ujiyasu's descendent in the twenty-ninth generation. His name was Konparu and his troupe was based at Enman'i in the province of Yamato. The demon mask made by Prince Hōsō is the secret treasure of this troupe.

There are four troupes in the province of Yamato. They are the Tobi, Yūzaki, Sakado, and Enman'i. They serve the Kasuga deity. There are three troupes in the province of Ōmi. They are the Yamashina, Shimosaka, and Hie. These troupes serve the Hie deity. In Kawachi there is the Shinza; in Tanba, the Honza; and in the province of Settsu, the Hōjōji. These three troupes serve the Kamo and Sumiyoshi deities. In the province of Ise, there are the Waya, Katsuta, and Shudō. They worship the deity at Daijingū.

Nobumitsu told me that although the art of sarugaku was popularized by Prince Hōsō and Kōkatsu, it originated during the age of the deities in the music played by the deities before the heavenly rock-cave. It again had its source in the time of the Buddha, when the venerable Sudatta constructed the Jetavana Vihāra hall for the Buddha and heretics tried to impede the service. The Buddha thereupon ordered Sāriputra to go to the back hall and play the flute and drum for the populace. Hearing the music, the heretics all gathered in the back hall, and the Buddha was able to complete the service in the front hall. Be it in the age of the Buddha or the age of the deities, sarugaku encompasses the ultimate of beauty, the ultimate of good.

To Nobumitsu I said that the performance of music before the heavenly rock-cave is clearly recorded in the sacred book, and it is not for me to comment on it. What you say [about sarugaku tracing its source to the time of the Buddha] corresponds more or less to what is recorded in the *Kengukyō* in the chapter on Sudatta's construction of the Jetavana Vihāra hall. Sudatta arrived at the land of Sarasvati and went to various places in search for an appropriate site. Hearing of this, the six heretic groups conspired to mesmerize him with magic. Sāriputra declared that even if the six heretic groups were to fill this world, as numerous as bamboo, they would not be able to touch even one hair on his leg. Among the heretics was one who excelled in illusion. Before those assembled he changed into a dragon, an ox, and then into a *yaksa* demon. Sāriputra thereby made himself into a golden winged *garuda*, lion king, and finally Vaiśravana [Jp. Bishamon]. The heretics all retreated and acknowledged defeat. If one thinks about this, it is no different from the performer, entranced, taking on the form of a deity or a demon, a woman or a warrior. Also, when the *gandharva* visited the Buddha and played the seven-jeweled sitar, Sāriputra began to dance despite himself. This fits exactly what you said about sarugaku originating in the time of the Buddha!

The religious name (*hōmyō*) of Nobumitsu is Sōshō, and his religious title (*hōgō*) is Taiga. He asked me to record the origins of his art and the beginnings of his family. I therefore wrote the above and also appended an inscription, which says:

His beard and hair gray;
a frequent visitor to the government offices,
and regular guest at splendid banquets.
In the Qin dynasty, Youzhan
used his art to remonstrate with the emperor.
And in the present era,
it is he who embraces the aims of the
worthies of old.
Great elegance enhances the beauty
of the pine.

When he took nuptial vows a second time,
fifty-three then he was.
May the couple both live a long life!
And as is often said,
may the age-old Kanze troupe bring forth
   longevity through its performance!

History of the Kanze Troupe

One large part of the *Nobumitsu Portrait Inscription* is the history of the Kanze troupe and the origin of sarugaku noh, as the noh theater was known at that time. It is actually this emphasis on the various "histories" that marks the inscription's most salient feature. Nobumitsu was by no means the first person to explain the historical origin of the Kanze family and the noh theater. Zeami, in "Jingi ni iwaku" (Divine matters), a section in one of his treatises *Fūshikaden* too has a detailed description of the same subject matter.

The accounts of the two Kanze noh practitioners should be similar—referring to the same historical figures, events, and time period. However, there is a subtle difference in the definition of the Kanze lineage, the noh theater and consequently, the meaning of "performance." The Keijō/Nobumitsu account demonstrates a new relationship between the practitioners and their theater, constructed within a social discourse that had changed in a positive way for the genre. We can also see that the two noh practitioners, Zeami and Nobumitsu, separated by approximately one hundred years, convey their different fundamental perception of the sarugaku noh theater.[16] This was only possible before the establishment of a dominant majority discourse on the noh theater, which would preclude a space for contesting voices.

---

16. In his writings, Zeami wanted the genre to be a blessing for one and all, which is reminiscent of the genre's religious origin. Nobumitsu, on the other hand, wanted to emphasize the nature of performance and indirectly an affirmation of the performers' professional status.

Zeami's account introduces Kōkatsu, a mythical figure who was supposed to be a reincarnation of the first Chinese emperor Qin Shihuang (Shi Kōtei in Japanese), and who had helped Prince Shōtoku structure a performance repertoire that blessed the land. Zeami then presents the family lineage of Hada no Ujiyasu, who is believed to be the ancestor of the Konparu lineage, in the following light:

> ... The descendant to whom this Kōkatsu had transmitted the arts of *sarugaku* was Hada no Ujiyasu. It was he who performed the sixty-six pieces in the Shishinden Hall. At that time, the acting governor of Ki was a man of high intelligence. He was the husband of Ujiyasu's younger sister, and he performed *sarugaku* with him ...
>
> Counting from Hada no Ujiyasu, the line extends twenty-nine generations to its distant descendants, Mitsutarō and Konparu.[17]

The Enman'i troupe later developed into the Konparu troupe, which enjoys fame as the oldest sarugaku troupe. In the *Nobumitsu Portrait Inscription*, we see a similar description of the mythological past, including the Hada legend. However, the Hattori clan from which Kan'ami was said to have originated under the instruction of the divine oracle, is identified specifically as the ancestor of the Kanze troupe. Hada no Kōkatsu and his descendents are then demoted to be the "ordinary performers." Hada no Kōkatsu was actually mentioned in the *Nihonshoki* as the one who built the Hachioka temple to store the statues of Buddha that belonged to Prince Shōtoku. Kōkatsu's relationship with sarugaku was probably fabricated by later generations so as to establish a strong lineage for the genre.[18] Even though both Zeami and Nobumitsu stated that

---

17. Hare 2008, 50.
18. Omote and Katō 1974, 39.

Hada no Kōkatsu was the first person to perform sarugaku noh and that he was the ancestor of the Konparu troupe, they differed in their attitude toward this legendary figure.

Zeami often signed his name as Hada no Motokiyo, establishing a lineage with the legendary name. Ōwa Iwao traces the Hada lineage and its relationship with Zeami and concludes with three reasons why, unlike his father Kan'ami who signed his name as "Hattori," Zeami opted for Hada. First, Zeami's mother originally came from the Hada family, and Zeami had, for unknown reasons, decided to use this name. Second, Zeami's son-in-law Zenchiku was also a descendent of the Hada family. Last, one of the powerful patrons of sarugaku in the Yamato region belonged to the Hada family. In short, Ōwa contends that several important people in Zeami's life were related to the Hada family.[19] Historical validation of this argument aside, it is also important to consider the specific background from which Zeami was working. Zeami's attempt to establish the family lineage arose from the anxiety of a theatrical practitioner whose art form was still in the early stages of development, confronted with keen competition from both other troupes, for example, the Hie troupe in Ōmi as well as from other performance genres such as the dengaku. By identifying with the Hada family, Zeami could claim a more acceptable social and historical standing for his own Kanze troupe. During Zeami's time, the sarugaku noh theater was still treated as an entertainment form of the lower social class, and Zeami made every effort to eradicate this unfavorable image. Katō Shūichi calls Zeami's treatises "military strategies" (*senjutsu*) and argues that one of the reasons for Zeami to write treatises was as a strategy to ensure troupe survival.[20] Quinn, in her detailed account of the development of Zeami's treatises, also suggests competition as one of the motivating factors in Zeami's writings.[21]

---

19. Ōwa 1993, 453–471.
20. Omote and Katō 1974, 515–541.
21. Quinn 2005, chapter 1.

The *Nobumitsu Portrait Inscription*, however, distinctly differentiates the Hada clan from the Hattori clan, and identifies the latter as the ancestor of the Kanze troupe. It called the Konparu troupe "the ordinary performers," while referring to the Kanze lineage as "divine." This section in the *Nobumitsu Portrait Inscription* not only clearly portrays the keen competition between these two oldest sarugaku noh troupes in the Yamato region, it also contrasts Zeami's more amicable relationship with the Konparu troupe with Nobumitsu's more confrontational stand. Nobumitsu had reaped the fruit of what Zeami had sown. No longer needing to reaffirm the general status of the genre, Nobumitsu's main concern was to be better than the Konparu troupe, rather than identifying with it. It was therefore important to accentuate the superior quality of the Kanze troupe, in this case with a clever reference to divine powers.

What Does "Performance" Entail?

The last few sections of the *Nobumitsu Portrait Inscription* are examinations of the historical origin and significance of the concept of "performance" via the discussion of several texts that included Buddhist sutras and legendary accounts. Again, similar accounts are seen in Zeami's *Fūshikaden*. Zeami presented the same stories of how Amaterasu, the Sun Goddess, was lured out of hiding by songs and dance, as well as how the Bodhisattva Sharihotsu diminished the distractions created by the heretics during the Buddha's sermon.[22] He concludes his section in *Fūshikaden* by referring to a certain "*Sarugaku Ennen no Ki*" record attributed to Prince Shōtoku. In this record, Prince Shōtoku praises sarugaku because, among other things, it "will chase away evil affinities, and will call forth happiness, so that the country will remain in tranquility, bringing gentleness and long life to the people."[23]

---

22. Rimer and Yamazaki 1984, 31–32.
23. Ibid., 35.

This is one of several places where Zeami tried to convey the beneficial power of the sarugaku theater in his treatises.[24] This assertion, however, is again presented through an authoritative figure, Prince Shōtoku, and then reaffirmed by yet another political authority, Emperor Murakami (926–967). The purpose of evoking the imperial rulers is the same as the reason for identifying with the Hada family—to acquire a more prominent status through associating with important and well-known personas. Zeami conveys the greatness of sarugaku noh in order to convince his audience that this is an important genre.

Less than a century later, a much less self-conscious Nobumitsu no longer required an agent to propagate the greatness of the noh theater. He was able to directly address "performance" as an independent art form through ostensibly discussing Buddhist teachings. In paragraph eleven and twelve of the *Nobumitsu Portrait Inscription* we see Keijō's response to Nobumitsu's comments on sarugaku as having originated from the sun goddess Amaterasu's heavenly rock-cave episode. Keijō provides his own version of sarugaku's relationship with Buddhism by detailing an account from *Kengukyō*, a famous Buddhist sutra. The parallel mentioning of the Shinto tradition together with the Buddhist hints at the universality of sarugaku—that whatever kind of religious tradition it was, sarugaku noh (and by implication, performance) had an important role to fulfill. Performance helped to save the day and restore order to a potentially chaotic situation. This is seen when Amaterasu decided to hide herself in the rock-cave or when the Buddha was trying to preach. From this, the abstract notion of the mesmerizing power of performance (or sarugaku) as encompassing the "ultimate beauty" and "good" is illustrated with concrete examples. The enchanting illusory nature peculiar to performance resembles the way Kisei praises On'ami's performance in the *On'ami Portrait Inscription*. The different roles that On'ami took up enchanted all

---

24. Elsewhere he also emphasized how the genre will bring peace and happiness to the land, such as in "Ōgi ni iwaku," see Omote and Katō 1974, 45–46.

members of the audience and left them with a deep impression. He was so skillful that whatever character he played the audience saw only this character. And On'ami's performance was similar to the different kinds of metamorphoses that both the heretics and the Buddha assumed—each transformation was a close enough imitation that it fooled its opponent. Nobumitsu's monomane has subtly reminded one of the aesthetic difference in performance style between his father On'ami and Zeami. Zeami warns of the danger of fully imitating any character, and prioritizes grace and elegance before realistic portrayal. Nobumitsu's evaluation of a realistic imitation approach to performance reiterates his lines of the Kanze family's aesthetic preference in noh.

From a broader perspective, mimicry or monomane, one of the important features of performance, has been accorded a status equal to that of the acts of deities in holy texts. Comparing the art of performance with that of the necessary illusions to defeat the heretics signified the importance of the sarugaku noh theater and implied that it is not plebeian or trivial. Speaking from the position of a cultural elite, Keijō's comment is significant because it represents a general acceptance of the genre.

A discussion of performance is not complete without considering the performers. The phrase that describes Nobumitsu as one who established himself as a famous performer is "yū wo motte naru mono 以優鳴者." The word yū 優, in its earliest usage in the Heian literature, refers to an elegant aesthetic.[25] It is also used with another character, hai 俳, to refer to actors (俳優 haiyū or wazaogi), which is a compound word of Chinese origin. Although it has a generally demeaning implication in the Chinese context, haiyū nevertheless identifies a distinct category of people

25. "Yū," as a recognized category of premodern Japanese literature, was first used by the Heian court poet Fujiwara no Shunzei (1114–1204). Hisamatsu 1978 defined it as "perfect or ideal" in the Heian context and "graceful and refined" as "a term in literary aesthetics" (112). Konishi 1991 describes it as "refined charm" (55). The Tokugawa period scholar and politician Arai Hakuseki (1657–1725) also has a short essay called "Haiyūkō" compiled in his anthology, detailing the various historical usages of the term in China and Japan. See Arai 1907.

whose occupation is performance. Other terms in the *Nobumitsu Portrait Inscription* that are used to describe the skill of the noh artists include *yū* 優, *gi* 伎, and *gei* 芸, words that are understood to be identifying noh as a special skill.[26] Here, sarugaku noh performers become professionals in their own right, no longer attached to the Buddhist temples as in earlier times. By using these terms to describe the sarugaku noh performers Keijō has shown a heightened awareness of the performer's professional identity. This is in sharp contrast to the treatment of their predecessors before Zeami's time who were known as the *kawaramono*, or people of the riverbed. The social inferiority of Zeami when he was young arose from this Heian period prejudice.[27] In Nobumitsu's time, however, performing noh became a cultural pastime, as illustrated by the various groups of people learning noh, and summarized by Keijō in *Nobumitsu Picture Inscription*. Being a noh performer—be it chanting or dancing—became an indication of one's cultural achievement.

Naming the Genre

In addition to identifying with a family name that had a concrete and stronger historical appeal, Zeami also redefined the name of the theater as an effort to affirm the status of noh in his treatises. During Zeami's time noh was called *sarugaku*, which was originally written with the characters meaning "monkey" (*saru*) and "music" (*gaku*). The original form of sarugaku, as seen in Fujiwara no Akihira's (989–1066) *Shinsarugakuki*, was indeed playful and often lewd.[28] In order to rid the genre of this image, Zeami in *Fūshikaden*

26. *Yū* and *gi* refer to performance, *gei* is often used as a compound word to mean proficiency in certain kind of artistic or martial endeavor.
27. See Ortolani 1990 and Kōsai 1979 for more details on the social status of the sarugaku noh performers before the medieval period.
28. Believed to be written between 1058 and 1065, this is an account of a fictive family's visit to a local carnival written by the court scholar-official Fujiwara no Akihira. See Fujiwara 1983.

used the character *"mōsu,"* which was pronounced *"saru"* when used to refer to the zodiacal year. Zeami further attributed the invention of this new character to Prince Shōtoku:

> ... These were *kagura* performances, so with a view toward posterity, Prince Shōtoku took the graph *shin* from the word *kagura* and removed the radical, leaving only the phonetic element. Read in the context of the calendar, this element is pronounced *"saru,"* so Shōtoku named the performance *sarugaku* because it "gives voice to" (申) "enjoyment" (楽). This is also because it derives from *kagura*.[29]

In the *Nobumitsu Portrait Inscription*, Nobumitsu followed a somewhat similar schema as Zeami in the naming of the noh theater. However, he also made an additional reference to a Chinese classic, the *Shuowen* (説文 *Setsumon* in Japanese), which he used to argue that the name *saru* actually refers to "deity."[30] On top of engaging political figures such as Prince Shōtoku, Nobumitsu refers to a text closely related to the institution of Chinese learning to give further legitimacy to his profession. This is not only an indication of the level of Chinese knowledge Keijō the Gozan prelate and Nobumitsu the noh practitioner both have, it can also be read as a gesture to share a common notion easily identifiable with the cultural elites of his time. Whereas Zeami used the mysterious and often divine accounts to explain the name

---

29. Hare 2008, 49.

30. This text was popular among the intellectuals of the Muromachi and Tokugawa periods. Completed around 100 CE, *Shuowen Jiezi* was compiled by Xu Sheng (*Kyoshin* in Japanese, 30?–124?) of the Eastern Han period. This fifteen-volume work is the earliest Chinese "dictionary" that systematically discussed and categorized Chinese characters. Xu proposed the *liushu* 六書 (*rikusho* in Japanese)—six types of character composition theory—to explain Chinese characters. These six categories are: indicative (*zhishi*), pictographic (*xiangxing*), associative (*huiyi*), picto-phonetic (*xingsheng*), notative (*zhuanzhu*), and loan characters (*jiajie*). Wilkinson 2000.

of his theater, Nobumitsu chose to relate the name of the genre to the Chinese classics, appealing to the intellectuals or the cultural elite who were familiar with the text. By referring to a Chinese classic, Nobumitsu was also able to demonstrate that he possessed cultural assets shared by other social elites.

More Than a Portrait Inscription

Even though we see traces of influence from two earlier texts— On'ami's portrait inscription and Zeami's *Jingi ni Iwaku*, the *Nobumitsu Portrait Inscription* is not merely a record of the personal history of its subject like its predecessors. A historical account of the Kanze troupe is presented to imply a more independent troupe identity; descriptions of the power and functions of performance—and by implication, noh—is illustrated with references to religious texts. The actual making of the portrait and its inscription, as well as the presence of the voices of the author Keijō and its subject Nobumitsu are all indicative of the reception and presentation of the noh theater in the late Muromachi period. In the following chapter I focus on the life and work of Nobumitsu, again engaging the broader historical background of his and his predecessors' time to see how sociohistorical elements interacted with the noh practitioner's life and compositions.

Chapter Two

NOBUMITSU

LIFE, CAREER, AND THE KANZE FAMILY

The analysis of the *Nobumitsu Portrait Inscription* in the last chapter provides insights into the intricate relationship between a noh performer and a Zen prelate—each representative of his own professional career and social circle. In this chapter I examine how the larger social and political background of the time function in the discursive construct of the *Nobumitsu Portrait Inscription*. I start with a discussion of the legacies of Nobumitsu's predecessors, situating the narrative within its specific historical context. The second half of the chapter focuses more on Nobumitsu and his noh plays—both as prefatory notes to the following chapters as well as a transitional narrative that brings our attention from the macro-level late Muromachi period (which has been the center of attention in this book so far) to its most important representative noh practitioner.

The Performer Who Came to Party

The main text (verse section) of the *Nobumitsu Portrait Inscription* summarizes Kanze Kojirō Nobumitsu's life and work in the regular metric verse style after the long "free prose" narrative. Written in *kanbun*, the classical Chinese–style writing, this part of the inscription is similar in format and content to the many other portraiture inscriptions composed during the medieval period. The emphasis on parallel structure and word play as well as the laudatory nature of the paragraph portray a man with a successful career and respectable social status. This last section of the inscription adheres most closely to the standard portraiture inscriptions found in the Gozan anthologies. Here, Nobumitsu is depicted as an honored guest at important occasions, and is alluded to an ancient Chinese figure who was courageous enough to put the benefit of the land before his own life—one virtue that qualified him as a sage.

Any reader who does not have previous knowledge of the subject of the inscription might wonder who this elegant elderly man was who befriended the socially important and powerful and who seemed to have a strong moral appeal. Other than the references to the ancient Chinese court performer Youzhan and to the Kanze troupe, it is difficult to associate the subject of the portraiture with a sarugaku noh *performer*, which during that time was a profession usually considered as belonging to the lower social classes. One illuminating example will be the portrait inscription of the dengaku performer Zōami, in which his performance was described as a form of "trivial art." Zōami was believed to be a little younger than Zeami, and he was described in his treatises as a good performer. It was at a time when dengaku still played an influential role in sarugaku, and when neither genre was well accepted as in later times. It is therefore not surprising to see a less positive evaluation of Zōami and the theatrical genre he represented.[1]

---

1. See Amano 2000, who introduces two portrait inscriptions of Zōami in his article, "Goyō yakusha Zōami wo torimaku kankyō: futatsu no *Zōami Gazōsan*." Zōami was patronized by the Ashikaga shogun Yoshimochi. Portraits of the two inscriptions are lost, but the inscriptions can be found in the anthologies of the writers. Amano deduces that the inscription was commanded by the Ashikaga shogun Yoshimochi, and that at that point in time dengaku and sarugaku were trivialized, reminiscent of Zeami's being called a "beggar child," and thus the "trivia art" comment. In other words, during this time dengaku and sarugaku were treated as socially inferior. Also see Ortolani 1990, 80–81.

Nobumitsu, however, had crossed the social boundary that often defined the status of performers in earlier times, and participated as an active member of the various elite intellectual circles, especially in the later part of his life. Not many historical records detail his participation in the cultural sphere of the social intelligentsia and elite, although the glimpses provided from historical documents such as diary records and temple accounts often back up what Keijō, the author of the portrait inscription, has presented. Nobumitsu's interactions with the Zen prelates or court elites were centered on sarugaku noh, including exchanges of views on noh artifacts such as masks, or views on noh chanting or composition. In other words, Nobumitsu the noh performer and the genre he represented had become part of the cultural life of the elite social circles. Not only had Nobumitsu assimilated himself into the social circles of the cultural elites but, in his noh plays too, he had created works that presented a different emphasis from those of the generation before him: including an expansion of the use of roles, an innovative use of play structure, and a more diverse set of sources from which plays were composed.

Fame and Awards

Nobumitsu's earliest recorded performance took place when he was about ten, at the Imperial Palace before the cloistered emperor Go-Hanazono (1419–1470, reigned 1428–1464). At this occasion Nobumitsu met Ashikaga Yoshimasa (1436–1490, reigned 1449–1473), the eighth shogun, who would become a critical patron of the Kanze troupe in the years to come. Nobumitsu put on an extremely good show; Go-Hanazono was so impressed by the youth's performance that he rewarded Nobumitsu with his fan. This event, described in the *Nobumitsu Portrait Inscription* as "an extreme honor that supersedes all things" aptly marked the beginning of Nobumitsu's performance career.

This reward from the cloistered emperor became an important source of status for Nobumitsu as a noh practitioner because of his ambiguous position in the Kanze troupe. He was never the official troupe leader like his father or elder brother, but had actually represented and managed the Kanze troupe for many years. The repeated emphasis in various texts on a reward from the emperor via the hands of the shogun serves as a way to justify Nobumitsu's leadership position in the Kanze troupe. Judging from entries in such documents as *Sanetaka Kōki* (Diary of Sanetaka) and *Inryōken Nichiroku* (The Inryōken journal), Nobumitsu was undoubtedly the most famous figure in the Kanze troupe during his time—probably more popular, even, than the official troupe leaders. But since he was fulfilling a position that was officially not his, there was a need to provide more evidence of his talents in order to legitimize his de facto leadership.

Another significant event that reaffirmed Nobumitsu's fame as a talented noh actor was his receipt of a gift from someone from China's Ming dynasty.[2] Since Ashikaga Takauji, the first Ashikaga shogun, started an official trade relationship with the Ming dynasty in the early 1300s, communication between Ming China and Japan increased, though not without some interruptions. The diplomatic relationship reached a peak when Yoshimitsu started sending envoys to China again in 1401 (first year of Ōei). Many Chinese cultural artifacts, books, and paintings, as well as religious ideas were imported from Ming China. Exchanges between Japan and China of religious personnel and texts also occurred during this period.

The gift Nobumitsu received was a piece of calligraphy lauding his excellent performance. The characters on it were *saika*, literally, "moved the flowers to bloom." Kōsai Tsutomu and Omote Akira traced the term to the tale of the Tang emperor Gensō (Xuanzhong in Chinese) beating a famous drum, the *Kakko*, on a spring day. His drumming was so beautiful that all

---

2. The Ming dynasty was established in 1368 and lasted until 1644. Ashikaga Yoshimitsu (1358-1408) initiated several transactions with Ming China and at one point subordinated Japan as a subject to the Ming government. See Imatania and Kozo 1992.

the spring flowers started to bloom.[3] Neither Kōsai nor Omote suggested any direct relationship between this tale and the calligraphy piece that Nobumitsu received, but the implication is clear: Nobumitsu's drumming skill was comparable to that of the Chinese emperor.

The calligraphy piece has a caption that also serves as a signature: "Inscribed for Kanze Kojirō of Japan by Yūbai from the land of the Great Ming." There is nothing else, not even a date, on this piece. Yūbai's identity will most likely never be confirmed, although by association, the name Great Ming indicates that Yūbai must be someone from Ming China. Another document, *Nōhonsakusha Chūmon* (An index of noh composers) provides yet another clue:

> Before long his fame as an expert performer
> in *ratsubu* dance had reached the Great Ming,
> and someone by the name of Yūbai sent a piece
> of calligraphy to Japan in praise of Nobumitsu.[4]

Yūbai is a common name for Zen monks. For example, Sesshun Yūbai (1290–1346) was a famous Japanese Zen monk from the Gozan tradition. However, he cannot be the creator of this calligraphy piece because Sesshun lived in a different era. Also, the name Yūbai in the piece is preceded by "Great Ming," and Nobumitsu was identified specifically as "Kanze Kojirō of Japan."

The origin of this gift, like several other issues in Nobumitsu's life, will remain a mystery. But one may conjecture that it could be something commissioned by a fan of Nobumitsu—probably a person who had good relationship with a Chinese Zen monk. One other possible explanation of Yūbai's identity could be that he was a Chinese Zen prelate who had heard of Nobumitsu's performance skill from his Japanese counterpart and sent the praise. It is also

---

3. Kōsai 1979, 212–213.
4. See *Shizayakusha Mokuroku*, Tanaka Makoto 1955, 9, for the source of this citation. *Ratsubu* (乱舞) is the name of a dance style which was practiced by Kan'ami and his peers. Yokomichi et al. (III) 1987, 121.

not unlikely that Yūbai actually lived in Japan and had witnessed and was mesmerized by Nobumitsu's performance. But whoever Yūbai was, the significance of the gift lies in the recognition of Nobumitsu as such an excellent performer that even someone from so far away as China would send a compliment. It also, yet again, reaffirms Nobumitsu as the noh performer par excellence.

Nobumitsu and His Family Lineage

Nobumitsu was closely related to the two arguably most important figures in noh history. His grandfather, Kanze Shirō (?–?), was the younger brother of Zeami Motokiyo (1363–1443). Nobumitsu's father, Motoshige Saburō (1398–1467) (who later adopted the better-known religious name On'ami), was said to be a great performer and once an adopted son of Zeami. But the situation changed for Motoshige when Zeami had his own children and when On'ami began to establish his own style of performance. Much tension and competition stemming from different aesthetic ideals that spilled over into patronage and succession issues existed between the Zeami and On'ami branches of the Kanze family.[5]

Whatever relationship Zeami and On'ami had, later generations remember these two sarugaku performers in a very different light: Zeami was an outstanding performer, but it was his treatises that had substantially influenced the direction of the development of noh. On'ami, as we will remember from his portrait inscription, was reputed to be an extremely captivating actor, most famous for his monomane style—loosely translated as "mimicry" or "imitation."[6] Unfortunately, this style has been mostly lost owing

5. See, for example, Dōmoto 1986, 470–494; and Quinn 2005, 39–42, for accounts of the relationship between the two Kanze families.
6. Zeami explains *monomane* in *Fushikaden*: "It is impossible to write about all the types of dramatic imitation. All the same, since it is of utmost importance to this vocation, you should take great care in this regard. Now, the main point is to present a comprehensive likeness of the object portrayed. But be clear on this: the degree to which imitation is appropriate depends on the object of imitation." Also

to a lack of systematic written documentation. While later generations were able to acquire a better understanding of Zeami's yūgen
noh thanks to his prolific writings and his father Kan'ami's plays
and performance style, On'ami's monomane can only be imagined,
based on historical documents, as simply a very popular style that
focused on character presentations. For instance, On'ami's first
performance at the Kiyotaki Shrine in 1434 (Eikyō 5) was described in *Mansai Juggō Nikki* (The diary of High Priest Mansai) as
"marvelous."[7] Other diarists also gave high praise to On'ami's performance in their writings. As discussed in the last chapter, On'ami
was such an extraordinary performer that the portrait inscription
of his son, Nobumitsu, devotes its first paragraph to an appraisal of
his performance.[8]

    Like most of the famous performers around his time, Inuō
(犬王   ?–?) and Icchū (一忠   ?–1413), for example, On'ami left
virtually no written work—plays or treatises—behind. The only
record that associates any noh play with On'ami is the *Nōhon
Sakusha Chūmon* (An index of noh composers) which attributed
the play *Sumiyoshi* (Sumiyoshi) to On'ami. Unfortunately, the play
is no longer performed and not much is known about it.

    On'ami became the third *tayū* (official leader) of the Kanze
troupe in the fourth year of Eikyō (1433), one year after the sixth
Ashikaga shogun Yoshinori (1394–1441) bestowed upon him the
position of Music Director (gakutō 楽頭) of Kiyotaki Shrine. To
celebrate the occasion, the Kanze troupe staged a subscription
noh performance (*kanjin nō*) at the riverbed of Tadasugawara the
following year. This was an enormous celebratory event believed to
have been been organized under Yoshinori's instruction. Physical
preparations for the event took two weeks to complete, with the
construction of sixty-two temporary viewing galleries. Other than
the commoners, the three-day performance was attended by the

---

see footnote 45 for more elaboration of the term. Hare 2008, 31.

    7. Mansai (1376–1435) was a high priest at the Daigoji Temple in Kyoto and an
important consultant to Ashikaga Yoshimitsu. His comments on On'ami are cited
in Nose 1938, 728–729, 774–775.

    8. See Nose 1938, 770–794, and Takemoto 2003, on the career of On'ami.

Ashikaga shogun and high-ranking court officials, as well as by members of the military quarters and religious institutions.[9] This performance was the pinnacle of On'ami's sarugaku noh career, and probably also an important time for the genre, as On'ami's aesthetic style was clearly well received by his military patrons and the general audience.

Nobumitsu was born two years after On'ami became the Kanze leader, around 1435.[10] Being the youngest of seven children is a reason often cited to account for his not inheriting the official leadership of the Kanze troupe, despite the promising talent he demonstrated from an early age. According to the *Nobumitsu Portrait Inscription*, Nobumitsu declined the position of troupe leader and specialized in drumming instead of learning to perform shite roles. He was identified as a stick drum player in *Shiza Yakusha Mokuroku*, implying that his "official" performance role in his earlier days was probably playing the stick drum.[11] The correlation between the troupe leadership and any designated role type during this period is unclear. The specialization of individual roles was certainly not as rigid as it is today, although during the medieval period most of the troupe leaders were trained to play shite roles, since the shite usually plays the protagonist who

---

9. Nose 1972, 774.

10. This birth date, calculated and presented by the noh researcher Kobayashi Shizuo (1909–1945) (Kobayashi 1942, 195–219), was challenged by noh historian Omote Akira. In a two-part article, Omote 1999 argued that Nobumitsu was born twenty-five years later than Kobayashi postulated. Omote based his arguments on various deductions from historical records, exactly the same method by which Kobayashi arrived at his calculation. In this sense, the birth date of Nobumitsu will always remain moot, although Kobayashi's argument seems more convincing to me. For instance, Nobumitsu's earliest noh play *Hoshi* was recorded as written around 1453, when he was eighteen. Based on Omote's calculation the play would have been written before Nobumitsu was actually born. On'ami's eldest son Masamori, whose birth date was unknown, died in 1470, in his forties. If Nobumitsu had been born in 1450, he would be about twenty years younger than his eldest brother. Even though there are five other siblings in between the two, a gap of twenty years seems less likely than a gap of ten.

11. Tanaka 1955, 7–8.

has the largest share in singing and dancing in a play.[12] In earlier generations of the Kanze family, eldest sons inherited the position of tayū, or troupe leader. Motomasa, Zeami's eldest son, was the troupe leader until his untimely death. On'ami then became the Kanze tayū, succeeded by his eldest son Matasaburō Masamori (?–1470). This practice continued into later generations.[13]

Masamori, Nobumitsu's Eldest Brother

At one time, On'ami and his sons Masamori and Nobumitsu were all actively performing. The historical record *Unjō Sangaku Kaien* (Sangaku performance and banquet in the court) details two occasions at the court that had the trio performing together. [14] The image of the enchanting actor On'ami performing with his two sons, who each specialized in different roles, conjures up a picture of the prosperous Kanze branch supported by the military rulers, who preferred On'ami's monomane approach over Zeami's music-oriented approach. Nobumitsu, though famous as a drum player at the beginning of his career, was a keen disciple of his father. His talent in performance was revealed to the world when in later life he often took up the waki and shite roles and won great acclaim for both. In other words, Nobumitsu was a versatile noh practitioner who was both an actor and a musician.

Nobumitsu's eldest brother, Matasaburō Masamori, on the other hand, specialized as a shite performer. His birth date is not

---

12. Some plays, as I will discuss later, attribute a smaller amount of stage time to the shite role, although it is nevertheless still a very important part in the entire play. On present-day noh stage, another well-known role of the shite is the *kōken* (stage assistant). The kōken's duty is to oversee the entire performance, ensure its smooth running, and be ready to take over any role whenever necessary, but this function only started during the Tokugawa period. Before that it was the *ai-kyōgen* who managed the stage. See Oda 1987, 98–104.

13. See Appendix 5 for a list of successive generations of troupe leaders.

14. Cited in Nose 1972, 785–789. *Unjō Sangaku Kaien* was edited by the fifteenth Kanze troupe leader Motoakira (1722–1774). The document is housed at the Institute of Nogaku Studies at Hōsei University, Tokyo.

clear, though it is postulated to be around the late 1420s. Masamori succeeded On'ami as the next Kanze tayū when On'ami turned sixty and took the tonsure. At that time the retired tayū and former troupe leader changed his name from Kanze Saburō to On'ami, a name in honor both of Kan'ami and Zeami. By putting together the first character of each of their names, the word "Kanzeon" (世音)—the Goddess of Mercy, is formed. Some commentators called this an illustration of On'ami's arrogance. Arrogance or not, this was undoubtedly a clear indication of On'ami's successful career, as well as that of his branch of the Kanze family. After his retirement, On'ami was able to concentrate fully on performance. Not only did he receive constant praise from his audience, but his presence was also advantageous in enhancing patronage for the Kanze troupe. The new troupe leader Masamori's name appeared together with On'ami in various important performances at both the military quarters and the temples. There were compliments for Masamori's performance, but his fame as a noh performer never reached the heights of his father's or brother's.

On'ami died in 1467, the year the Ōnin War (1467–1477) broke out. This civil war, which was triggered directly by a succession dispute of the Ashikaga family, was indicative of the weakening status of the Ashikaga shogunate. Individual warlords participated in this civil war, making allies and attempting to expand their political and financial power. Communication between the capital, Kyoto, and the provinces—often including the manors (shōen) belonging to the aristocrats—was often disrupted. The financial situation of the court nobles therefore grew worse as time went by. Although they did not stop organizing cultural activities such as poetry meetings or attending sarugaku noh performances in the court or at their residences, they did so less frequently and less lavishly.[15]

The imperial court was not the only victim of the civil war. The religious institutions, which had been the major patrons of

---

15. See Haga 1960, 90, for accounts of the court nobles and their lives during this war. Also see Berry 1994 for accounts of life in Kyoto during this time.

sarugaku troupes, were also adversely affected. The sources of traditional financial support of the noh troupes were thus critically challenged. In Kan'ami and Zeami's times, the Kanze troupe sometimes traveled from Nara where they were based to the capital Kyoto and its vicinity for performances.[16] At times some troupes had to flee even further away from the capital and its environs to avoid the war, and it was during these brief sojourns to the provinces that they were exposed to elements that later manifested themselves in the noh dramaturgy. Unfortunately, no concrete records detailing the troupes' travels in the provinces have been found—not surprising at a time when warfare and arson reigned, although one finds occasional references to troupes' visits to the provinces in diaries or temple records.[17]

It would be a misconception to imagine, however, a war-torn capital where life came to a standstill. Various records show that the noh troupes, like the court elite who continued with their cultural pursuits, still performed at military headquarters and at temples and shrines, though not as frequently. It was during one of these performances that Nobumitsu's eldest brother Masamori suddenly died. The *Daijōin Jijazōjiki* (Miscellaneous records by the regent priest of Kōfuku Temple, 1450–1508) described the incident as follows:

> There was a sarugaku performance at the Muromachi shogun's residence. Kanze Matasaburō was rewarded with plenty of treasure, in addition to expensive fabric. After the noh performance he returned to his quarters and passed away. A sudden death. What an unfortunate occurrence. They said it was a punishment from the formidable Deity.[18]

16. Quinn 2005, 28–29.
17. For instance, Sanjōnishi Sanetaka recorded receiving a gift from Nagatoshi after the latter returned from a visit to Izu in the first month of the third year of Tenmon (1534; *Sanetaka Kōki*). Also see Geinōshi 1993, 21–22, on exchanges between the provinces and the capital.
18. Cited in Nose 1972, 795.

People believed that Masamori's inexplicable death was related to the wrath of the great deity (Kasuga Daimyōjin) at Kasuga Shrine.[19] The diarist and scholar-monk Jinson (1430–1508), who was also the head priest of Kōfukuji Temple and son of the court official Ichijō Kaneyoshi (1402–1481), expressed his dismay at the fact that in recent years noh performers had been neglecting their duties and focusing only on material gain. From today's point of view Masamori's death could simply have been caused by heart failure, but popular belief at the time was that the military rulers and the court elite were rewarding the noh performers too handsomely, and there was something unsettling about this state of affairs. The accusation was somehow reminiscent of the infamous entry from an earlier period in *Gogumaiki*, in which Zeami was compared with a beggar child, though now it took the loss of a life under mysterious circumstances to engender a critical view of a noh performer.[20] This incident and people's reactions to it hint at the elite courtier's latent and ambivalent attitude toward the sarugaku troupe. Although their popularity was much higher than in earlier times, when challenged by extraordinary occurrences, the performers and their troupes were still placed under strict scrutiny.

Even though he was the official troupe leader, Masamori was never as famous as his brother Nobumitsu, because of his premature death and the fact that he did not leave behind any noh plays or treatises. As a noh performer, Masamori did receive some praise but as he often performed with On'ami he was overshadowed by his father. The many entries in medieval documents that recorded his performances paid more attention

---

19. The Kasuga Daimyōjin is the key patronage deity of sarugaku noh in the Yamato area. The Kasuga Shrine and Kōfuku Temple (Kōfukuji) were closely related during the medieval period and were the most important patrons of sarugaku noh, especially before Yoshimitsu's time. See Omote 1995, 41.

20. Sanjō Kintada (1324–1383) showed his exasperation when he described in his diary, *Gogumaiki* (後愚昧記), how a certain sarugaku noh child performer had become the military leader's favorite. Kintada considered sarugaku noh "the occupation of beggars." See Sanjō 1984, 267.

to On'ami, leaving behind a less distinct image of Masamori. He died when Nobumitsu was in his mid-thirties. Sandwiched between his father and his talented younger brother, there is very little for later generations to remember of Masamori. Even in *Shiza Yakusha Mokuroku*, the historical record that was compiled closest to his time, one finds only a two-phrase description that identifies Masamori as On'ami's son and Nobumitsu's brother.[21]

Masamori did leave behind a young heir for the Kanze troupe, Yukishige (?–1500). Because this designated leader was very young, and because Nobumitsu was the most outstanding performer in the Kanze troupe and probably an excellent leader himself, he assumed leadership of the troupe without ever becoming the official troupe leader. He did take up the title of *gonnogami*, although scholars have different interpretations on what the term really mean.[22] Masamori's son Yukishige had a relatively smooth career thanks to Nobumitsu. But like his father, Yukishige also died at an early age. Nobumitsu's son, Yajirō Nagatoshi (1488–1541), reputedly repeated his father's role in assisting Yukishige's young successor although the two branches of the family began to drift apart around this time.

The Civil War and Its Aftermath

Masamori died at a time when the Kanze troupe faced one of its most difficult periods. Social unrest triggered by the outbreak of the Ōnin War put the traditional patrons—the religious institutions and the military houses—in limbo. As mentioned earlier, the military leaders and shrines had not altogether stopped sponsoring noh performances, but the schedule of such

---

21. Tanaka 1955, 31.
22. The term *gonnogami* seemed to be a regular title used in noh troupes. It originally referred to some higher-ranking personnel involved in a religious ceremony that performed "Okina." Although it is understood that Nobumitsu was the de facto leader of the Kanze troupe, the precise meaning of the title remains unclear.

performance opportunities became irregular, and the scale of performances was reduced. One way for the troupes to ensure their survival was to expand beyond the usual territory around the Kyoto area and go to the provinces.

This expansion would have occurred one way or another when the genre reached a certain stage of development or when the audiences from the provinces began to become interested in noh performance. But the outbreak of the war forced the troupes to seek alternative sources of revenue, and this turned out to be fruitful in terms of new sources of income as well as in finding new subject matter for new plays. Yamanaka argues that with more interaction between Kyoto and the provinces, the city dwellers grew to become even more interested in the provinces. This kind of interest is reflected in some of the noh plays composed during this time.[23]

Without written documentation one can only speculate which plays have features that were not found in plays produced earlier, such as a locale that is not related to the established literary conventions before Nobumitsu's time, or depiction of subject matter that includes customs and practices of faraway provinces. Some scholars postulate that Nobumitsu's play *Momijigari* (Autumn excursion) is one of the products of this interaction between the capital and the provinces. The play takes place on Mt. Togakushi—a mountain in present-day Nagano Prefecture where the legend of Koremochi's slaying of the female demon originated.[24] It is possible that Nobumitsu learned of this story during his troupe's visits to the province in Ōshū and developed it into a play. Two other Nobumitsu plays, both no longer performed, that take place outside the familiar geographical landscape within the poetic convention of noh are *Hikami* (The Hikami River), set in Mutsu (modern Aomori and Iwate region), and *Kameyama* (Kameyama), set in Sanuki, present-day Shikoku.

It is important to note that the Kanze troupe was not the

23. Yamanaka 1998, 144–167.
24. Komatsu 2004, 58–63.

only one to travel between the Yamato area and the provinces. Practitioners from other troupes and in other artistic genres, such as *renga* (linked verse), also went beyond their usual geographical boundaries as a means for survival in a difficult time. This went two ways: not only did performers and artists travel but we also find records of wealthy provincial rulers visiting the capital and learning about the cultural activities of Kyoto.[25]

Around this time, another untimely death occurred within the Kanze troupe—that of the waki actor Torakiku. This further aggravated the crisis that confronted the troupe. Although Nobumitsu, the versatile performer, could have taken up the waki role after Torakiku's death, the lack of a designated performer was still a great strain. The problem was eventually resolved when the Ashikaga shogun Yoshimasa commanded two Konparu waki performers, Hie Genshirō and Morikiku Yashichirō, to join the Kanze troupe. This move was a welcome one for Nobumitsu and his troupe, but it also worsened the antagonistic relationship between the Kanze and Konparu families. As scholars such as Ishii and Quinn have observed, the Konparu leader Zenpō's sense of rivalry toward Nobumitsu can be detected in the plays that he composed as well as in his comments on the latter's work. The dynamics between the two troupes took a more positive turn only when Konparu Zenpō's daughter married the next Kanze troupe leader during Nobumitsu's son Nagatoshi's time.[26]

After the Civil War

Commanding actors from another troupe to shore up the Kanze performers was not the only favor Yoshimasa bestowed on the Kanze troupe. One year after the Ōnin War ended, he sponsored a large-scale subscription noh performance at the Seiganji temple

25. For instance, Sanjōnishi Sanetaka recorded in his diary that there were visitors from the provinces who were surprisingly proficient in matters related to *renga*. Cited in Haga 1960, 67–68.

26. See Ishii 1998, Chs. 1 and 2; Yokomichi et al. 1987, 280; Quinn 2005, 39–42.

in Kyoto. This was a great boost for the Kanze troupe, which was struggling to recover from the destructive effects of the civil war. And following Yoshimasa's lead, his wife Hino Tomiko (1440–1496) continued to patronize noh even after his death and when their son Yoshihisa (1465–1489; shogun: 1473–1489) became the ninth shogun.

The Kanze troupe recovered from the shock of the civil war in an impressive manner. After the performance of the subscription noh at Seiganji, they were able to secure additional performance opportunities. Nobumitsu continued to play the role of the troupe leader and was also an active member in the elite cultural circles, which included members such as the court official Sanjōnishi Sanetaka and other Gozan Zen monks. Interacting with these members probably secured more performance opportunities for the Kanze troupe. In the ninth month of the third year of Bunki (1503), for instance, Nobumitsu performed a noh play by Sanetaka at the Ashikaga shogun's residence.[27]

Meanwhile, civil unrest continued to plague Japan. New power centers occupied by smaller warlords began to develop, as well as new kinds of trades and professions. Members of these new social groups proved to be the new patrons of the noh theater, not just simply attending the performances, but also becoming ardent students of the genre. This trend became clearer during Konparu Zenpō's time, as we can tell from many of his treatises dedicated to a much wider, enthusiastic audience. Again, without written documents, it is hard to discern if, like Zenpō, Nobumitsu had amateur disciples. It is revealing, however, that there were intelligentsia like Sanetaka who became friendly with Nobumitsu and other noh performers and had composed plays that were performed at official functions held at the Ashikaga shogun's residence. Other members of the cultural elite who participated actively in the practice, and at times composition, of noh included *renga* master Ichijō Kaneyoshi (1402–1481) and Takeda Hōin

---

27. Elsewhere I have discussed the significance of this kind of social interaction between noh practitioners and court elites. See Lim 2004.

Jōsei (1421–1508).[28] The sarugaku noh theater by this time had acquired the status of a genuine cultural asset.

In addition to the major noh troupes in the Yamato area, many smaller semiprofessional groups and some individuals also performed sarugaku noh during the late Muromachi period. For instance, in the seventh year of Kanshō (1466), female sarugaku noh performers were invited by Yoshimasa to his residence to perform.[29] Other individual performers who claimed to be amateurs were considered just as skillful as members of the major sarugaku noh troupes. Many factors encouraged the aristocrats and military houses to engage these performers, including a smaller remuneration and a smaller-scale of performance. It was within such a competitive and complex environment that Nobumitsu remained the pillar of the Kanze troupe until the young leader, Yukishige, came of age.

Nobumitsu's Later Life

Nobumitsu remarried in his fifties. This second marriage was first mentioned in the *Nobumitsu Portrait Inscription*, stating his age to be fifty-three. No information is available regarding his first marriage. We do know from the *Nobumitsu Portrait Inscription*, however, that Nobumitsu had three male children from his second marriage. And like most women related to noh (as in premodern historical texts in general), the identities of both Nobumitsu's first and second wives are unknown. It is also not clear if he had any daughters. Women entered historical texts mainly when they enjoyed extraordinary political power, like Ashikaga Yoshimasa's wife Hino Tomiko, or more commonly, if a nuptial relationship was involved.

In the noh world, marriage arrangements among the various

28. See Yokomichi et al. 1987, 292–295, for a brief introduction of these elite practitioners.
29. Sakurai 2001, 233–234.

troupes were common. Examples include Konparu Zenchiku (1405–1470), who became Zeami's son-in-law. The eighth generation Kanze tayū, Motohiro Dōgen (?–1550?), married Konparu Zenpō's daughter. A member of the Kongō family married the daughter of the Hōshō tayū. Relationships formed through marriage were a form of convenience in the guise of social liaison, as they often were in previous eras and continued to remain so in other sectors of society, such as among the military leaders and court nobility. In earlier times, Zeami had transmitted some of his treatises to Zenchiku, and after Kanze Motohiro Dōgen married Konparu Zenpō's daughter, the earlier friction between the two troupes eased and more combined performances were staged.[30] Meanwhile, the women in most cases remained anonymous.

The three sons from Nobumitsu's second marriage, Yajirō Nagatoshi (1488–1541), Matajirō Nobushige (?–?), and Yasaburō Mototomo (?–1529?), are better documented.[31] All three were trained to be noh practitioners; the first two children took up acting, while the youngest son, Yasaburō, specialized in drumming. Nobumitsu no doubt had a profound influence on his children, especially on the eldest son, Nagatoshi. Nagatoshi composed many noh plays, some of which resembled his father's works, while others were in a style that differed greatly from any noh plays before his time. Although there are more than twenty plays attributed to Nagatoshi, only about five are still performed today.[32] One common characteristic that can be found in Nagatoshi's plays is large cast of characters, which often confused the functions of designated role types. The commentary on *Kasui*, a play in the anthology *Yōkyokushū*, summarizes the characteristic of this play as "its extremely large number of characters would probably create

30. Nose 1972, 831.

31. Birth and death dates are from Tanaka 1955.

32. Different anthologies identify different plays as remaining in the contemporary repertoire so there seems to be no consensus. The major plays that are attributed to Nagatoshi include: *Ōshiro, Shōzon, Chikatō, Rinzō,* and *Kazui.* See Yokomichi 1987.

confusion on a normal noh stage."[33] If one were to argue that there is a legacy as a noh composer that Nobumitsu has passed on to his son, it would have to be the penchant of composing plays with large casts and, by association, dramatic narrative. However, one can only claim it to be a partial legacy because the relatively "experimental" nature of Nagatoshi's plays crossed the subtle line of the recognizable limits of the genre, and it is exactly in this respect that we see the significance of Nobumitsu as both a noh actor and composer. Nobumitsu was able to experiment with different kinds of creative approaches in noh composition but never transgressed beyond the defining features of the genre.

Like his father On'ami, Nobumitsu's skill in performance improved as he aged. During different times in his life Nobumitsu's name was connected with different roles, the most famous being the spirit of the willow tree in *Yugyō Yanagi* (The willow tree and the priest) which is discussed in detail in Chapter Five. The play, believed to be his last and commonly held to be one of his best, features an old man who is the spirit of an ancient willow tree. Nobumitsu performed this role when he was in his eighties and again won wide acclaim for his finesse. In one sense, this is reminiscent of his father, On'ami, whose advanced age contributed to rather than impaired his performance skill.

Although Nobumitsu excelled as a troupe manager, a captivating performer, and a prolific playwright, what seems to be lacking in his credentials is the presence of treatises. By the time he died, Nobumitsu had only a surprisingly small number of treatises to his name, unlike his predecessors Zeami and Zenchiku. There are two known treatiselike works by Nobumitsu, the *Koetsukaukoto* (On singing, 1511)[34] and *Kanze Kojirō Gonnogami Densho* (The

---

33. Four Nagatoshi plays are included in this anthology. The commentaries on these plays highlight the main characteristics of these works, including the emphasis on visual elements such as dances and the use of props, and the attribution of equal dramatic significance to the different roles. See Yokomichi and Omote, 1960–1963, vol. 2, 195.

34. See Omote 1972, 566–570, for a transcription and discussion of the text.

teaching of Kanze Kojirō Gonnogami, 1492).[35] The former is an extremely short discussion on methods of manipulating fans and ways of singing, while the latter is on the teaching of drumming. It is also important to note that rather than a philosophical contemplation of what noh performance means, these two short writings are basically manuals for anyone who would like to improve their performance skill in specific aspects of the genre. In a sense these two short treatises share a similar characteristic with *Zenpō Zōdan* (Miscellaneous comments of Zenpō), a treatiselike compilation of teachings by Konparu Zenpō.[36] Zenpō's work discusses various aspects of noh ranging from subject matter in the plays to ways of chanting and dancing—both Nobumitsu's and Zenpō's writings therefore focus on the practical aspects of perfecting one's skill in noh, rather than on the exploration of the more philosophical or spiritual aspects of the art form such as are found in Zeami and Zenchiku's writings. Relative to the number of noh plays that Nobumitsu composed, the number of treatises that he wrote is disproportionately low. It is obviously not the case of a lack of literary ability or practical experience that hindered this kind of writing, but the fact that the noh practitioners of the late Muromachi period lived in a different cultural environment from their predecessors meant that there was no imperative to create treatises.

Noh treatises during the late Muromachi period lost their significance as a secret strategy in the survival of the troupe, as they had been during Zeami's time. Competitions among noh troupes and challenges from other semiprofessionals such as the *tesarugaku* noh performers remained keen. But the audience during this period demonstrated a more open attitude toward the genre, and many of them took pleasure in practicing noh chanting and/or dancing as an avocation. The function of secret treatises—to transmit secret strategies to outdo other competitors—was no longer as important. With the popularity of amateur study of and

---

35. Omote and Itō, 1969.
36. The text is compiled by a person named Fujiuemon, one of Zenpō's disciples. See Omote and Takemoto, 272–280.

involvement in the genre it became more important to expand the scope of one's intended audience, who were likely to be potential pupils and patrons. The status of the noh theater as a socially sanctioned entertainment form was firmly established. This explains why Konparu Zenpō's treatises, unlike his grandfather Zenchiku's works, focus mainly on specific aspects of the theater rather than on profound philosophical explanations of the genre. And it is probably one reason why Nobumitsu did not leave behind many treatises despite his prolific noh play output.

Nobumitsu died in 1516 at the age of eighty-one. Like Zeami and On'ami, Nobumitsu had been an active member of the Zen community. It is believed that the ground in which he was laid to rest was in one of the major Gozan Zen temples, Shōkokuji in Kyoto, although the exact spot is unknown.

As Keijō described in *Nobumitsu Portrait Inscription*, Nobumitsu had a successful life and career, combining the identities of noh practitioner, literati, and lay religious practitioner. Perhaps in this sense Nobumitsu was indeed the equal of many others who had the Zen prelate compose inscriptions for their portraitures, despite the fact that he was just a sarugaku performer.

Nobumitsu's life and career illustrate an important transitional period in the history of Muromachi noh theater. After Zeami's initial assiduous efforts in establishing the sarugaku noh theater as one that was loved and respected by all, Nobumitsu and his contemporaries were able to venture out and create another noh stage with more expansive sources of inspiration and styles of presentation. *Kan no Kōso*, the noh play that has been attributed to Nobumitsu as his first play, is an intriguing piece that serves as a good illustration of this late Muromachi trend.

Nobumitsu's Debut Work and Its Significance

According to various historical records, over thirty plays have been attributed to Nobumitsu.[37] This is second only to the number attributed to Zeami, whose work constitutes a significant portion of the contemporary noh repertoire. Nobumitsu's earliest play, known by various names such as *Kan no Kōso* (Emperor Kōso of Kan), *Kōso* (Emperor Kōso), and *Hoshi* (The Star), was performed at the *takigi nō* (noh performed by bonfires) at the Kōfukuji temple in Nara in the second month of the first year of Kyōtoku (1452). On'ami played the shite role in this play.[38] Nobumitsu was then in his late teens, and this play, which was inspired by the tale of the Chinese historical figures Han Gaozu (Kan no Kōso), Xiangyu (Kōu), and Hanxin (Kanshin), embraces some of the characteristics that distinctly mark Nobumitsu's later plays.

The play begins with the waki Kanshin's introduction.[39] He explains that his general, Kōu, the shite, has attempted to attack the capital of the Qin emperor, though without much success. While Kanshin is discussing possible strategies with his colleague Kishin (tsure), he receives divine instructions that Kōu should pray to a certain military deity in order to win the battle. In Act Two of the play, Kōu offers a prayer and eventually wins the battle. The play ends with Kōu commanding the deity to become his guardian angel.

Critics label *Kan no Kōso* as among the "immature" plays produced during Nobumitsu's earlier years, citing the somewhat awkward arrangement of the characters and excessively "dramatic" plot, as well as the emphasis on the waki character, Kanshin.[40] There is, however, an important feature that escaped the critics' attention—the play's frequent references to Chinese subject matter and poetic sources. Visually, the play, especially the scene where Kōu offers prayers to the deity of war, contains more pageantry than

37. See Appendix 1 for the synopsis of works attributed to Nobumitsu.
38. Nose 1972, 1261.
39. Tanaka 1993, 99–100, 386–389.
40. Nishino 1975, 47.

many other plays already in existence at that time. Even though the spectacle displayed has come to be viewed as undesirable in modern-day noh discourse, at the time when it was performed it did exert an impact on later productions. Konparu Zenpō's later plays *Kurogawa* (River Kuro) and *Yakamochi* (Yakamochi the poet) exhibit similarities to *Kan no Kōso*. Both plays present grand prayer sessions as part of their main plots, and *Kurogawa* also has a battle scene that ends with a victory aided by heavenly beings.[41] The visually oriented characteristic of noh plays refreshed and in a sense re-created during the late Muromachi period was beginning to take shape at this time, and *Kan no Kōso*, which was performed throughout premodern times, is undoubtedly an early model of this style. This is the deciding element of furyū noh in modern-day noh discourse: plays that leaned toward the spectacular, including performers, stage props, music, plot, etc.

Kan no Kōso is not the first noh play that is situated in wartime. In fact, war is a popular topic in noh plays. The Genpei War (1180–1185) that took place between the Minamoto (Genji) and Taira (Heiji) families not only brought down the Minamoto family and weakened the power of the court, it also propelled Japanese history into the medieval period. This extremely important historical event has a strong presence in many literary and performance genres. In the contemporary noh repertoire, there are various famous plays of the defeated Taira warriors, categorized mainly under the warrior noh plays (*shura nō*). Compared to Nobumitsu's *Kan no Kōso*, which attempts to represent war preparation scenes, these warrior noh plays have their protagonists, the aggrieved souls of dead warriors, return to narrate their tragedies.[42] Scenes from these warrior

---

41. See Nishise 1986 ,15–30, for a discussion of Zenpō's plays, especially 23–27.

42. One of the more representative plays in this category is *Atsumori*, attributed to Zeami, where the ghost of Atsumori confronts Renshō, the Taira general who kills him during the battle at Ichinotani. See Brazell 1998 for a translation of the play. Other examples include *Kiyotsune, Sanemori,* and *Yorimasa*, all attributed to Zeami.

noh plays are usually more introspective, referring constantly to the psychological landscape of the warriors. Even the dance reenacting the battle scene by the warrior protagonist at the end of the play is often contemplative. In *Kan no Kōso*, however, the emphasis is on the presentation of a boisterous battle, coupled with a prayer scene in which large stage props are believed to have been used.[43] The dramatically more significant role of the waki Kanshin—as messenger between the gods and his general— foretells the emphasis that Nobumitsu would eventually place on the waki and other auxiliary roles, such as the tsure (followers) and the kokata (child performer). This play is no longer performed today, and it has never been considered as either important or interesting by practitioners or academics, as evidenced in the very scarce and often negative comments on it. Nevertheless, *Kan no Kōso* marks an important transition in the composition and production of noh in the late Muromachi period.

The Noh Practitioner on Another Stage

Nobumitsu composed many other noh plays that surpassed *Kan no Kōso* in terms of aesthetic presentation, technical achievement, and acclaim received. Nevertheless, characteristics such as a wider allusion to Chinese sources, an expanded cast, the emphasis on the present rather than on the past, and the use of more props heralded some of the representative features in his later plays. And as I will illustrate in the following chapters, one other very important feature of Nobumitsu's noh plays is his ability to follow the conventional style of noh composition such as the use of poetic allusions and intertextuality, while simultaneously incorporating uncommon or novel elements, such as a silent shite character.

---

43. This is reminiscent of the performance at Tōnomine in the first year of Eikyō (1429), in which actual horses and helmets were used on the stage, illustrating the versatile and multifaceted nature of sarugaku noh of the Muromachi period. See Nose 1972, 724–725.

Kanze Kojirō Nobumitsu was a talented noh practitioner who lived in a time when the noh theater had achieved a more stable social status and practitioners had more access to different sources for their compositions. Noh audience in this period joined the rank of amateur performers by participating in not only chanting and dancing but also composition. Nobumitsu, coming from a family with two generations of important noh practitioners who had contributed significantly to the development of the theatrical form, further expanded the genre with his own creativity, leadership, and engagement with his audience. Nobumitsu's career as a noh practitioner and his reception by later generations were as much a legacy of the Kanze noh school as the political and cultural specifics of his time. The social and political chaos caused by the Ōnin War and the importance of the Gozan institution in the cultural and political realms are two such examples. Equally important is the fact that the time when Nobumitsu was alive almost directly preceded the Tokugawa period, when noh started to be transformed into an official state ritual. These historical intersections and their impact on noh are all parts of the discursive construct of present-day noh discourse, to which I will return in the last part of this book.

It is from this very complicated background, one that combines the individual noh practitioner's innate characteristics with external circumstances, that we see the making of an important noh practitioner whose plays are still enjoyed by many today. In the following chapters I present a close reading of Nobumitsu's noh plays both to introduce the reader to an interesting corpus of work that is representative of the late Muromachi period as well as to illustrate Nobumitsu's skill and talent in noh composition.

Part Two

之慷動蕩于其肉以天下奇觀也
偉光克傳父後然而推讓於為
父之後者而不為髴但以撃皷
為之能萬韻既揚大小皷色應
送于如電劃々十皷再皷報音皆
絶美人皆眩耳目矣加之後人
有才智而能向本朝神化以俤
之故夔俊窺和歌之歌諷詠者
羣搜泉潰閇與慶故寡而尠之
於歌飄度之於曲諷以作新色
貴義畜三衆工之中無出其右
者歳甫十五未冠　先帝懷花
圍虎呂之上廠佛手賜扇時卷
那有公侍上前加々乎以今拜其
賜栄軏大於々等偉光其先出自
服部氏乃伊賀列之甲族也
繁有三子男春日大明神祇其々

Chapter Three

Deciphering "Furyū"

As I mentioned at the beginning of this book, the late Muromachi noh plays are often referred to as furyū noh. Oda Sachiko attributes the development of furyū noh to practitioners such as Nobumitsu, Konparu Zenpō, and Kanze Nagatoshi, who were active during the Ōnin War (1467–1477) period.[1] Other scholars seem to agree on the general association between this period and furyū-style noh, examples include Ishii Tomoko, who entitled her book on Konparu Zenpō's plays *The Period of Furyū Nō* (Furyū nō no Jidai). Yamanaka Reiko identifies furyū-style deity plays in which numerous deities would appear in a play, as being characteristic of the time.[2] In his works on Nobumitsu, Nishino Haruo, too, often identifies elements of furyū in Nobumitsu's noh plays.[3] Many Japanese writers on noh share the position that works by Nobumitsu, Zenpō, Nagatoshi, and the mysterious Miyamasu could all be identified as sharing the furyū characteristic.

In these writings, furyū is defined by the stylistic (and predominately visual) characteristic of these plays. In short, furyū-

1. See Oda Sachiko's entry "Furyū nō" in Nishino and Hata, 328.
2. Yamanaka cites two other articles to substantiate this argument, further illustrating the general consensus among noh scholars on the relationship between late Muromachi period and furyū-style noh. See Yamanaka Reiko 1998, 162.
3. See Nishino Haruo 1975 and Yokomichi et al. 1987, 258–260.

style plays are marked by the use of more stage and hand props, elaborate costumes, and the number of performers present on stage; often also with more dramatic significance given to role types other than the shite. Other components include a more complex narrative structure as well as an expanded range of sources of inspiration. Another important characteristic of the furyū-style plays is the shift of focus from an internal emotional landscape of the characters to external drama.

These features have contributed to a certain degree of difficulty and confusion when these plays are considered under the *Gobandate*, or "five types," categorization paradigm. Most of Nobumitsu's and his peers' noh plays have been categorized as either fourth or fifth category in the Gobandate, since they do not really fit into any category because of the various stylistic features they often have. The Gobandate, a system of dividing noh plays into five categories—the deity, the warrior, the female, the miscellaneous, and the demon plays—evolved as a result of the Tokugawa shogunate's effort to transform the genre into its own official entertainment form.[4] The Tokugawa government worked to construct a repertoire of noh plays that has a "ritual aura," one that befits the solemn or perhaps majestic demeanor of the Tokugawa military government. By accessing and imposing strict limits on placing noh plays in a structured manner, those plays that do not really fit neatly into these categories tend to be given less weight, and placed under either the fourth or fifth category—miscellaneous or demon plays. A look at present-day noh anthologies will show that these are the two most common categories.

In this chapter I examine closely some of Nobumitsu's best-known furyū-style plays, highlighting the various factors that contribute to their being labeled as *furyū*.

---

4. Gerry Yokota adeptly summarized the establishment of the Gobandate as the start of the official canonization of noh plays during the early Tokugawa period. See Yokota 1997. Other scholars have also discussed about the institutionalization of noh. See footnote 10 in the Introduction.

The Enchanted Warrior's Adventure in *Momijigari*

Nishino Haruo comments that *Momijigari*[5] and *Funabenkei* are the noh versions of the "luck of the mountain" and "luck of the sea," alluding to the *"yamasachi umisachi"* from Japanese mythology.[6] *Momijigari* is a tale of deceptions that unfolds during an unexpected encounter on a mountain. *Funabenkei*, on the other hand, has its most critical moment at sea. There are many parallels between the two plays, considered as the two most representative furyū-style plays in Nobumitsu's repertoire. Both plays feature warriors as their protagonists, and in them we see a metamorphosis of the shite characters: in Act One, elegant females, and in Act Two, vengeful spirits. Significant dramatic roles attributed to the waki and ai-kyōgen and a renewed approach to musical and dance tempos are also believed to be Nobumitsu's innovation.[7]

Furthermore, *Momijigari* does not open with the usual announcements made by the waki. Instead of a matter-of-fact monologue that spells out the details of the journey and its destination, we see an entourage of beautiful women enjoying an autumn excursion in an unknown location. This feature, even

---

5. This play has been translated into English as *Autumn-Leaves Viewing* in *Nippon Gakujutsu Shinkōkai*, 1985. Another translation by Meredith Weatherby, *The Maple Viewing*, can be found in Ernst 1959.
6. Nishino 1998, 187. The mythologies are *Kojiki* and *Nihonshoki*. *Kojiki* is an imperial-ordained three-volume account of Japanese deities and emperors compiled around the early eighth century. *Nihonshoki*, also known as *Nihongi*, is a thirty-volume compilation of similar subject matter, except written in kanbun (Chinese-style writing). Both books present descriptions of the beginning of Japan and the initial deities responsible for its construction. The mythology sections of both works have an especially strong presence in the noh theater, especially in first category deity plays. See Philippi 1968, esp. 148–155, and Aston 1972, esp. 92–94, for a translation of *Kojiki* and *Nihongi*, respectively. Examples of noh plays with characters from these works include *Awaji*, which features Izanagi as its shite, and *Ema*, which has Amaterasu as its main character; *Kusanagi*, *Kuzu*, and *Gendayū* feature mythological characters, including Yamato Takeru, the Tenmu Emperor, and the old couple Ashinazuchi and Tenazuchi, who are also characters in Nobumitsu's *Orochi*.
7. Nishino 1998, 187.

within Nobumitsu's repertoire, is uncommon. Many noh plays performed today usually provide their audience with plenty of information about the setting of the play and the waki's intention at the outset—suspense or drama (as we understand them today) are not the most important considerations.[8]

Drama and suspense are more regularly seen in noh plays composed by the first generation of practitioners. Some of them are mentioned in Zeami's treatises, such as *The Sarugaku Dangi*, and are referred to as *Kosakunō* (Early Noh) by Zeami. Examples include *Aoi no Ue* (Lady Aoi) and *Jinen Kōji* (Priest Jinen).[9] *Aoi no Ue* tells of the mysterious disease of Genji's wife Lady Aoi, which was revealed to be caused by her love rival Lady Nijō, while the priest Jinen in *Jinen Kōji* bargained for the return of a child from slave traders by presenting them with various forms of entertainment. Both plays sustain the audience's curiosity, wanting to know what the next development in the plot will be. Who or what is causing the illness? Is Lady Aoi going to die? And, while enjoying the priest's songs and dances, the audience wonders if the priest will be able to win over the slave traders and rescue the poor child. But most such "dramatic" elements, which relied more on the monomane style of performance, were subsumed in plays produced by the second generation, mainly by Zeami who instead chose to focus on literary and musical elements such as poetry and music. Into the late Muromachi period, renewed attention was paid to this style of performance, and the results are plays such as *Momijigari*.

Nobumitsu's *Momijigari* focuses on the multiple levels of deception between the beautiful woman (shite) and the warrior

8. It is true that in many two-part noh plays the revelation of the identity of the first shite, who is often being of the supernatural world (ghosts or deities), is "climatic" in terms of the way it is presented: the libretto, chorus, and dance steps all call for special attention to this moment of revelation. But in terms of the flow of the narrative, the shite's identity is often hinted at right from the beginning when the waki and shite start exchanging words so it is hardly any surprise who he/she is when the identity is revealed.

9. See Goff 1991, 134–139, for a translation of *Lady Aoi*.

Koremori (waki), which leads to the climatic final battle scene. Allusions to literary classics from both Japan and China, as well as to religious ideology, are deployed in the play to both intensify the drama and convey beautiful imagery. In this sense *Momijigari* is an important work, perhaps more so than *Funabenkei*, as a representation of another kind of noh play. *Momijigari* opens with the entrance of an unusually beautiful woman (shite) and her several attendants (shite tsure)—all in gorgeous autumn dresses that befit the entourage of an elegant high-ranking noblewoman. The mystery shrouding her identity thickens in the *shidai* section after she introduced herself as a "woman who lives in the vicinity":

> My transient life in this melancholy world
> the dense catch-weed
> that surrounds my humble hut,
> unnoticed by one and all,
>> the arrival of autumn
>> just like the white chrysanthemum fading
>>> from its prime
> is my sad life.[10]

The image is of a woman as beautiful as a white chrysanthemum, wasting away and waiting in vain for a lover who fails to appear at her doorstep. These opening lines immediately capture the attention of the audience, who are able to identify with a lonely and forlorn beauty, and perhaps even unconsciously wish to see her agony resolved as the play unfolds. This melancholic mood presents a sharp contrast to the bright autumn foliage, as sung by the entourage and visually emphasized by their colorful outfits. Additional contrasts keep surfacing, contributing greatly to the pleasure of the play.

---

10. 実やながらへて憂き世に住むとも今ははや、たれ白雲の八重葎、茂れる宿の淋しきに、人こそ見えね秋の来て、庭の白菊うつろふ色も、憂き身の類いとあはれなり。Nishino 1998, 188.

Even without venturing further into the play, we see that this opening section showcases features that subtly distinguish themselves from other plays. First, it is not a common practice to have the shite character appear before the waki. The entrance of the elegant noblewoman and her entourage creates a visually attractive scene. In other noh plays we usually see the entrance of one lone waki character at the beginning, or at times accompanied by the waki tsure, often a group of traveling priests or court officials. Neither of these groups is able to create a visual impact as strong as the opening of *Momijigari*. The woman's opening melancholic monologue serves as a contrast to her lively entrance. In fact, the play's mood often oscillates between two extremes: rowdiness versus melancholy, romance versus thrills, fine weather versus a tempest, etc. This skillful interweaving of visual excitement, literary sophistication, and dramatic intensity is one of Nobumitsu's signature characteristics and can be found in many of his other works, including *Kochō* (The butterfly), *Tamanoi* (The jeweled well), and *Funabenkei* (Benkei on board).

Although unusual, the introduction of the shite character before the waki is not unique to *Momijigari*. Several other plays in the current repertoire present the shite first. For example, in *Kantan* (Kantan) and *Kanyōkyū* (The Kanyō Palace), the shite characters introduce themsleves after the ai-kyōgen characters explain the situations in which the narratives will unfold.[11] Neither play has an identified composer nor a creation date, and both are "Chinese plays," i.e., they take place in *Morokoshi* (the Chinese land). Another play, *Kosode Soga* (Soga brothers bid farewell), one of the many Soga brothers' revenge tales believed to have been created in the late Muromachi period, also opens with the shite character singing the *shidai*.

Miidera (The Mii Temple) and *Zegai* (Zegai the Tengū) are two more noh plays that start with the shite characters introducing themselves and explaining the purpose of their travels—taking over the role usally assumed by the waki characters. *Miidera*,

---

11. See Tyler 1992, 133–141, for a translation of *Kantan*.

composer unknown, is identified as a work created during Zeami's time. It has a relatively large cast, which is one of the furyū-style noh characteristics, and I believe its relatively complex narrative of a mother reuniting with her lost child resonates more with the early noh.[12] While the focus of *Miidera* is the shite's psychological turmoil in finding her lost child, we see a different approach in *Zegai*. *Zegai* centers around a battle between a *tengū* (shite)—a Japanese mythological creature with magical powers—and a high ranking Buddhist prelate (waki). The composer Takeda Hōin Sadamori (1421–1508) was a contemporary of Nobumitsu and an amateur noh practitioner.[13]

Still, even among the plays that begin with the shite character's entrance, *Momijigari* stands out with its calculated visual design of the shite's entrance and elaborate presentation of the character. The sophisticated *and* mysterious woman with an entourage that hints at her nobility is not a regular feature in noh plays since many female characters usually first simply appear as an unidentified local villager in Act One and only reassume their original identity in Act Two. In this play, the noblewoman's laments on her life add a melancholic sentiment, perhaps even a hint of possible romantic development. Those who are familiar with noh dramaturgy, however, probably suspect something else, as *enacting* romantic encounters is hardly a part of the noh repertoire.[14]

---

12. Nishino 1998, 482.

13. Takeda Hōin Sadamori was a descendent of a family who had been imperial physicians for three generations. He was Ashikaga Yoshimasa's doctor and thus acquired the official rank of Hōin. Takeda also won high acclaim as an amateur noh practitioner. The play *Zegai* tells the tale of a Chinese *tengū* forming an alliance with his Japanese counterparts to challenge the top-ranking Budhdist prelate. It is consistent with other plays of that time in which unusual characters ranging from dragon princess to one-horned wizards were employed.

14. This is not to say that romantic narratives do not exist in noh repertoire. Another example that comes to mind is Nobumitsu's *Tamanoi*, where the Heavenly Grandchild Hohodemi first meets the Dragon Princess and falls in love. In fact, a large number of plays under the third category, "women's play," are about romantic love: the protagonist reminiscing about an unforgettable affair (e.g., *Matsukaze*), unrequited love with a tragic ending (e.g., *Ominameshi*), or the reunion of lovers (e.g., *Hanjo*). But very few of these plays actually enact the ini-

The woman and her party set up a tent in the woods to admire the beautiful fall colors. At this juncture, the waki, Taira General Koremochi, enters. He is presumably on a deer hunting trip, and his entrance is much more boisterous than that of the woman's.[15] The chorus sings,

> The brave hunters with their Azusa bows
> with their Azusa bows they stride
> through the dew-layered path of silver grass
> to the mountain depths they head.
> Descending dangerous deer-trap paths
> the deers' cries are carried by the wind.
> Listen carefully to follow their trace!
> Listen carefully to follow their trace![16]

There are significant contrasts between the entrances of the noblewoman and the warrior: one is elegant while the other is gallant; one seems melancholic while the other is in high spirits. The contrast in the successive introductions of the two main characters serves to heighten the drama that is about to unfold.

As expected, Koremochi is surprised by the presence of the women. Although the noblewoman will not reveal her name, her sophisticated air makes Koremochi decide that he should not be boorish when his group passes the party. Hinting that he is about to confront great danger, the chorus describes his action:

---

tial romantic encounter onstage. The usual method of presentation is to narrate it *retrospectively* through the words and dances of the characters.

15. As in some plays, the ai-kyōgen, a deity from the Hachiman shrine, reveals more detailed information about the play, including the venue of the event. It is not until he appears that Koremochi's visit to the woods is accounted for. Different kyōgen schools, however, provide different explanations for his excursion. I have adopted the text in Sanari's anthology *Yōkyoku Taikan* (Sanari 1982), which explains that deer hunting is actually a pretext and that his real intention is to hunt down the demon who has been haunting the place.

16. 丈夫が、弥猛心の梓弓、弥猛心の梓弓、入野の薄露分て、行方も遠き山かげの、鹿垣の道の険しきに。落ち来る鹿の声すなり、風の行方も心せよ、風の行方も心せよ。Nishino 1998, 188.

He dismounts from his horse and removes his
   riding shoes.
He dismounts from his horse and removes his
   riding shoes
      with undivided attention,
through the dangerous pebble path under the
mountain shade
he strikes forward
      with undivided attention.[17]

Tension builds with every step he takes, as suggested by
the chorus' running commentary. But the play takes another
unexpected turn when the noblewoman shows an interest in the
brave warrior and invites him to join her party. Koremochi tries
to resist the temptation of the beautiful woman, but alluding to
an ancient saying that karmic connections exist even between
strangers, she manages to convince him that their meeting is
chigiri, a predestined connection beyond one's control. The
relationship between a couple that is defined by chigiri can be
explained at two levels. The first refers to the present time in
which the two people have committed themselves to each other,
regardless of circumstances. The second, which is at least equally
important if not more so, rationalizes this relationship as one that
is predestined, and therefore by implication extremely powerful
because it is beyond the control of any human.

Chigiri is not an unfamiliar concept in noh plays. In *Kiyotsune*,
the ghost of the disheartened Heike warrior appears in his wife's
dream to accuse her of refusing to accept his memento—the only
keepsake he left for her before killing himself. His wife chides him
for dying without her, thus breaking their vows (*chigiri*) to die
together. It is this broken vow that enrages the wife and makes
her discard Kiyotsune's only memento, which then leads to the
appearance of Kiyotsune's ghost and the unfolding of his tale. After

17. 馬より下りて沓を脱ぎ、馬より下りて沓を脱ぎ、道を隔てての、
岩の懸路を過ぎ給ふ、心遣ひぞ類なき、　心遣ひぞ類なき。Ibid., 189.

the husband's vivid elaboration of his thoughts and feelings leading to his death, his wife is finally convinced that she should keep his memento. However, this does not stop her from calling their vow "regretful" (*urameshi kari keru chigiri*). The term "chigiri" in *Kiyotsune* has two important functions: it is a plot device around which the play unfolds, and it is also an important motif through which the main theme of the play is conveyed: the strong love that binds the husband and wife.

Another play, *Ikkaku Sennin* (The wizard Ikkaku) by Nobumitsu's contemporary Konparu Zenpō, also makes use of the chigiri motif. In this play, the dragon kings who are responsible for producing rain have had a fight with the wizard Ikkaku Senin and have been imprisoned by him. The land, as a result, is in crisis because of the lack of rain. A beautiful woman is sent by the emperor to rescue the dragon kings. She offers the wizard wine and invokes a similar rhetoric of a predestined connection to relax his wariness and eventually gets him drunk.[18] The play ends with the successful release of the captured dragon kings, who can then produce rain to end the drought. Here we see a woman who sets out to seduce a man (or in this case a wizard) and his succumbing to her beauty. The use of chigiri as an important motif remains from Zeami's time, although its use has expanded in plays produced by practitioners such as Nobumitsu and Zenpō. The original meaning of a long-lasting relationship based on mutual trust has now become a deceptive device to facilitate a more dramatic plot.

In *Momijigari* the idea of chigiri is evoked several times, and each time its scope expands further. First, the mysterious woman alludes to the natural phenomenon of rain falling on trees to argue that their meeting is inevitable. She then makes a second reference to an anecdote of a drinking session of three famous Chinese hermit poets. Finally, when Koremochi admits his attraction to her, she reassures him further by claiming that there is indeed a karmic connection between them from their previous lives.

This exchange between the two, presented in the *kuse* section

---

18. Sanari 1982, 281.

of the play, is full of beautiful poetic imagery. The chorus sings what is in Koremochi's mind and introduces a new concept: the five commandments (*gokai*) in Buddhism.

> Indeed the hearts of men are fickle
> just as the dew-covered bamboo leaves evoke
> thoughts of good wine.[19]
> Without even touching the sake cup
> I am already drunk by its sight.
>> But as it is,
>> among the various Buddhist command-
>> ments
>> I have committed the sin of drinking,
>> lewdness, and lying.
>> My mind is confused, and I am tipsy.
>> What would the world think, if they
>> were to see this drunken me?[20]

This guilt-ridden confession from the lovestruck man is followed by the mesmerizing woman's reply:

> But upon contemplation, nothing can be done.
> The karmic connection from our former lives
> here on this random mountain path with
> tiny dew drops on the grass
> which speak my thoughts
> Men's hearts, just like the floating clouds,
> are unpredictable.

---

19. Nobumitsu uses a pun here from a linked-verse text which is quoted in Itō (vol. 3) 1988, 307, footnote 19. The derivative meaning of the line is that being in the company of such a beautiful woman, Koremochi has already lost his composure even without any influence from alcohol.

20. さなきだに人心、乱るる節は竹の葉の、露ばかりだに受けじとは、思ひしかども盃に、向かへば変はる心かな、されば仏も戒めの、道はさまざま多けれど、ことに飲酒を破りなば、邪淫妄語ももろともに、乱れ心の花鬘、かかる姿は世にも、類嵐の山桜、外の見る目もいかならん。Nishino 1998, 190.

Worrisome
is the future of this vow. [21]

Koremochi admits that he has fallen for the woman and broken three of the five commandments in Buddhism: drinking, lewdness, and untrue words. The first two faults are clear, but one wonders what untrue words Koremochi has uttered? And has the woman committed the same offenses? She refers to the well-known Buddhist concept of a karmic link from a former life. And as the play unfolds the audience realizes that the woman is not lying, since she does have a previous connection with Koremochi. While they thus sing, dance, and drink away the beautiful autumn day, evening falls. Now that Koremochi is drunk, the woman bids him farewell:

The unbearable sight of autumn leaves on the
moss-laden ground
The unbearable sight of autumn leaves on the
moss laden ground
now the chilly evening wind
from the darkening sky comes the falling rain.
In the depth of this desolate mountain you should
lie and wait for the moon
Lie on your folded sleeves, dampened by dew.
Fall asleep and wake not from your dream.
Fall asleep and wake not from your dream.[22]

In this last segment, sung before the woman's disappearance, are allusions to two poems from *Wakan Rōeishū* (和漢朗詠集)

---

21. よしや、思へば是とても、前世の契り浅からぬ、深き情の色見えて、かかる折しも道のべの、草葉の露の託言をも、かけてぞ頼む行末を、契るもはかなうちつけに、人の心も白雲の、立ち煩へる気色かな。 Nishino, 1998, 190.

22. 堪ず紅葉、青苔の地、堪ず紅葉、青苔の地、又これ涼風、暮行空に、雨うち注ぐ、夜嵐に、物凄しき、山陰に。 Nishino 1998, 190–191.

and *Kinyō Wakashū* (金葉和歌集), respectively.[23] The Tang poet Hakurakuten's (Bai Juyi, 772–846) poem about a sad autumn evening has turned into a warning of danger that the warrior is about to encounter. The drama vacillates between suspense, romance, then back to danger and suspense, producing an unsettling feeling throughout the entire play. In the first half, Nobumitsu presents what appears to be a woman seeking love. By alluding to poetic images in famous anthologies as well as presenting an elegant female dance—the *chū no mai*—an icing of elegance is added to the pseudo-romance. The vivid image of a beautiful woman parallels many other protagonists in plays such as *Yuya* (Lady Yuya) or *Eguchi* (Eguchi).[24] A somewhat familiar character type relaxes the audience and the readers, although in the last part of the *chū no mai*, the tempo of the dance picks up quickly and turns into a fast-paced performance, *kyū no mai*, indicating the emergence of something more surprising. The elegant woman who looks like a noblewoman is indeed a metamorphosis of a demon—awaiting an opportunity to slaughter the brave warrior.

Demons disguised as human beings also appear in *Yamanba* (Yamanba the mountain witch) and *Kurozuka* (The dark mound, also known as *Adachigahara*, The field of Adachi). In *Yamanba*, the pseudo-demon appears before a group of pilgrims to expound on the philosophy of enlightenment based on Buddhist teachings.[25] In *Kurozuka*, a demon disguised as an old woman lives in the deep mountains. Her lonely existence is upset when a group of lost traveling priests ask her for lodging. This play, produced around Zeami's time or earlier, has a relatively simple plot. The priests are shocked by what they learn about the "old woman,"

---

23. *Wakan Rōeishū* is an anthology compiled by Fujiwara Kintō (藤原公任 966–1008) (see Ōsone and Horiuchi 1983). It is a collection of Chinese poems, mostly couplets, composed by both Japanese poets who were mainly Kintō's contemporaries and by poets from China whose works were transmitted to Japan. *Kinyō Wakashū* is a ten-volume imperially ordained waka anthology compiled by Minamoto Toshiyori (源俊頼 1055?–1129?).

24. See Shimazaki 1976 and Tyler 1992 for a translation of *Yuya* and *Eguchi*, respectively.

25. See Brazell 1997, 207–225, for a translation of this play.

though the emphasis of the play, like *Yamanba,* ultimately lies on the protagonist's agony as a demon and her desire to attain enlightenment. In contrast to its counterparts in these two earlier plays, the demon in *Momijigari* has a very different agenda, and desire for enlightenment is simply not on it.

The ai-kyōgen, a local deity at the Hachiman shrine, emerges after the women exit, and brings with him more surprising information: the elegant woman is actually a demon who has disguised itself in order to kill Koremochi. We learn also that Koremochi has come to the forest precisely to search for this demon. The lies of both Koremochi and the beautiful woman are revealed gradually with each new development of the play. At this point the audience realizes that not only are the characters deceiving each other with fictive accounts, the audience too has fallen into the same trap. The tales of deception by both the warrior and the demon are presented on two complementary levels: literary allusions, puns, and poetic imagery on the one hand, and song and dance on the other.

After Koremochi wakes with a start, the chorus foretells the imminent ferocious fight:

> Awakened by the dream,
> flashes of lightning and claps of thunder
> pierce the sky
> powerful wind howls near and far from the mountain.
> How dreadful;
> how frightening![26]

With this announcement, the demon, after much anticipation, appears. The beautiful and melancholic woman in Act One has now metamorphosed into a ten-foot-tall demon soaring through the sky in frightening red flames to attack Koremochi. Koremochi, after all a competent warrior, pulls out the sword he

---

26. 驚く枕に雷火乱れ、天地も響き風をちこちの、たつきも知らぬ山中に、おぼつかなしや恐ろしや。 Nishino 1998, 191.

receives from the Hachiman deity and starts an intense battle with the demon. This battle scene is similar to the endings of several other Nobumitsu plays, including *Kōtei* (The emperor), *Rashōmon*, *Funabenkei*, and *Orochi* (The serpent). With rapid drumbeats and a shrilling flute, the play ends quickly when Koremochi finally slaughters the demon.

Momijigari can be identified as an important representative furyū-style play in Nobumitsu's repertoire. All aspects, from the visual presentation of the characters and the unexpected plot development, to the poetic imagery in the text and sudden changes of tempo, indicate a play identifiable with the formulaic stylistic preference of noh. In a sense we can argue that the aesthetic preference of both the first- and second-generation noh practitioners can be detected in this play—the elegant female and the ferocious demon characters performed by the shite is an excellent showcase of monomane, while the literary allusions that underscore the Zeami generation's preference for lyricism. In this play, Nobumitsu has successfully created a new level of novelty by combining the two important stylistic features of his predecessors On'ami and Zeami: monomane and lyrical.

The Brave Warrior Versus the Silent Demon at *Rashōmon*

Similar to *Momijigari*, *Rashōmon* (sometimes known as *Tsuna*, the name of the protagonist) is a warrior-versus-demon play. Not only does the play embrace all the defining features of the furyū plays, ranging from the many characters to the presentation of a journey to combat a demon, it also has a shite role whose performance focuses on a singular battle dance. And like *Momijigari*, *Rashōmon* is also imbued with poetic imagery and other literary techniques that greatly enhance its lyrical nature. The most salient characteristic of *Rashōmon* is that the shite appears only in Act Two and speaks no lines. Critics claim this play to be a challenge to the shite role—undermining him, since in addition to having no spoken (or chanted) lines he has very little stage time. This criticism, however, is valid only if one's access to the play is strictly through the play's text. The waki character, indeed, has a lot of dramatic significance, and his action and psychology can be much better understood than those of the shite character when one *reads* the play. On the noh stage, however, when one can actually *see* the breathtaking dance performed by the shite, his image as a ferocious demon is actually further strengthened by his silence. The belated introduction of the shite character in this play produces a carefully calculated dramatic moment that is the climax of the play. Again, we see similar treatment of the shite character in several plays produced during this period, including Konparu Zenpō's *Yakamochi* and *Kurogawa*.[27]

Rashōmon opens with a party scene at the military general Minamoto Raikō's (wakizure) quarters on a rainy spring evening. Among the party guests are Raikō's retainers, which include Watanabe no Tsuna (waki) and other warriors. The first lines, in praise of the peaceful time, suggest a relaxed and celebratory mood. But as in *Momijigari*, the tempo builds up very quickly as the play progresses. During the banquet one of the guests mentions a rumor that a demon is residing in the Rashōmon Gate. Tsuna questions the authenticity of the rumor, and is in turn challenged to investigate. He takes up the challenge without any hesitation, despite objections from the other retainers. Bringing along a placard to prove his visit, he promptly departs for the haunted gate.

Tsuna leaves while the chorus chants the following lines, answering the worries and concerns of the other retainers, and showing the determination and bravery of Tsuna the warrior:

> Tsuna received the placard from Raikō.
> While retreating from the general
> he stops and says to one and all,
> "Although this is not the Field of Adachi at Michinoku,

---

27. *Yakamochi* is not in the current repertoire. See Lim 2005 for a discussion of this play. See Ishii 1998, 38–46, for a discussion of *Kurokawa*.

if I cannot capture the demon,
I will not face you again."
He grasps his *azusa* arrow and whisks himself out
of the hall.
Awesome is the brave heart of the warrior.
Awesome is the brave heart of the warrior.[28]

Our brave-hearted warrior thus travels through the streets of the capital while the chorus presents an eerie description of the surroundings:

The sound of the spring rain
deepens with the night,
deepens with his passing by the Eastern Temple
where the impending dawn will be hailed by its
        morning bell.[29]
Crossing over to Ninth Street
Rashōmon Gate comes into sight.
The sound of the torrential rain, accompanied by
        a sudden gust,
the screeching horse freezes, and will proceed no
        more.[30]

In this section Nobumitsu has skillfully used the different kinds of *sounds* and their reverberating effects to highlight the spooky path on which Tsuna travels to accomplish his mission.

---

28. 綱はしろしを賜はりて。御前を立つて出でけるが。立ち帰り方々は。人の心を陸奥。安達が原にあらねども。こもれる鬼を従へずは。二度また人に。面を向く事あらじ。ころまでなりや梓弓。ひきはかへじ武士の。やたけ心ぞ、恐ろしきやたけ心ぞ恐ろしき。　Sanari 1982, vol. 5, 3351–3352.

29. I have translated *Tōji* as Eastern Temple. Also known as Kyōōgokokuji, Tōji is an important Shingon sect Buddhist temple in Kyoto.

30. 春雨の。音も頻りに更くる夜の。鐘も聞ゆる暁に。東寺の前をうち過ぎて。九条おもてにうつて出で。羅生門を見渡せば。物凄しく雨落ちて。俄に吹きくる風の音いん。駒も進まず。高嘶きし。身ふるひしてこそ立つたりけれ。　Sanari 1982, vol. 5, 3354.

The level of eeriness heightens each time with the introduction of a new image. The spring rain in question seems to be getting heavier as more objects come into sight—first the temple, then the temple bell, which is associated with the dawning sky. The sound of the bell cannot be heard because dawn, the usual symbol of hope and brightness, fades as Tsuna proceeds. By the time the Rashōmon Gate comes into sight, the spring drizzle has turned into a heavy downpour. Even the stallion shivers and refuses to advance further in the face of such an ominous storm. The abstract fear is concretized by the escalation of the rain and the kinds of sounds that it makes. The prancing of the horse punctuates this segment of Tsuna's trip, while one anticipates more frightening developments in the shite's quest.

Act Two begins with the stagehands setting up a platform on which sits an enclosed structure representing the Rashōmon Gate. The stage prop indicates a change of scene; the introduction of different stage props is one important cue to scene changes, especially in Nobumitsu's plays when the setting usually changes quickly between Acts One and Two.

Tsuna, upon successfully attaching the placard to the top of the gate, turns and prepares to leave. At that moment the demon launches an unexpected attack from within the Rashōmon Gate, grabbing Tsuna's headpiece in order to stop him. The two begin to engage in a fearsome fight—in the form of a carefully choreographed dance. This scene is a technical challenge for both the waki and shite. The demon has to attack Tsuna at the precise moment when he turns after placing the placard on top of the gate, but the constraint of the mask, the prop, and the relative position of the two actors make the attack difficult to execute.

Some scholars argue that designing difficult dance move-ments is another feature of Nobumitsu's plays. In *Chōryo*, a *karamono* play, the waki has to jump into an imaginary river to retrieve an old man's shoes as soon as he discards them. In *Haen*, a play no longer performed, two deities jump out from a magical fruit. Both jumps require precision. It is small wonder that *Dōjōji*, the tale of a vengeful serpent's revisit to the Dōjō temple, was long attributed to Nobumitsu.[31] In this play the shite has to leap up into a bell as it is descending. This kind of leap is not usually seen in noh plays.[32] Just as the silent shite character, whose dramatic significance can be much better understood if one witnesses the actual performance, this special move is also best appreciated on the noh stage.

In addition to the visual effects, structurally speaking, the play quickly develops from a peaceful and relatively mellow beginning to heightening suspense and a fast-beat finale. This suspense, especially intense at the beginning of Act Two when Tsuna heads toward the Rashōmon Gate, continues until the end of the play when Tsuna finally cuts off the hand of the demon. It manages to escape but does not forget to leave behind a chilling threat:

> Just you wait,
> I'll be back for this![33]

As I will explain further in Chapter Five on the use of time in late Muromachi plays, the promise of a future return is not a common gesture in noh plays produced in earlier generations. This is because the concept of time and progressive temporal development were treated differently in many of the earlier noh plays, where the focus of the protagonists is usually on a regretful

---

31. See Keene 1970, 237–252. *Dōjōji* was attributed to Nobumitsu, although it is currently identified as "composer unknown," probably because it is not mentioned in *Shizayakusha Mokuroku*, which has been credited as the most reliable record pertaining to Nobumitsu's works. However, I am inclined to believe that Nobumitsu, though not the composer of the play, must have been involved in editing it. The markedly inconsistent lines and almost fragmented narrative development can only be explained as a result of multiple editions. Also see Klein 1995 for an analysis of the play.

32. One other famous leap on the noh stage is in *Kantan*, composer unknown, where at the final section the shite wakes from his dream and has to leap from a standing position to a lying position. See Tyler 1992, 133–141, for a short commentary and translation of this play.

33. The noh text is "時節を待ちて。又取るべしと"—a direct citation of what the demon says. Sanari 1982, vol. 5, 3356. I have translated it as including a hint of revenge for "toru" (to take or claim). See Yokomichi and Akira, 1960–1963, 167.

past deed (warfare or romance) that inhibits them from achieving enlightenment. Religious enlightenment is therefore often the closest one gets in terms of a "future" venture in these earlier plays. Some other plays that are set in the present focus on the turmoil felt by the protagonist searching for a loved one (usually a child, sometimes a spouse) who has gone missing or is dead. Temporal flow in this kind of play is also restricted within the immediate *present* in which the protagonist lives—the mother of the missing child wanders around for an eternity until she finds an answer to her quest, or one spouse finds the other after being apart for some reason. But in *Rashōmon*, when the demon threatens to return, we see a distinct reference to the future, albeit an unidentifiable one.

In fact, we can see that temporal element has more varied functions in plays by Nobumitsu, Zenpō, Nagatoshi, and other practitioners of the time. This new, and more versatile, approach to time is a by-product of the gradual shift of focus in noh plays— from the internal psychology of the protagonists to the external milieu. The next two plays that I will discuss, *Tamanoi* (The jeweled well) and *Orochi* (The serpent), are felicitous plays that celebrate happy events presented in a festive manner. Both plays are situated in the dramatic present, although each follows the structure of having the waki character appears first to introduce the events leading to his trip. We can again see at the concluding parts of both plays reference to future events.

Tales from a Long Time Ago: *Tamanoi* (The jeweled well) and *Orochi* (The serpent)

Both *Tamanoi* and *Orochi* are plays based on characters and events from the Japanese mythologies *Kojiki* and *Nihonshoki* (a.k.a. *Nihongi*). Like other plays inspired by these two mythologies, Nobumitsu's *Tamanoi* and *Orochi* demonstrate a delightful, festive mood. In terms of structure, they are less compact than other Nobumitsu plays that I have already discussed, but this is compensated for by their visual presentations. We can also find additional performance elements that are identifiable as furyū characteristics.

The tales of the heavenly royal family members Susanoō (in *Orochi*) and Hikohohodemi-no-mikoto (in *Tamanoi*) are popular as "sources of inspiration" *(honzetsu)* for noh plays.[34] On the one hand, Susanoō, the rebellious yet powerful brother of the Sun Goddess Amaterasu, was expelled from the Heavenly realm because of the havoc he had created. *Orochi* tells the story of what happened after his exile. As soon as he descended to Earth, he discarded his wild temperament and turned into a gallant knight who came to the rescue of a beautiful princess. On the other hand, the heavenly grandson Hikohohodemi-no-mikoto is one of the two brothers identified with the tale of the "Luck of the Mountain" and "Luck of the Sea." The play *Tamanoi* is an account of the adventure of Hikohohodemi-no-mikoto after he lost his brother's treasured fishing hook while at sea. In order to pacify his brother, he ventured to the bottom of the sea to search for it.

In *Tamanoi* and *Orochi* Nobumitsu retained most of the original mythological narratives. At the beginning of both plays, detailed accounts of what had happened are summarized and presented by the waki (Hikohohodemi-no-mikoto and Susanoō in *Tamanoi* and *Orochi*, respectively). As mentioned earlier, such an approach is not uncommon in noh plays: the waki character provides a prefatory, sometimes detailed, account of his journey, then the drama unfolds with the emergence of other characters. Compared with *Momijigari* and *Rashōmon*, however, such a rendition seems cumbersome. Nevertheless, this is the best way to introduce the ensuing plots, which are themselves complex.

In *Tamanoi*, the waki Hikohohodemi-no-mikoto enters and starts to tell of his unfortunate encounter with his brother's fishing hook. We learn that his effort to find his brother's lost fishing hook leads him to a certain old man who in turn advises him on where

---

34. *"Honzetsu"* is an important concept in plays produced by Zeami and his peers. Mitake Akiko outlines the meaning of the term and postulates that most of Zeami's mugen noh plays are dependent on the literary sources. See Chapter 4, footnote 20, for more detail.

to go and what to look for. The usual traveling song (*michiyuki*) is made more colorful with the description of a leak-proof vessel and the final destination of the Dragon Palace, and is presented in a performance technique that is uncommon in noh plays.[35] At the end of his journey to the sea, Hikohohodemi-no-mikoto arrives at the gate of the Dragon Palace. Finding the jeweled well and a laurel tree as the old man instructed, he decides to hide behind the tree when he sees the two Dragon Princesses approaching.

    Princess Toyotama (shite) and her sister, Princess Tamayori (tsure), have come to fetch water from the jeweled well. While drawing the well's magical water, they sing praises to it.[36] Their peaceful task, however, is disrupted when Princess Toyotama suddenly sees the reflection of a stranger in the water. Hikohohodemi-no-mikoto comes out of hiding and they exchange introductions. The Heavenly Grandson reveals his intention to visit the Dragon Palace, and the princesses offer help by bringing him to the Dragon King. In the final section of Act One, before the mid-play entrance (*nakairi*), the chorus describes the events:

"The fishing hook I borrowed from my elder brother
is swallowed by fish in the sea.
My regretful explanation calmed not his rage,
and I am at a loss as to how to placate him," said
    the Prince.

---

35. The waki's opening lines are not presented in the usual *shidai-nanori-ageu-ta* style in first category deity plays. Instead the waki uses a *hankaiko* style that replaces the *nanori* with "*sashi*-singing." The other play that uses this presentation technique is the karamono play *Hakurakuten* (composer unknown). In the present-day Kanze school only *Tamanoi* and *Hakurakuten* are presented in this way. Nishino 1974, 7; *Kanze* [1974], 15.

36. The tale of two sisters drawing water may well bring to mind another famous sister couple, in the noh play *Matsukaze*, attributed to Kan'ami and edited by Zeami (see Keene 1970 for a translation). Although both *Tamanoi* and *Matsukaze* share some common motifs such as water-drawing and reflections in the water, the latter is a mugen play expounding on unrequited love, while Nobumitsu's *Tamanoi* is decidedly a lively celebratory play.

Consoling are the Dragon King's kind words:
"We should first find your fishing hook, and then
   send you home."[37]

Shite:

And when your brother gets angry again,

Chorus:

The two treasures *Shio-mitsu* and *Shio-hiru* will
   be presented to you
so you will rule the land the way you want to.[38]
                  Then the Heavenly Descended Prince
will marry Princess Toyohime
   and father my grandchild.
Days and nights pass quickly
in no time three years have gone by.[39]

   Time passes very quickly after the initial meeting of the prince

---

37. われ兄の釣針を。かりそめながら波ま行く。魚に取られてなき由
を。歎き給えどその針に。あらずは取らじととにかくに。せうとを痛
め様々に。猛き心の如何ならんと。語り給へば父御心安く思召せ。ま
づ釣針を尋ねつつ御国に帰し申すべし。Sanari 1982, vol. 3, 1979.

38. The two treasures are the tide-controlling jewels: one for pulling tide in and
one for pushing it out. With these two complementary jewels the owner possesses
great power when it comes to battles. The original lines are: 潮満潮涸の。二
つのたまを尊に奉りなば御心に。任せて國も久方の。Sanari 1982, vol. 3,
1979.

39. The description of the Heavenly Descended Prince at the end of this section is extremely compact in the original Japanese. This small section can be
translated into "From Heaven descends (天より降る) / becomes the grandfather of a deity (御神の外祖となりて) / Princess Toyotama gets pregnant (豊
姫もただならぬ姿) / sight of the bright sun and moon, and in no time three
years have gone by (有明の月日程なく三年を送り給へり)." It is impossible
to translate such compact lines into grammatical English without drastically
adding information. I compromised by changing the perspective of the speak-
ers and using line breaks: the lines "Days . . . gone by" are spoken/sung from
the perspective of the omniscient narrator (chorus); and identify the speaker of
the two phrases "*ama yori kudaru / on-gami no gaisō to narite*" as the Dragon
King who will be the *gaisō*, or material grandfather. Sanari 1982, vol. 3, 1980.

and princesses, and it is three years later before one realizes it. During these three years Hikohohodemi-no-mikoto marries the Dragon Princess, fathers a child, and acquires the tide-controlling jewels of the Dragon Palace before heading home. Within the space of the last few lines sung by the chorus, time is fast-forwarded. The present is glossed over; the future is announced and realized in the concrete form of the birth of a child and the action of moving back to Hikohohodemi-no-mikoto's home—the land.

Act Two is a farewell party for the Heavenly Grandson and his family. Rather than presenting dramatic events, this section showcases music and performance: a short dance by a female deity (*tennyo no mai*), by the two Princesses (both tsure, at times kokata), and a finale dance by the stately Dragon King (nochi-jite). As in many Nobumitsu plays, the shite plays two characters: Princess Toyotama in Act One and the Dragon King in Act Two. The change in sentiment of the two characters is not as extreme as in *Funabenkei*—where the first character is a heartbroken woman bidding farewell to her lover and the second an angry ghost seeking revenge—although the styles of the dances performed in the two parts are still very different. Unlike Shizuka from *Funabenkei*, Princess Toyotama appears again in Act Two, played by the tsure. This more flexible character-role allocation again allows for a more expanded cast, a distinct characteristic of a furyū-style play.[40] Nishino also identifies the style of the short female dance as a novel practice in the late Muromachi period—probably a new dance form created by Nobumitsu.[41]

In synchronization with this visually oriented furyū presentation is the ai-kyōgen section in earlier versions of the play. During the mid-play entrance, ai-kyōgen characters would assume the roles of different kinds of seashells and perform a celebratory "*kai-zukushi*" (All-seashell) dance.[42] This practice of having various

---

40. Other noh plays that have the first shite character played by a tsure role are Zenpō's *Arashiyama* and Nagatoshi's *Rinzō*.

41. Nishino 1975, 42.

42. According to Sanari, there were at least five kyōgen performers assuming

ai-kyōgen characters perform short dances during the interval was extant until the Tokugawa period, though it is not clear when was it replaced by the monologue of one ai-kyōgen performer. Still, with or without a lively shell dance, it is not difficult to see that *Tamanoi* is a lighthearted, festive piece replete with colorful legendary characters and happy events, emphasizing the musical and visual aspects of the play.[43]

Orochi has a stronger story line than *Tamanoi*. In this play, Susanoō-no-mikoto (waki), the rebellious brother of the Sun Goddess Amaterasu, slays the eight-headed serpent. Along the way he acquires a wife and earns credit for composing the first ever waka in Japan. The play starts with Susanoō's account of his journey from his heavenly abode to Izumi no Kuni, where he encounters a grieving old couple, Tenazuchi (shite) and his wife, Ashinazuchi (tsure). Susanoō hears of the cause of the old couple's deep grief and offers to kill the eight-headed serpent, which has already devoured seven of their daughters. In the first half of the *sashi* section, Tenazuchi, the father, refers to himself as a weakening

roles of different sea creatures, and they would perform a dance together, though different noh schools have some variations (Sanari, 1982, vol. 3, 1980–1982). Unfortunately this particular version is no longer performed in the modern-day repertoire. This kind of performance technique is known as *zukushi*—where a long list of similar items such as flowers or seashells, or performance genre, such as different kinds of dance and singing, is performed in one song or dance. *Yugyō Yanagi*, another Nobumitsu play that I discuss in Chapter Five, presents an extensive list of references to willow-trees, ranging from the individual kinds to their different presence in different literary works, using Japanese and Chinese literary sources. In some of the very early plays that were adapted or edited by Kan'ami and Zeami, we can see some traces of this performance technique, either in actual performance or in the lines sung. The long list of cherry blossom–related accounts in Zeami's *Saigyō Zakura* and the list of fruits in *Kayoi Komachi* immediately comes to mind as an example of the latter. *Jinen Kōji*, which was attributed to Kan'ami, has the protagonist Priest Jinen performing various acts in exchange for the release of a child. Similarly, *Kagetsu*, a play already existing before Zeami's time, also has a section where the shite engages in different kinds of performances.

43. Gerry Yokota-Murakami presents a very different reading of the play in her book on noh canon. In short she identifies a new form of hierarchical relationship among the characters in the play using masks, costumes, and parts of the libretto as evidence. See Yokota-Murakami 1997, 133–134.

aged crane, mourning the loss of a young loved one:

> Despite a long life I now live in regret
> Sadness is the life I know
> We are not the only couples who will
> Separate from our beloved child
> But alas! I can do nothing
> except to cry like an aging crane.[44]

Susanoō offers to help the inconsolable parents. In exchange, he asks for the hand of their daughter, to which the old couple gladly agrees. Then the chorus continues to narrate:

> Susanoō turns Princess Inatabime into a comb
> and pins it to his hair.
> Henceforward he becomes ruler of the land.
> He constructs the two pillars of the royal palace,
> together with his wife from the faraway land of
> the eight-layer cloud,
> they build the palace with an eight-sided hedge,
> and he composes the poem about the eight-fenced
> palace—
> —the very first thirty-one syllable waka![45]

Again, within the span of several lines the chorus has narrated a magical transformation, the setting up of a palace, and announced the author of the very first waka. The compression of time and action within such a small section is especially impressive,

---

44.　ながらへて生けるを今は嘆くかな。憂きは命の科ならず。とは思へども思ひ子の。別れを慕ふ世の習ひ。我等夫婦に限らめや。身は老鶴の音に立てて。泣くより外の。事ぞなき。The line on the sadness of life is an allusion from *Zoku Shūyishū* 1201, vol. 17, Misc. II, Sanari 1982, vol. 5, 3506.

45.　やがて尊は稲田姫の。湯津の爪櫛とりなして鬢づらにさし給ふ。そのまま治まる國津神。ここに宮居の二柱。立つや八雲の妻ともに。八重垣造る言の葉の。三十一文字の詠歌の始めなるべし。 Sanari 1982, vol. 5, 3509.

and it strikes a similar chord with the closing section before Act One of *Tamanoi*. A close examination of the lines reveals that they describe events that occur much later—*after* Susanoō slaughters the great serpent—when he finally settles down and becomes the ruler residing in the palace that he has so famously built. After the chorus presented these lines, the progress of the play reverts back to the dramatic present, where the old man asks Susanoō of his strategy for killing the serpent. Susanoō describes his plan, and while they prepare for it, the ai-kyōgen enters to reiterate the plot.

Act Two starts with the entrance of Susanoō and the young daughter of Tenazuchi (sitting in a palanquin). They hide in a corner to observe the serpent while it enjoys its alcohol. Susanoō battles the serpent after it shows sign of tipsiness. Upon successfully slaughtering the serpent, he finds inside its stomach a sword, which becomes one of the three imperial treasures.

The fast tempo, accentuated by the shrill-sounding flute and quick beating of the drums, produces not a ferocious fighting mood but a delightful, festive atmosphere instead, with the finale performed by the eight-headed serpent and Susanoō. Like *Tamanoi*, this play emphasizes lighthearted and feliticious events, including a wedding, poetry writing, and the discovery of a treasure.

In addition to sharing a similar emphasis on the visual and musical aspects in the form of celebration, *Orochi* also has several different role types. In Act Two, the waki performs the final *maibataraki* dance with the nochi-jite—the eight-headed serpent. Not surprisingly, in this play the shite again plays two different characters. In Act One, he is the old man Tenazuchi, the desperate powerless local deity facing the threat of having his last surviving child devoured by an eight-headed serpent. His description of a helpless parent lamenting the impending death of a child is sad and moving. In Act Two, however, the shite has to present a very different role as the serpent, performing a powerful dance without uttering a word. The silent second shite is reminiscent of *Momijigari* and *Rashōmon*. The shite in *Orochi* stands out among these plays in that his first challenge is to convey intense emotion mainly through singing, while in the second half of the play he uses only his body to perform the powerful and drunken serpent. The audience enjoys these two different presentations, and the expansion of character-roles facilitates a much more dramatic performance.

As plays that focus on creating a music-oriented ambience supported by a dramatic narrative line, less effort seems to be invested in the literary aspects of *Tamanoi* and *Orochi*. Still, where a poetic image is called for, we usually find one. For instance, Tenazuchi, the father who is about to lose his daughter, is compared to a weakening, aged crane about to lose its young ward. The young potential victim is alluded to as the cherry blossoms under the attack of a powerful gust of wind. In these sections, where the ambience is sad and heavy, corresponding literary techniques convey these emotions. In other words, it is not the case that furyū noh plays have an inherent lack of literary quality. The literary specificities of these plays are a function of their nature: furyū plays embody a more dramatic narrative and a broader range of sentiments that demand different forms of literary and theatrical expression.

About Furyū Noh

In this chapter I examine what is probably the best-known category of noh plays in Nobumitsu's repertoire: the plays that are labeled as furyū.[46] Furyū's most salient feature is doubtless its visual aspect: the number of characters actually appearing on stage, the variety and significance of props, and the different kinds of dance performed. Closely related to this feature is the much expanded range of sources, and the probable emphasis on monomane as On'ami would have advocated.[47] Nobumitsu, however, while incorporating these different approaches in his plays, also pays

---

46. The issue of furyū is addressed in more depth in Chapter Six.

47. It is unfortunately not possible to reconstruct the use of monomane on On'ami or Nobumitsu's stage for obvious reason. I can only use conjecture here to describe what I perceive to be one of the many features of furyū.

close attention to other conventional practices in noh plays. We therefore see in these plays poetic imagery, wordplay, and other familiar literary devices in the lines. One important characteristic of Nobumitsu's role-character use is that, despite the increased dramatic significance attributed to the various role types the importance of the shite character is always prioritized by assigning to him the finale dance.

Although present-day scholars examine furyū noh against Zeami's aesthetic paradigm and postulate it to be an inferior cousin, it is important to realize that the spectacular, the flamboyant, and the extraordinary are very much a part of the late Muromachi period plays. These features are perhaps not prioritized in Zeami's aesthetic schema, but they do not necessarily compromise or detract from the artistic value or pleasure of the plays as either independent readings or performance texts. It is also important to note that even though the spectacular style seems to be the *only* important feature ascribed to the furyū noh repertoire, it is really a combination of the various factors (such as the more dramatic plots and different kinds of dance) mentioned above that contribute to the appealing characteristics of this particular subgenre. *Funabenkei* and *Momijigari* are both popular plays, not simply because of their spectacular presentation, but also because of their *entirety* as plays that embrace both conventional and more unusual elements including the introduction of tales into the structure of the plays, the clever literary and dramatic devices used to enhance suspense and mystery, and the literary allusions.

What also informed these plays, and to a certain extent facilitated the use of the more dramatic elements and devices, was the changing religious and cultural discourse of the period. The nostalgia toward the Heian court culture had diminished, together with the gradual loss of power of the major military families such as the Ashikaga.[48] Zeami's focus on an "appropriate" source of

---

48. Some scholars have argued that the nostalgia for the Heian period and the desire to become more "cultured" like the Heian courtiers has influenced the aesthetic preference of such early Ashikaga military leaders as Yoshimitsu. See, for example, *Nihon Geinōshi* 3 (Nihon Geinōshi Kenyukai 1983), 157–168; Murai

composition from the classical canon had been replaced by a wider range of choices, which allowed for the creation of more dramatic plays. Also, the emergence of the new Kamakura Buddhism introduced a greater variety of approaches to enlightenment.[49]

In the next chapter I examine some of Nobumitsu's noh plays that, more than just exhibiting a spectacular visual presentation, also incorporate "Chineseness," which are both familiar and not familiar to the noh repertoire.

2001, 22–23.

49. See Ōsumi 1990, 544–582, and Weinstein, "Rennyo and the Shinshū Revival," in Hall and Toyoda 1997, 331–358, for a description of Rennyo's religious movement during the Muromachi period.

Chapter Four

PERFORMING THE OTHER

"KARAMONO"

In the last chapter I discussed some of Nobumitsu's well-known plays that are identified as furyū plays. These plays involve warriors engaging in battles such as *Momijigari* and *Funabenkei* and figures from the Japanese mythologies *Kojiki* and *Nihonshōki* such as *Tamanoi* and *Orochi*. Even though they each have a different story to tell, the characters in these plays share one common characteristic, which is that they are all from Japanese sources.

This chapter presents another category of Nobumitsu's plays, the *karamono* or the Chinese plays—ones that either take place in China or feature Chinese characters.[1] There are six noh plays that

---

1. It is very interesting to see how "Chineseness" is presented in noh plays. Chinese subjects, including characters, events, venues, not to mention Chinese literary references, are often found in noh plays. Zeami's *Fushikaden* discusses how to perform "Chinese subjects" (唐事 *karagoto*): that the effect of Chineseness should be created by conveying something exotic or "extraordinary" (異様し たる) Omote and Katō 1974, 26–27; also see Hare 2008. As illustrated in this section of Zeami's treatise, learning to perform Chinese subjects is similar to learning to perform other kinds of characters, ranging from females to priests to demons. The Chinese subjects, however, have been identified as "exotic" or different. We see the same in Nobumitsu's plays, there are regular references to Chinese literary and historical sources, and the emphasis lies on the "exotic" nature of the subject matter, such as the setting, the outfit, or sometimes the plot. While there

are about Chinese subjects among Nobumitsu's extant plays. These karamono plays exhibit some characteristics that distinguish them from other Nobumitsu plays that are inspired by Japanese sources. Out of the six, *Haen* (The Ha garden), *Idaten* (The deity Idaten) and *Kan no Kōso,* which I discussed in Chapter Two, are no longer performed. In this chapter, I focus my discussion on the other three plays, *Chōryō* (General Chōryō), *Kōtei* (The emperor) and *Ryōko* (The dragon and the tiger), which are still being performed today.

These plays share some common features: Two of the three plays are named after a character. All these characters are figures in Chinese history but greatly mythologized and dramatized according to their various textual transmissions both temporally and geographically. In terms of structure, these plays are all *genzai* (現在 present) noh—their narratives are all situated in the dramatic present and are generally more complex. The focus of these plays is to present dramatic events through multiple characters and stage props. All three plays present some form of interaction and power negotiation between different social institutions, like the superior-subordinate relationship and hierarchical ranking between Buddhist (仏法 *buppō*) and sovereign laws (王法 *ōhou*). *Ryōko* least alludes to institutional power relationships, although it uses Buddhism as part of its motif and later on comments on the power struggle that living beings often engaged in. In *Chōryō*, the involvement of Kannon (Bodhisattva of Mercy) in Chōryō's quest for a secret military treatise highlights the importance and power of religion. And in *Kōtei*, the exorcist who possesses supernatural power offers to subjugate himself to the seemingly incompetent emperor.

---

are no conscious attempts to identify China as a specific foreign country different from other foreign sources such as Tenjiku (天竺 an old name of modern India), there is the implication that *karagoto* is different from the usual Japanese subject matter. The difference is not one of nationhood or state of course, but perhaps more of a self versus other. That said, I am not insinuating that the use of Chinese subjects does not shed light on the cultural relationship between the continent and Japan. A more meaningful discussion will have to take into consideration the specific cultural, historical, and political factors in which Japan encountered China in history during the medieval period.

Dragon versus Tiger: *Ryōko*

Ryōko (The dragon and the tiger) is a play that tells of the events
that happened when a Japanese priest travels from Japan to China.
This play has some unusual features, including the sources of
inspiration and the plot development, although it was not a very
popular piece especially when compared to other Nobumitsu
plays such as *Funabenkei* and *Momijigari*.[2] According to Oda
Sachiko, the earliest performance record of this play was in the
third and twelfth months of the ninth year of Keichō (1650), both
by the Kanze troupe.[3] It was not until the time of Tokugawa
Tsunayoshi (1646–1709) and his successor Ienobu (1662–1712)
that the play was performed more regularly.[4] Omote categorized
Ryōko as a "rare piece" (*kikyoku*) and recorded a total of seventeen
performances of this play during the reigns of these two shoguns,
a period of approximately thirty years.[5]

   Ryō in the title *Ryōko* refers to dragons and *ko*, to tigers.
Although a dragon is a mythological creature while a tiger is real,
they are both accorded extraordinary status in traditional Chinese
and Japanese beliefs, probably because tigers are not native to
most parts of these two places. Both creatures are believed to have
supernatural powers, and are regarded as ferocious yet auspicious
animals. Nobumitsu's knowledge and interest in Chinese literary
and historical traditions is clearly illustrated in this play, especially
in the frequent allusions to Chinese poetry and tales.

----

   2. Nose Asaji compiled a performance record from various historical documents and calculated the total number of performances of noh plays between
1429 and 1602. *Ryōko* is not found in Nose's list, whereas other Nobumitsu plays,
including *Funabenkei* and *Yugyō Yanagi*, were recorded as being performed 43
and 11 times, respectively. See Nose 1972, 1312, and 1314.

   3. Oda 1985, 32.

   4. Tsunayoshi and Ienobu are, respectively, the fifth and sixth shoguns during the Tokugawa period (1600–1868). Tsunayoshi is particularly famous for
his preference of "rare plays," and because of this special liking, many plays that
were not performed before his time were restored and continued to be performed
today. *Ryōko* is one such example. See Omote and Amino 1987, 116–117, for a
detailed list of plays that were revived by these two military generals.

   5. Omote 1990, 45.

The waki of the play is a Japanese priest who believes he has exhausted all places of Buddhist-learning in Japan so he decides to visit China and India to further pursue the Buddhist Law. He encounters an elderly Chinese woodcutter (with whom he discusses Buddhism) before leaving the old man to witness a battle between a tiger and a dragon. This seemingly straightforward plot, however, is full of beautiful poetic images and subtle dramatic turns. The play starts with the waki and his companions' speedy crossing of the seas and passing by the islands of Japan. The *michiyuki* (traveling song) sung by the chorus vividly describes both the Japanese and Chinese landscapes. This section alludes to poems from anthologies such as the *Santaishi* and the *Wakan Rōeishū*, creating a beautiful introduction to the play:[6]

> Under the heavenly plains, as we row by the
>   numerous islands,
>   as we row by the numerous islands
>   into the distance Tsukushi disappears.
> Continuing toward the ocean divide where the
>   clouds meet the mists
>   mountains come into view in no time.
>   Very quickly we have arrived in the land
>   of Cathay.
>   Very quickly we have arrived in the land
>   of Cathay.[7]

---

6. *Santaishi* or *Santeishi* (三体詩) is an anthology of Chinese poetry compiled by the Song poet Zhou Bi (周弼 Shūhitsu) around 1250. It was called "*santai*," or "three styles," because the collection is divided into three different styles (7 character *jue*, 7 and 5 character *lu*) of Tang poetry. It was transmitted to Japan around 1332 and became one of the most important Chinese poetry collections in the Gozan Zen tradition.

7. 天の原。八十島かけて漕ぎ出づる。八十島かけて漕ぎ出づる。船路の末も不知火の。筑紫を跡になし果てて。行くへに続く雲の波霞を分くる海原に。又山見えて程もなく。はや唐土に着きにけりはや唐土に着きにけり。 Sanari 1982, vol. 5, 3362.

As they admire the Chinese landscape, the company spots some woodcutters. The *sashi* segment sung by the woodcutter (shite) and his companions (shite-zure) praises the beauty of early spring, but the follow-up segment sung by the elderly woodcutter laments the quick passage of time. The imagery thus progresses from the external to the internal: from the vast sea voyage (during departure) to the Chinese landscape (upon arrival), and then from the early spring to the melancholic lament of an old man whose daily woodcutting is taking a toll on him.

At this juncture a seasoned noh audience may expect the play to unfold in the structure of a mugen dream play—one that will be enacted by the spirit of the old woodcutter. This may perhaps be reminiscent of the opening of Zeami's warrior play *Atsumori*, in which the waki runs into a group of woodcutters, including the shite.[8] But what follows in *Ryōko* is a surprising twist. The Chinese woodcutter learns from the priest that he and his company have crossed the ocean all the way from Japan. The priest then provides further explanation of the purpose of his trip and his future plans:

> You are indeed observant. I have traveled from the land of the rising sun to this country in order to trace the transmission of the Buddhist Law. From here I want to travel further, to the faraway land of Tenjiku.[9]

The woodcutter, however, feels that what the priest has been doing is futile, and the chorus continues to comment:

---

8. See Brazell 1997, 128–142, for a translation of this play.

9. げによく御覧じて候ものかな。われ日の本よりこの國に渡り。仏法流布の古跡を尋ね。これより渡天の志あるにより。遥々思立ちて候。Sanari 1982, vol. 5, 3363–3364. "Land of the rising sun" (日の本 *hi no moto*) refers to Japan, while Tenjiku is the old name of India. The concept of country, if it existed at all, was very different in Nobumitsu's time from what it is today. In my translation I try to stay with the earlier meaning as much as possible, which is why "Cathay" or "Chinese land" is preferred over "China."

You said you are traveling to the kingdom
   of the stars.
You are traveling to the kingdom of the stars,
   you said.
Alas, the human heart understands no vanity,
   pursuing the transient clouds.
It is there in your heart, that very moon you are after.
     Seeking the Truth from afar
A futile search that bears no fruit.
A futile search that bears no fruit. [10]

In this exchange the moon is a metaphor for Buddhism, which is presented neither as a doctrinal teaching nor a means to salvation. The priest's intent to find the traces of the transmission of the Buddhist Law—basically an intellectual quest—is a far cry from the usual treatment Buddhism receives in earlier noh plays. In other words, Buddhism in this play has become an object to be pursued, much like knowledge or treasure. Here the theme of shedding a sinful attachment to reach enlightenment, as seen in the mugen dream plays, or the theme of praising the virtue of religion in plays that celebrate the deities, is missing. Examples of noh plays with these themes are numerous: Zeami's Atsumori in the play of the same name seeks enlightenment in order to rid himself of the attachment to hatred of his murderer, Renshō; or the courtesan in *Eguchi*, attributed to Kan'ami, who is an incarnation of *Fugen Bosatsu* (Sk. *Samantabhadra*). In *Ryōko*, the secularized image of Buddhism is emphasized, and this unusual perception of the religion is further underscored in the continued exchange between the priest and the woodcutter. The priest, after listening to the woodcutter's lengthy lecture about the futility of traveling afar when he should be looking inward for Buddhist

---

10. 星の國にと行く雲の。星の國にと行く雲の。はてしはあらじ人心。心せよ胸の月。よその光を尋ねても。何にかはせん目のあたり。見るを尋ぬる。はかなさよ見るを尋ぬるはかなさよ。The "land of the stars" (星の國) refers again to India. The metaphor implies the distance and hardship involved in the travel. Sanari 1982, vol. 5, 3364.

teaching, abruptly interrupts their conversation and starts out on a totally new topic:

> You have indeed interesting thoughts. But I have something else to ask you. It is a great pleasure to look at the panoramic view of the mountains and rivers from here. And at the foot of the misty mountain is a bamboo grove. It looks like it has suddenly just been shrouded by ominous clouds. Could you tell me what is happening, please?[11]

Polite as the priest's question may be, he has clearly dominated the discussion by launching a new topic. There is no further mention of either Buddhist doctrine or Buddhism as a source of enlightenment in the rest of the play. At this juncture, the play totally abandons the Buddhist theme and develops a second thread: the battle between the two mighty creatures.

This unexpected twist may strike one as awkward and as evidence of inferior composition. What this change actually reveals, however, are the important features that constitute the fundamental framework of late Muromachi noh plays. The secularization of Buddhism is clearly demonstrated in the shift of focus in Buddhism from being a means of salvation to being a form of knowledge to be pursued intellectually. Many of the noh plays created during this period diverged from the theme of seeking enlightenment through religious rituals. In plays composed in earlier times, especially in the mugen dream play categories, we often find the mention of shūshin 執心 or mōshū 妄執, which can be loosely translated as attachment or obsessive delusion.[12] But a

---

11. かかる面白き御答へこそ候はね。まづまづ尋申したき事の候。見え渡りたる山河の気色。いづれも妙なる眺めのうちに。あれに霞める遠山もとの。向ひに見えたる竹林に。俄かに雲のうち掩ひ。風凄しく吹き落ちて。さながら気疎きその気色。これは如何なる事やらん。Sanari 1982, vol. 5, 3365.

12. Examples are many: *Tamakazura* (玉鬘 Tamakazura), *Teika* (定家 Teika), *Matsukaze* (松風 Matsukaze), *Ukifune* (浮舟 Ukifune), *Tadanori* (忠度 Tadanori), *Sanemori* (実盛 Sanemori), *Kinuta* (砧 The fulling block), *Yorimasa*

look at the contemporary performance repertoire shows that these two terms do not appear in any plays by Nobumitsu, Zenpō, or Nagatoshi. The number of plays featuring spirits seeking religious enlightenment decreased in Nobumitsu's time, and the connection between religion and the afterlife was replaced by either a more secular attitude toward religion or a more rational, and at times intellectual, approach toward religion. In these plays, Buddhism is more than something that offers salvation. We can see stronger secular elements in these plays. For instance, in Konparu Zenpō's *Yakamochi*, the emphasis of the play is on the staging of an exorcist exercise. The shaman's religious power is showcased in concrete action, putting more emphasis on the visual than the spiritual.

This is the same in *Ryōko*. The priest and his companions pursue the Buddhist Law not to achieve enlightenment, but as a quest in and of itself. It is therefore necessary to travel afar. And because the party is on a trip to explore, they naturally change the topic of conversation when they see something more interesting such as the sudden appearance of unusual clouds. Before they part ways, the woodcutter explains to the priest the appearance of the distant eerie black clouds—it is a result of the constant battle between the dragon and the tiger. The chorus then comments:

> Just as futile as a battle within the snail's bulging antenna[13]
> human beings
> ceaselessly fight over trivial matters.
> This being the practice of the world

(頼政 Yorimasa), and *Obasute* (姨捨 The deserted crone). In these plays we see the protagonists yearning to clear their strong and often sinful attachment to the living world and reach enlightenment. The characters seek help from Buddhist monks that happen to cross paths with them.

13. Found originally in a poem, *Dui jiu* (对酒 Drinking together), by the Tang poet Bai Juyi, "Wo niu jiao shang zheng he shi, shi huo guang zhong ji ci sheng" (蜗牛角上争何事，石火光中寄此生). Literally, "What is there to fight for on the antenna of the snail? Our lives are like sparks from a flintstone." These two lines address the transient nature of human lives metaphorically and advocate a more relaxed manner toward competition in life.

Beasts, too, will only act the same.
Beasts, too, will only act the same.[14]

Amazed by what he has heard, the priest asks the woodcutter for more details of the battle and receives the following teaching about life:

Well, any creature that is blessed with life
will struggle for more power.
This is not restricted to the dragons and the tigers.
We humans, too, are no different from them.[15]

In this short exchange one sees a didactic commentary on human behavior and an attempt to explain it logically. There is also a hint of criticism that any form of battle is meaningless. This comment on life is uncommon, as the noh theater does not usually deliver moralistic teachings. Within the noh dramaturgy, until Nobumitsu's time, if any noh play were to include didactic teaching, it was usually of a religious nature. The most commonly known are the themes of killing and its formidable consequences. Killing here refers to the taking of life from both human beings and animals, for instance, the "sin" (*tsumi*) of warriors such as Kagekiyo (in the play *Kagekiyo* 景清) or the fisherman in *Ukai* (鵜飼 The cormorant fisher).[16] Closely related to this is the realization of the ephemeral life and the rejection of worldly attachments, especially strong emotions that will only cause suffering. Many plays that portray young females, such as *Matsukaze*, present

14. 蝸牛の角の上にして。はかなや何事を。争ひは人の身も。変らぬものを世の中の。習ひなればや畜類の。戦ふことも、理や戦ふことも理や。Sanari 1982, vol. 5, 3366. The first two lines are an allusion to a couplet by Hakurakuten in Osone and Horiuchi, ed., *Wakan Rōeishū*, vol. 2, no. 791, 1983. See the couplets in the preceding footnote.
15. それ生を受くる者。その身の威勢を争ふこと。人間以てこれに同じ。必ず龍虎に限るべからず。Sanari 1982, vol. 5, 3366.
16. Ienaga Saburō discusses the different kinds of punishments related to the various types of killing (殺生 *sesshō*) as identified in earlier noh plays. See Ienaga 1980, 174–181.

anguished female ghosts failing to attain enlightenment because of their strong earthly attachments to a lover. There are also plays in which the protagonists become deranged as a result of the loss of a loved one, *Miidera* (The Mii Temple) and *Sumidagawa* (Sumida River)[17] are such examples. In these plays, if any moral teaching is to be found, it will have to be one that is based on belief in Buddhism. Perhaps plays that depict warfare will illustrate this point best. Among Zeami's six most famous warrior plays, battles are a key element, though they are mostly presented as a source of suffering from which one needs to escape. In *Ryōko*, however, we find an objective evaluation of battles, which are explained as basic human nature and not defined as illusory or undesirable within the Buddhist cosmology.

Act Two of the play takes yet another twist from this objective observation of warfare. The play now focuses on the two creatures in action and is devoted fully to the presentation of a fearsome fight between two powerful creatures as witnessed by the waki priest who has arrived at the other side of the bamboo shrub. The play ends with the following lines:

> The golden dragon ascends to its heavenly abode,
> the ferocious tiger leaps to its boulder and
> with a rueful look at the dragon
> dives back again into the bamboo grove,
> into the bamboo grove, and returns to the rock
> cave.[18]

So the spectacular battle between two powerful and ferocious creatures ends with lines that provide neither closure nor any suggestion that this will be the final battle between them.

In terms of structure, then, the play resembles many mugen

---

17. See Brazell 1997, 160–178, and Tyler 1998, 251–163, respectively, for translations of these plays.

18. 金龍雲居に遥かに上れば。悪虎は勢い巌に上がり。遥かに見送り無念の勢ひあがりを払ひ。又竹林に飛び帰り。又竹林に飛び帰て。そのまま巌洞に。入りにけり。Sanari 1982, vol. 5, 3371.

(dream) plays in which the final lines hint at a repetition of a similar event in the future. But other than that, this play bears little similarity to the many other noh plays with nonhuman beings as their protagonists. In these plays, the nonhumans are usually either members of the heavenly pantheon or spirits of creatures and plants that are often presented with anthropomorphic traits—especially emotions. But in *Ryōko*, all we see are the nonhuman or beastly characteristics of the two creatures. Oda Sachiko identifies this "lack of humanity (人間性 *ningensei*)" as one of the play's characteristics. She points out that the narrative of the battle is presented without value judgments, such as branding the creatures as good or bad.[19] This particular way of presenting his characters also demonstrates Nobumitsu's creativity. Again, as suggested by Oda, Nobumitsu's ability to transform abstract ideas such as a poetic line describing movements of the dragon and the tiger into dramatic movement is a clear indication of his talent in noh composition.

There are a few noteworthy aspects related to character-role relationship in this play. Like many of his counterparts in other late Muromachi plays, the waki character in *Ryōko* is given more dramatic significance. The waki initiates the flow of the play by asking the shite questions, then brings forward a second theme instead of letting the shite take over. By having the waki cut the shite short in his comments, the power relationship of the two roles is more equal: both role types share similar dramatic significance.

The most intriguing feature about the shite is not his relationship with the waki, however. Rather, it is the identity of the character. Who is this elderly woodcutter appearing in time to answer the waki's questions? Is he someone or something else, such as the tiger, in disguise? This assumption follows the structural development of a conventional mugen play: the protagonist appears in the form of "a person living in the vicinity"

---

19. The other significant traits as identified by Oda are the skillful compilation of information on the two creatures and the poetic presentation of the imagery. See Oda in *Kanze* (June 1985): 20–49.

before showing his or her real identity in Act Two. In some of the plays that I have discussed, it is very clear that the shite role plays two different characters in Acts One and Two, respectively, but we find no plausible hints that suggest one way or the other in *Ryōko*. Taking into consideration the basic structure of the play, which is its segmental nature, one may argue that the two characters are not related. What is even more interesting in this assertion is that *Ryōko* therefore embraces most of the characteristics of the late Muromachi noh plays, including one that challenges the performers to a greater extent by demanding two different modes of performance in one play. Again, it also demonstrates the effort of Nobumitsu to compose plays that are extraordinary: a play that shares the structure of the mugen plays while providing a surprising twist later.

This twist in the narrative structure of the play would have baffled anyone who wanted to ascertain the sources of inspiration, or *honzetsu* (本説). If we examine the issue of honzetsu with reference to Zeami's treatises, this play clearly lacks an appropriate source.[20] The absence of reference to any canonical literary works, characters, or texts, creates—paradoxically—both novelty and alienation. There is also one other explanation for the inspiration of the play. In his introductory comments to this work, Sanari Kentarō identifies paintings of a battle between a dragon and a tiger as a possible source.[21] From the perspective of the play's structure, this is certainly a plausible explanation. Unlike *Taise Taishi* or *Rashōmon*, in which the dramatic plot is an important element, the emphasis in *Ryōko* lies more in the battle between the tiger and the dragon, epitomized in the finale dance. Both the painting and this play share a similar emphasis on visual elements.

---

20. Appropriate source (本説正し) is one of the important ideas related to noh composition in Zeami's *Fushikaden*. Omote and Katō 1974, 29–30, 47–49. It basically refers to the need to allude to certain literary texts or sources that enjoy a "cultured" status. Mitake 2001, 87–109, explains Zeami's use of the term and goes as far as to state that *honzetsu* is a critical component in Zeami's mugen noh. Also see Chapter Six of this book for more discussion of this concept.

21. Sanari 1982, vol. 5, 3360.

Not only are the possible source(s) of origin difficult to identify, the specific locale in which the narrative unfolds is also somewhere unfamiliar to the Japanese imagination. Oda Sachiko explains that it is necessary for the waki to travel all the way to China before the story can be enacted because of the exotic nature of the battling creatures.[22] In other words, because of the unusual nature of its protagonists, the narrative can only be situated in an unusual setting. This echoes the definition of karamono or Chinese characters (as something exotic) in Zeami's treaties, which I mentioned at the beginning of this chapter.

One other ambiguous feature in this play is its seemingly insipid plot, although this is not an uncommon feature in noh plays. Many deity plays, for instance, are odes celebrating rulers, while women plays display the beauty and elegance of female-style dance. These plays often have a very thin plot. Other plays that extol Buddhism or Shinto deities, too, enact or reiterate a miraculous deed by the religious subject in question and focus on music and lyrics in the play. But, be it celebration or elegance, the thematic concerns of these plays need no deciphering. *Ryōko*'s central theme of battle, however, is more mystifying.

Nishino Haruo, focusing on the stylistic presentation of the play, classifies it as an exemplary representation of the furyū noh category of Nobumitsu's plays.[23] Shirakawa and Oda both associate the theme of battles between the dragon and the tiger with the political situation during the late Muromachi period when there were constant power struggles among the different warlords, which were manifested in the incessant civil warfare that marked especially the second half of the medieval period. While it is impossible to deny any suggestion of a political inspiration for the play, it is also somewhat simplistic to propose that the historical backdrop provides a full answer to the problem of the thematic source for *Ryōko*.[24] It may even be argued that the association

---

22. Oda 1985, 24.
23. Yokomichi et al. 1987, 260
24. See Shirakawa 1985 and Oda 1985.

between a dragon and an emperor, as mentioned in the chorus's lines (the emperor's face is *ryūgan* or *ryōgan* 龍顔, also dragon face, and his conveyance, the *ryōga* 龍駕 or dragon carriage), may suggest the emperor is the power center. One should remember first, however, that the power of a Chinese emperor is very different from that of his Japanese counterpart; and second, in view of the apolitical nature of many other Nobumitsu plays and the conventional indifference toward current affairs in noh plays in general, it is more probable that rather than an explicit political implication, this usage reflects Nobumitsu's expanded sources of inspiration as well as his proficiency in Chinese classical learning.

As a final observation in the discussion of this play, Oda also argues that the late Muromachi period was a time when the people were beginning to anticipate a more peaceful era after a long period of warfare. The audience then was more open to noh plays that were more this-world-oriented rather than those that dwelled on nostalgia or sinful existence. This remark highlights the importance of the audience. It is definitely true that the demands and preferences of the audience can never be underestimated. Oda is therefore correct in highlighting the audience's preference as one of the possible considerations behind the composition of *Ryōko*, although audience preference, again, cannot be the only explanation accounting for authorial intentions. The fact that this play was not often performed indicates that in spite of its appealing features, audiences in the late Muromachi and subsequent periods had not really developed a taste for it. The stylistic features and the thematic presentations of *Ryōko* exhibit many features that are different from other more popular noh plays that the audience would have found it difficult to appreciate.[25]

---

25. It would be interesting to use modern Western theatrical theory to explain this phenomenon of audience reception. Keir Elam uses a theatrical semiotics approach to explain interactions between the performance and the audience during a performance, although some of the features (theatrical codes, dramatic codes, and cultural codes) he identifies as crucial in theatrical communication can also be used to explain the communication between a particular play and its audience over a stretch of time (Elam 1993, 32–97). *Ryōko*'s late Muromachi period audi-

The Emperor Who Wins It All

Kōtei is also called *Myōōkyō* or the Lord Myō's Mirror, the name of the magical mirror that is used to conquer the illness demon who has tormented both the romantic emperor, mentally, and the fragile consort Yōkihi, physically.[26]

The play starts with a court official (kyogen) explaining to the audience that the emperor is very worried about his consort Yōkihi (kokata). We then hear from the Emperor Gensō (waki) that his favorite consort Yōkihi, whom he loves dearly, has suddenly developed a mysterious disease. Then an old man (shite) appears in the court from out of nowhere and claims that he will be able to help Gensō by identifying the source of Yōkihi's illness and curing her. The old man turns out to be Shōki, a famous exorcist who declares that he has come to repay past kindnesses that he received from one of Gensō's predecessors. Shōki offers the emperor a magical mirror to find out where the illness demon is hiding. But even though Gensō is able to see the demon, he is not able to approach it, let alone kill it. In Act Two Shōki enters in full battle attire and cuts the demon to pieces in no time. The play ends with Shōki requesting Gensō's permission to become the protecting deity of the emperor and Yōkihi.

Like some of the furyū-style plays discussed in the last chapter, this play includes characters of almost every possible role-type, ranging from the child role (kokata) who plays Yōkihi to the auxiliary role (waki-zure) who plays the court ministers accompanying the emperor when he enters. The shite plays only one character, although he changes from an ordinary-looking old man at his first appearance to a majestic and sword-wielding warrior riding on a magical horse during his second appearance. Finally, the evil illness demon, which is the cause of all the

ence might have problems decoding the various ideological, historical, or cultural significations that the play exhibits. The treatment of Buddhism, for instance, could be one of these significations.

26. The text is based on Itō 1983–1988, vol. 2, 72–78.

consternation, and which nevertheless performs two dances with
the emperor and then Shōki, respectively, is performed by the
shite-zure.

The stage is relatively well adorned. In Act One the center
of the stage is occupied by a small platform behind which Yōkihi
sits. And halfway through the play Gensō orders his attendants
to bring out the stand that holds the magical mirror, which is
then placed on the front part of the stage. The dance sequences
in the play, too, contribute to the visual aspects of the play. There
are two quick-paced dance sequences that involve active dance
movements on the stage. The first is when the emperor tries to kill
the illness demon and ends up chasing him around Yōkihi's chamber.
The second is when Shōki arrives in his battle attire and eventually
kills the illness demon after yet another round of pursuit.

The visual elements in this play, most of which can also be
identified in many other Nobumitsu's plays, are clearly abundant
and entertaining. The creation of a play that is based on Chinese
sources also means that the characters will have costumes (and
probably hand props) different from those in noh plays based on
Japanese themes. For instance, the nochi-jite wears a red-colored
wig (*akagashira*), a Chinese crown with a red-golden satin
headband (*kindan hachimaki*), a colorful flowery brocade robe,
a hunting cloak (*kariginu*), and red divided skirts (*hangiri*).[27]
Other characters, too, wear some kind of "Chinese"-type costume
that identify them as being non-Japanese.

Structurally speaking, this play is more complicated than the
average noh plays produced before Nobumitsu's time. Instead of
letting the characters narrate the events that lead to the dramatic
present, events are *enacted* on stage, and therefore presented
with more dramatic intensity. The kyogen's introduction at the
beginning of the play is also relatively rare in noh plays. Usually
an ai-kyogen appears, like the one in Nobumitsu's *Momijigari*,
to reiterate the story and give the nochi-jite a chance to exit
and transform. But in this play the shite exits after his initial

27. Itō 1983–1988, vol. 2 (1986), 72.

appearance without the use of a formal *nakairi* (mid-play entrance), and the usual explanation by the ai-kyogen is replaced by an exchange between the waki and the kokata. Even within the group of plays that are situated in the dramatic present, to have the shite enter without a proper *nakairi* seems to be more the exception than the rule.

Such an arrangement gives the narrative a very smooth flow—and consequently encourages the audience to pay more attention to the drama that is unfolding before their eyes than they would to the musical and poetic elements that some other noh plays (both by Nobumitsu and other noh composers) prioritize. This kind of presentation of the narrative—beginning with the announcement that Yōkihi is sick, developing as unexpected help arrives, and ending with the slaughtering of the illness demon—presents a more "modern" structure to contemporary readers and audiences. This structure marks a different kind of noh presentation, compared to other categories of noh plays where events are narrated through the words of the characters and the visual elements are minimized so that the audience's attention is induced to focus on the solo dance and the lyrics.

There is, of course, more to *Kōtei* than just the structural and visual effects that make for an interesting noh play. Below I present a close textual reading of the play, highlighting the literary aesthetics and the possible interpretations of the text. This play, unlike the rest of Nobumitsu's karamono plays, alludes heavily to the famous Tang poem *Changhenge* (长恨歌 *Chōgonka*, "Song of Everlasting Regret") by Bai Juyi. Therefore a brief historical account of Bai and the original poem, *Chōgonka*, is in order before I examine the play.

Bai Juyi is one of the representative Chinese poets from the Tang dynasty. In his long career he wrote many poems and prose essays on a myriad of subjects. He compiled a collection of his works into the sixty-seven-volume *Baishi Wenji* (白氏文集 Bai's anthology) in 839 (Kaicheng 4),[28] which later was brought to

---

28. See Zhang 2005, 290–294, for a brief biographical account of Bai's life.

Heian Japan by Buddhist monks. Thanks to this anthology, which is called *Hakushi Monjū* in Japan, Bai became the most influential Tang poet in premodern Japan through to the end of the medieval period.

One of Bai's most famous works is the long narrative poem *Changhenge,* which depicts the rise and fall of Yang Yuhuan (719–756), more commonly known as Yang Guifei after her court rank.[29] The poem can be divided, very broadly, into three sections: the emperor Tang Xuanzong's (Gensō, 685–762) discovery of Yang and their happy days together, the army's rebellion, and Yang's death. The final section describes the brief encounter between the Taoist priest sent by Xuanzong and the spirit of Yang. It is certainly not inaccurate to argue that the poem presents an idealized, almost perfect, romantic relationship between the emperor and his consort.[30] But no interpretation of the poem is complete if the element of political criticism is not taken into account.[31] The opening line of the poem that summarizes the emperor's desire to find a beautiful woman at all cost is clearly an expression of dissatisfaction with the sovereign. In short, Bai Juyi's poem is not simply an account of romantic love but also a critique of the emperor and the imperial institution that he represents.

Zhang presents a detailed analysis of the narrative poem *Changhenge* in this book, arguing that the romantic relationship between the star-crossed lovers proves to be a very effective way to critique the political situation then.

29. See Kroll 1991 for a commentary and an annotated translation of this poem.

30. There are many examples. For instance the last two couplets, "天长地久有时尽、此恨绵绵无绝期" (Heaven and earth will end in time to come, but our regret will stay with eternity), arguably the most famous lines in the poem, describe the lovers' desire to be always with each other in whatever form of existence they may be, and therefore the agony and sorrow of failing to do so will last beyond eternity. Other episodes in the poem, such as the emperor's singular passion for Yang earlier on and his persistence in finding Yang after her death, are all indications of the romantic relationship between the two protagonists.

31. Chen Hong (?–821?), a literati and Bai's contemporary, wrote an introductory free verse called *Changhenge zhuan* (长恨歌传), a preface to the poem. In one version of this piece, he mentioned that one of the intentions of the article is to record this historical event as a lesson for later generations to remember. Cited in Zhang, 282.

Besides Nobumitsu's *Kōtei*, there is at least one other noh play in the active repertoire that is based on *Song of Everlasting Regret*. The play, *Yōkihi*, presents the episode where the Taoist priest finally tracks Yōkihi down and conveys a message from Gensō.[32] Attributed to Konparu Zenchiku, this play focuses on the psychological agony that the spirit of Yōkihi suffers and her reminiscences of good times with the emperor. The play alludes frequently to the poem, even though the focus of this play is the internal turmoil that Yōkihi experiences and her desire to achieve enlightenment so as to rid herself of suffering once and for all.

Unlike *Yōkihi*, Nobumitsu's *Kōtei*, which also frequently alludes to Hakurakuten's long narrative poem, does not focus on the sad beauty. As mentioned earlier, the play is a drama that involves anguish over Yōkihi's life, repayment of past kindnesses, a ferocious battle between supernatural beings, and a happy ending (except for the demon). The play has condensed the narrative into a much smaller scale both spatially and temporally. Other than the literary descriptions and poetic lines, Nobumitsu developed a plot that is independent of the poem, incorporating characters and episodes from other sources and probably his imagination. This highly intertextual play is an excellent indication of Nobumitsu's creative talent and knowledge of Chinese traditions, while its relatively complicated narrative also reflects the trends in the noh plays produced in the late Muromachi period.

The first allusion in the play to the poem is sung by the waki character Emperor Gensō describing his own passion for Yōkihi:

> Indispensable is her attendance at parties and feasts
> Inseparable are they on spring days and spring nights
> There are three thousand beauties in the palace,
> The passion and love meant for all is bestowed on
> her alone.[33]

---

32. See translation in Keene 1970, 210–217.

33. 春は春遊に入つて夜は夜を専らとし／後宮の佳麗三千人／三千の寵愛一身にあり (Itō 1983–1988, vol. 2 [1986], 73). These three lines are very similar to Bai Juyi's *Song of Everlasting Regret*: 承欢赐宴无闲暇、春从春游夜

These lines are sung at the beginning of the play, announcing its temporal setting (spring), which is one of the important tropes in the work. It is usually important in noh plays to indicate the seasonal and temporal settings in which the narratives unfold. Here, Nobumitsu has aptly appropriated the second half of one couplet in the Chinese poem. Rupturing a couplet in a regulated Chinese poem could be awkward in view of the nature of Chinese regulated verse, but Nobumitsu has skillfully maneuvered the lines to serve his purpose of fulfilling the requirement of a noh play and wringing new meanings out of the couplet for the play. In addition, the seasonal marker is also clearly conveyed. The lines are sung by Emperor Gensō himself rather than by the chorus, which can be read as a disinterested narrative voice. This arrangement greatly reduces the political tension that is implicit in the Chinese poem.

In this play, Nobumitsu is often able to reinvent the characters and plot from other forms of narrative. For instance, Emperor Gensō who has been turned into an embodiment of great romantic love while his political misdeeds (as indicated in the poem and later on in other Japanese sources such as the *Taiheiki*) have been greatly diluted. Also, using a kokata to play Yang Guifei alleviates the conventional accusation of her as being the beauty who is the indirect cause of civil war. The fact that she is the object of rescue instead of being a culprit is also very different from Bai's poem or any other later tales about her. Even though the play alludes heavily to the poem, it presents very different thematic concerns.

One of the ways this presentation can be achieved is through the modes of narration. The poem is told by an invisible and omniscient narrative voice that not only describes but also comments on and critiques the situation. This use of an omniscient narrative voice distances the readers from the text while it

专夜、后宫佳丽三千人、三千宠爱在一身 (Required is her attendance at parties and feasts / Inseparable are they in the spring days and nights / There are three thousand beauties in the rear palace / The passion and love meant for all is bestowed on her alone.). Qiu 1999, 110.

manipulates the presentation of the text from the vantage point of the voice. The chorus in the play, whose lines often overlap with those of the characters, performs a somewhat similar function as the narrative voice, especially when it speaks in the third person. But often it also speaks the lines of the characters, and in this play the chorus does not critique the emperor or his consort as does the poem's narrative voice. As a result, the complex political undertone of the poem is greatly reduced—the play becomes a depoliticized romantic account with vivid literary imagery and a spectacular stage presentation.

Immediately after Gensō's declaration of his love for Yōkihi, he continues to describe her ill state of health:

> The peerless impassioned blush of Yōkihi
> The impassioned blush of the lotus blossom is
>   fading
> Not even the strength of a willow bough at Biyō
>   Palace has she.[34]

Here the lotus blossom is a metaphor for her beauty while the willow bough suggests her fragile state. The abstract idea of a beautiful but weak woman is presented using the concrete images of the lotus flower and the willow bough. These two metaphors are both allusions from the Chinese poem, although Nobumitsu has inserted "*kōshoku*" (red color) between "flower" and "willow" which again gives a meaning most suitable to the play but very different from the original poem. In the poem, these lines describe the emperor's sad reminiscences of the past after his return to his palace from the coup d'état that killed Yang Guifei:

> Nothing has changed upon return—not the
>   garden nor the pond

---

34. かく類ひなき貴妃の紅色／芙蓉の紅色かへて／未央の柳の力もなし。Itō 1983–1988, vol. 2 (1986), 72.

> the lotuses and willows of old
> Lotus blossoms that are like her face, the willow
>   boughs her brows
> Seeing all these, tears he cannot hold back.[35]

Not simply metaphors for beauty, the plants are also the only things that remain from happier times. The contrast between the past and the present creates a tremendous sense of sadness in the poem, although this is not the case in the play. Here, the beautiful image of Yōkihi is intensified with the introduction of the color red (*kōshoku*), and her state of being is emphasized by the use of the gerund "is fading" (*kaete*)—the beloved consort may be sick, but she is still alive. The willow boughs that were originally a metaphor for her eyebrows now become a metaphor for her entire being instead. The geographical and temporal transition that takes place in the poem, marked by the lines that I have just cited, is also missing in the play since its narration has so far been centered on the illness of Yōkihi.

In the first part of the *kuse* section, the chorus continues to introduce the emperor and his relationship with Yōkihi:

> However mighty the Emperor may be,
> with the world in his hands, enjoying all glory,
> because of his desire for beautiful women,
> he pledges, to the peerless beauty Kihi,
> vows so deep that for years and months, he,
> annoyed by the quick passing of the spring nights
> rises only when the sun is high,
> sparing no thoughts for anything else,
> Neglected are both his official duties and other
>   court ladies.[36]

---

35. 帰来池苑皆依旧、太液芙蓉未央柳、芙蓉如面柳如眉、対此如何不泪流。 Qiu 1999, 111.

36. しかるに明皇／栄華を極め世を保ち／色を重んじ給ふゆゑ／類ひなき貴妃に斯く／契りをこめて年月の春宵短かきを苦しみて／日高く起き出で／朝政り事も絶え絶えに／移る方なき仲なれ

This section alludes to two different parts in *Song of Everlasting Regret*. The first part is the opening couplet in the poem:

> The amorous Han Emperor, yearning for a beauty
>   who may upset a kingdom,
> Fails to find one, over many years of his reign.[37]

This first four characters in this opening couplet literally read as "Han Emperor desiring beautiful women (汉皇重色)." It accuses the emperor of his desire for women, and hints that the kind of beauty (倾国) that the emperor is after has the potential to cause havoc in the country. The lines in the play, however, not only emphasize the emperor's desire for a beautiful consort, but also emphasize that this is a powerful emperor who is simultaneously a great lover, one whose every action, including neglecting his official duties, is quickly dismissed as a manifestation of his love for the beautiful Yōkihi. Nobumitsu has skillfully made use of the first half of a couplet that has a political undertone and depoliticized it—the amorous desire has been valorized as romantic. In this play the emperor does not need to suffer any political consequences for his actions because even though similar lines are used to describe his desire, by changing the order of the couplets, and by focusing on a short time frame and one singular incident, Nobumitsu simply tells the story of a romantic couple that has a bad start but ends well.

In the play, when the emperor asks Yōkihi how she is feeling she replies by describing her state of being as:

> Indeed I have not the strength to pick up my robe
>   or to push aside my pillow.[38]

The act of picking up a robe and pushing aside a pillow is

ど。Itō 1983–1988, vol. 2 (1986), 75.

37. 汉皇重色思倾国、御宇多年求不得。 Qiu 1999, 110.

38. げにや衣をとり／枕を推すべき力もなく。Itō 1983–1988, vol. 2, (1986), 75.

presented in Bai's poem in the final section, when the emperor's messenger, the Taoist priest, finally locates the spirit of Yang Guifei. Yang has joined other ranks of female celestial beings at a faraway mysterious mountain in the middle of a sea. She hastens from her nap to meet with the emperor's messenger:

> Picking up her robe and pushing aside her pillow,
> she walks in quick and hurried steps,
> Curtains of pearl and silvery screens give way.[39]

Even though Yang Guifei is hasty in getting dressed and coming out from the inner chamber of her sojourn, the poetic lines still present her as an elegant woman. The many screen doors and passages she has to go through represent the irreversible distance from the emperor and the human world—something that comes up a few lines later in the poem. In the play, however, the elegance and grace of the beautiful consort is retained but the focus has shifted to the fact that the ill consort is so weak that she is not able to perform a simple chore. Here, instead of the distance, it is the illness that is underscored.

We see here in the first part of the play a pair of star-crossed lovers appearing differently from their counterpart in the poem, even though several of the lines are almost word-for-word allusions. The play has reduced the temporal and geographical scale of the poem, nullified the destructive power of the beautiful Yōkihi and her relationship with the emperor, and romanticized and depoliticized the emperor.

In Act Two, the focus shifts to the shite character Shōki's heroic battle with the illness demon.[40] Shōki is not an unfamiliar character in medieval Japanese narratives. *Shōki,* a noh play attributed to Konparu Zenchiku features the spirit of the famous

---

39. 揽衣推枕起徘徊、珠箔银屏迤逦开。 Qiu 1999, 112.

40. Itō has detailed the major Japanese premodern sources that involve the character Shōki in his commentary to this play in his anthology. See Itō 1983–1988, vol. 2 (1986), 439–480. Also see Graham 1998, 151–153, for an account of the other texts in which Shōki appears.

Chinese exorcist as its protagonist. In this play, Shōki wants to pass a message to the emperor regarding his desire to exorcise all demons and evils in the land in order to make amends for his mistake in tenaciously wanting to pass the Imperial Examination. This insistence on a worldly achievement causes his untimely death. In Act Two of the play Shōki performs a demon-quelling dance. This play is one of Zenchiku's famous works because of its melancholic style and heavy dose of Buddhism.

But who is Shōki (Zhong Kui)? It is believed that Zhong Kui lived in the beginning of the Tang period. He was famed as a superior scholar, but for some reason he did not win first place in the Imperial Examination. Feeling ashamed, he killed himself by crushing his head against a pillar at the main palace hall. After his death, for some unspecified reasons and at some time in the early Tang period, he was believed to have been posthumously awarded an official position. He is best known as a supernatural being, at times a deity, who protects people against diseases and plague. Among other texts that are related to him in Japan, Shōki is seen in the Hell Screen Picture Scroll (地獄草紙 *Jigoku zōshi*) as a deity who is about to tear apart a small creature believed to be a disease-causing demon. To summarize, then, Shōki is a benign supernatural being who uses his power to protect human beings.

The image of Shōki as an exorcist certainly informed Nobumitsu's creation of the play—after all, the highlight of the play is the final battle between the two supernatural beings. And on close scrutiny, we can argue that Shōki's power in defeating the illness demon is an important tool to signify the power relationship between the three main characters. In short, despite his supernatural power, his final voluntary subjugation to the emperor indicates the importance of sanction by the ruling institution, here represented by the emperor. This is a feature also shared by the other Shōki in Zenchiku's play mentioned earlier. Shōki is mentioned in another noh play, *Kokaji* (小鍛冶 composer unknown), and again, the exorcist's name is mentioned side by side with the emperor's as "Minister

Shōki who serves Emperor Gensō."[41]

What about the Shōki in Nobumitsu's play? Other than the final act of volunteering to become the emperor's guardian deity, what is his relationship with the sovereign? He first introduces himself as someone who had received the great favor of being bestowed with a posthumous official rank from Gensō's predecessor. In order to repay this *kyūon* (former kindness), Shōki has come to save Yōkihi's life. Then in Act Two he appears in style: arriving in gorgeous trappings on a horse; sword in hand, he chants a secret spell, a prelude to his heroic rescue. The demon is more than terrified at this unexpected challenge: it first loses its power to disappear and, after a pathetically unsuccessful attempt to escape, is quickly slashed to pieces by Shōki. This scene contrasts markedly with the earlier scene when the emperor tries in vain to challenge the demon: after flying around the palace compound as if teasing the emperor, the demon simply disappears behind a pillar, leaving the emperor totally perplexed. The emperor's powerlessness when confronting the illness demon needs no further elaboration—it is demonstrated not only through the fight but also through his inability to relieve Yōkihi's suffering.

Shōki, on the other hand, is a conglomeration of might and humility. Besides his supernatural powers, he is also in possession of the magical mirror and sword, both of which are instrumental in killing the illness demon. These two items are also similar to two of the three regalia of the imperial family, even if they may not be exactly the same. That it is the exorcist rather than the emperor who is in possession of these items suggests the confusion and instability of the power relationship between the two. There is, however, no conflict between them as Shōki is more than willing to surrender himself to the hierarchical paradigm of subject/lord vis-à-vis the emperor. Both his opening and closing comments are

41. The first line, the beginning of the sashi section, is sung by the shite, and followed by the chorus: その後玄宗皇帝の鐘馗大臣も劔の徳に魂魄は君辺に仕へ奉。A literal translation: "Then, the minister Shōki serving Gensō Emperor, too, with the virtue of the sword, his soul serves besides the sovereign." Sanari 1982, vol. 2, 1117.

related to the imperial family: first a return of gratitude, and then an offer to be the guardian deity of the emperor and his beloved consort. These requests redefine the power relationship that existed earlier in the play. Shōki, despite his supernatural power and possession of mighty magical weapons, lacks only an official sanction to practice the good deeds he so desires. At the end of the play, he manages to legitimize his position by offering his services to the imperial institution while the emperor's superior position is reaffirmed. All's well that ends well.

Chōryō: The Tale of the Chinese General[42]

Chōryō (General Chōryō) is a play based on a famous tale about a well-known Chinese general, Zhang Liang, from the Western Han period. This play, which at first glance seems like an ordinary genzai noh that tells the story of a military man's adventures, again displays features that illustrate both Nobumitsu's characteristic style in noh composition, and a general indication of a trend that late Muromachi noh plays were developing toward.

The play opens with the self-introduction of the waki, Chōryō. It is not yet dawn, but he is hurrying along to meet an anonymous old man who promises to give him a secret treatise.[43] The treatise is vital to Chōryō's military career because it promises a strategy that will help him and his generals defeat a strong and tenacious enemy—the first emperor of Qin who built the state that

---

42. Chōryō (张良 Zhang Liang, ?–168 BCE) was a subordinate of Liu Bang (刘邦 256?–195 BCE), a general who rose against the rule of the first emperor of Qin (秦始皇帝 Qin shihuangdi). Liu successfully defeated Qin and became the first emperor of the Han dynasty. This political struggle was recorded in various Chinese historical accounts such as the Shiji (史记 Records of the Grand Historian) and Hanshu (汉书 History of the Former Han Dynasty), and some of the tales became legendary in the course of transmission. The story of Chōryō is one of them.

43. The old man is Kōsekikō (黄石公 literally the "Yellow Boulder Elderly"). He appears in Chinese historical texts such as Shiji and Hanshu as the elderly man who eventually gave Chōryō the secret military treatise.

became China's first dynasty. Upon reaching their meeting place, an upset old man is already awaiting Chōryō. The elderly man chides the young general for coming late, and before he stomps off in indignation, he offers a second opportunity for Chōryō to meet him in five days. Chōryō, although feeling that he has been wrongfully accused because it is the old man who was early, decides to follow his instruction and returns in five days. Act Two starts five days later, after the ai-kyōgen, Chōryō's attendant, explains the general's intriguing adventure. This time Chōryō has left for the appointment long ahead of time. When they meet, the old man puts Chōryō through a second test: to retrieve his shoes from a river where a huge serpent (shite-zure) is waiting to challenge him. Chōryō calmly battles the serpent and successfully retrieves the shoes. He is awarded the secret military treatise and also wins himself a guardian deity in the process.

In the *Shiji* (Records of the grand historian) the original source of the brave general's adventure, General Zhang Liang has to endure three humiliating encounters with the old man before he is able to gain the latter's trust and receive the secret military treatise. In the noh adaptation of this story, Nobumitsu introduced two novel features. The first is Chōryō's initial encounter with the anonymous old man Kōsekikō. Instead of meeting Kōsekikō in person, the play has moved the meeting place to a dream. This encounter is in turn narrated by the waki in his opening speech (*kaikō*), thus complying with the more common noh narrative structure in which the events that lead to the (dramatic) present are summarized orally at the introduction. The play then unfolds as a performance of the events that follow. The second twist that Nobumitsu has made to this famous tale is the final test that Chōryō is put through. Before Chōryō can be trusted with the military treatise, he has to battle a fearsome serpent in a river, which turns out to be an apparition of the Goddess of Mercy (Kannon).[44] After

---

44. The "original" tale of Chōryō and his military treatise is less dramatic. Chōryō has to endure humiliations designed by Kōsekikō owing to the consequences of their encounter; Kōsekikō is to present the young general with an important military treatise that will help him fight the battle against the First

Kōsekikō reveals the true nature of the frightening serpent, he announces that the Kannon will become Chōryō's protecting deity from then on—adding an extra dimension to the brave general's story. In his commentary to the play, Sanari has dismissed this extra episode as redundant in the eyes of the modern audience, even though it was not uncommon to incorporate religious elements at the time when the play was composed.[45]

There are certainly more implications to this addition to Chōryō's legend—it is more than a religious belief manifested on the stage as Sanari suggests. For one thing, it enhances the dramatic effect of the play—one that is premised on a motif that most late Muromachi audiences were familiar with. Just like the changes made to Chōryō's encounters with Kōsekikō, the addition of a serpent and a struggle between the two in a narrow river over a shoe becomes a visual and boisterous highlight to a play that already has an exotic flavor to it. It is somewhat uncommon for the shite not to perform the *maibataraki*—a dance that is performed with a quick tempo—although he sings the last section and hands the scroll to Chōryō before the play ends. In this way the shite still has a significant dramatic role while the waki and tsure, too, enjoy a fair share of the stage. The addition of the serpent episode is therefore not simply a reflection of the popular Buddhist belief of *rishō* (利生 divine favor), but rather a calculated move that demonstrates characteristics of Nobumitsu's noh plays.

Kanako addresses this issue of the different functions of the shite and waki by arguing that rather than viewing the waki as stealing the limelight of the shite, this play should be viewed as

Emperor of Qin. Chōryō has to pass the test of picking up Kōsekikō's shoes and putting them on his foot three times to prove his humility and perseverance so as to qualify as the suitable recipient of the treatise. In the noh play, however, more dramatic twists are added to the story with the more concise plot, the introduction of a dream and the serpent-turned-Kannon. This kind of liberty is common in the composition of Nobumitsu's noh plays. For instance in *Kōtei*, which I have discussed earlier, the Chinese sorcerer Shōki from the early Tang dynasty also becomes the guardian deity of another Tang emperor generations later.

45. Sanari 1982, vol. 3, 2045.

presenting two contrasting sentiments: the waki represents the active and the dramatic, while the shite represents solemnity and grandeur.[46] It is true that ascribing separate sentiments to the shite and waki implies, again, a more equal dramatic sharing between the two roles. The tsure's role as the serpent in the river who challenges Chōryō when he retrieves the old man's shoe is yet another example illustrating Nobumitsu's ability to distribute dramatic significance to different role types. Here we recall Nogami Toyoichirō's comment that noh is the kind of play that focuses on the shite and the shite alone—*shite ichinin shūgi*—referring mainly to the *mugen* noh plays that were composed by Zeami and his contemporaries.[47] If we contrast this style with the plays produced by Nobumitsu and his peers, we will be able to see that there is a changing trend in these later noh plays to expand beyond the practice of focusing on the shite. There are, of course, advantages and disadvantages to this new trend. The obvious advantage is the possibility of enacting the events as they unfold, although at times this is done at the expense of the poetic aesthetics that are especially essential when the shite performs "solo." The dramatic role of the serpent-turned-deity character is clearly important, as it accentuates the heroic nature of the protagonist Chōryō. The significance of the shite character, however, is not eclipsed in this method. The bigger cast simply increases the dramatic action of the play.

Closely related to the use of the tsure role as a silent serpent who battles the waki Chōryō is the spectacle that such an arrangement produces. The entrance of the shite, Kōsekikō, during Act Two, exemplifies one general feature of the late Muromachi shite roles: strong visual effect. He wears a special old man mask, a Chinese-style hat with two white flowing streamers, and a golden hair band indicating his Chinese origin. With his robe, travel cloak and Chinese fan, the shite makes a grand entrance, holding the scroll of military strategies in his hands.[48] Even in Act One when

---

46. Kanako 1991, 21.

47. Nogami 1948 argues that the shite is the most important performer on the noh stage. See Introduction, footnote 22, for a more detailed explanation.

48. It is difficult to determine exactly which mask(s) was (were) used during

his costume is less elaborate, Kōsekikō, with his fiery temper and authoritative presence, has his fair share of dramatic spectacle. Nevertheless, it is easy to miss the visual significance ascribed to the character if the play is experienced as a reading text—his ostentatious attire and majestic style of entrance cannot be easily conveyed in writing. In fact, we see this kind of very stylized entrance regularly in plays by Nobumitsu and his peers—usually at the beginning of Act Two when the shite enters as his or her real self. This particular part, when the shite reenters, is usually an important chance to showcase the unique nature of the shite, be it beauty or frightfulness or elegance.

A close look at *Chōryō* will reveal one other characteristic: the play unfolds through the regular use of spoken lines (both conversational or monologue) rather than poetic imagery or lyrical libretto. It therefore has a low level of allusions to any literary source, unlike the other two plays, *Ryōko* and *Kōtei,* that are discussed in this chapter. Perhaps the intense visually oriented presentation in the play is a deliberate strategy to compliment this feature, and it can be understood as yet another indication of the general trend of the noh plays composed in the late Muromachi period. Act One has no allusion to any known literary texts, and Act Two has two allusions to describe the early morning landscape when Chōryō starts out very early to meet Kōsekikō. Chōryo sings this at the beginning of Act Two:

> Traveling along the frost-layered land of Outai,
> a lone crane squalling through the autumn sky
> Passing by the gorge of Ha,
> the melancholic monkeys howling at the dawning
>   moon
> how desolate, this mountain pass.[49]

---

the late Muromachi period when the play was first performed, because of the lack of reliable sources. Anthologies that I have consulted have all describe Kōsekikō's mask as some kind of old man (尉 jō) mask, although different texts indicate different versions.

49. The noh text: 瑶臺霜満てり。一声の玄鶴空になく。巴峡秋深し。

This is followed by the chorus's comment:

> The dawning moon shining over the mountain gorge
> The dawning moon shining over the mountain gorge
> Under the bridge at Kahi that I cross,
> a river ripples under,
> undisturbed is the white frost on it.
> How happy I am, the first one to cross,
> My wish will be fulfilled
> like the rising tides at the break of the day, from afar
> From afar is the hurried sight of a man on horse.[50]

The waki has first started his journey in the early morning where no human traces can be found, and where the atmosphere seems to be sad and frightening. Even though this particular section does not seem to match the basic atmosphere of the play, which is upbeat and positive, the section which follows clarifies the emphasis of the poem—that the hour is still too early for any human being other than the determined general. The second allusion is to a poem from the *Shinkokinwakashū*, a waka by the Manyōshū poet Ōtomo Yakamochi (大伴家持 717?–785). Together these two segments of the play describe a quiet, almost solemn early morning hour, where the only sources of noise are animals, and the only light is from the moon. The undisturbed frost on the bridge is a reassurance to Chōryō that this time

---

五夜の哀猿月に叫ぶ。もの凄しき。山路かな。This section alludes to a poem by the Tang poet Xie Guan (谢观 Shakuan, ?–?), which is anthologized in *Wakan Rōeishū* vol. 2, "Monkeys," no. 454. The original poem is: 瑶臺霜満／一声之玄鶴唳天／巴峡秋深／五夜之哀猿叫月。

50. The noh text is: 有明の。月も隈なき深更に。山の峡より見渡せ ば。所は下ひの川波に。渡せる橋に置く霜の。白きを見れば今朝はま だ。渡りし人の跡もなし。嬉しや今ははや。思ふ願ひも満つ潮の。 暁かけて遥かに。夜馬に鞭打つ人影の。駒を早むる気色あり。Part of this *ageuta* segment: "wataseru hashi ni oku shimo no shiraki wo mireba," is loosely based on a poem in *Shinkokinwakashū*, no. 620 (winter) 鵲の／渡せ る橋に／おく霜の／白きを見れば／夜ぞふけにける。

around he has reached the meeting place earlier than the old man, indicating that he is a step closer to the much sought after military treatise.

Other than these two sections, however, there are no further allusions to any other poetic sources. Both Nishino and Sanari, in their respective annotated anthologies *Yōkyoku Hyakuban* and *Yōkyoku Taikan*, identify various texts that could be possible sources of inspiration for this play. These sources include Japanese material such as Otogizōshi and commentaries of poetry anthologies, as well as Chinese sources such as *Shiki*. In this play *Chōryō*, we see an interesting approach to intertextuality in noh compositions: a stronger emphasis is put on dramatic presentation rather than on lyrical presentation. Within Nobumitsu's active noh repertoire, this stylistic feature is not common. However, it does seem like a more preferred trend in plays by Zenpō and Nagatoshi who started to compose noh plays perhaps about a decade later than Nobumitsu.

Karamono Plays and Their Possible Meanings

In this chapter I present a close reading of three of Nobumitsu's *karamono* plays, highlighting the different emphases in presentation and themes these plays demonstrate. *Kōtei* and *Chōryō* are titled after the waki characters who, like their counterparts in many other Nobumitsu plays, are instrumental in propelling the development of the plots. In *Ryōko*, the two creatures, the dragon and the tiger, both of which the title refers to, are performed by the shite-zure and the nochi-jite, respectively. One can argue that if Nobumitsu were to have written a treatise on noh composition, the major development in the character-role relationship would have been to expand the dramatic significance of the other role type, although the shite would still be allocated the most important role such as performing the final dance as the tiger does in *Ryōko*, or being visually impressive such as Kōsekikō in Act Two of *Chōryō*.

There are other important characteristics in these karamono plays that are not as commonly found in other Nobumitsu
plays. The first is the liberal adaptation of Chinese sources. The best
example is *Kōtei*, which skillfully reworked a complicated poetic
narrative into a simple episode that allows for the introduction of
a new character in Act Two. The story of Chōryō too, shows a more
compact tale of adventure injected with a dose of late Muromachi
religious belief. Both plays introduce the Chinese subject matter
visually and through allusions to Chinese poetry.

The allusions to Chinese poetry serve two functions: an
emphasis on the setting of the narratives, as well as the producing
of a different aural effect when chanted, given the need to use
the "Chinese pronunciation" more. These factors contribute to
the "exotic" as well as the "furyū" effects of the plays, although
as I argued earlier, while there is consciousness of *kara* being a
cultural other, the concept of China as another state had yet to be
formed.

We also see, in this group of plays, references to warfare and
power negotiation among different social institutions. In *Ryōko* the
shite character gives everyone a lesson on the futility of warfare,
while the other two plays end with a reaffirmation of political
hierarchy. The emperor in *Kōtei*, although somewhat incompetent,
has his world back in order by the time the play ends. Chōryō's
quest is sealed and approved by the promise of protection from
the Bodhisattva of Mercy. In all these plays, then, we see a more
complicated treatment of the interactions among political and
religious institutions, although they end in conformity with the
ruling institutions.

Other non-karamono Nobumitsu plays are different,
often ending with the successful completion of a mission like
that in *Momijigari* and *Rashōmon*, or the enlightenment of the
protagonists like that in *Yugyō Yanagi* and *Kochō*. In *Tamanoi*,
the Dragon King seems to have conceded his powerful position
to the Heavenly Grandchild Hikohohodemi-no-mikoto as
Yokota suggested, but the two parties have their own designated

space to rule when Hikohohodemi returns to land.[51] Another representative of a political institution is Susanoo-no-mikoto in *Orochi*, who slaughters the evil human-devouring serpent and claims ownership of a sword found in the serpent's stomach. Perhaps a hint of a power struggle can be detected in this play, although Susanoo's legitimized position is not questioned at all. Relatively speaking, the discussion of power and hierarchy seems more explicit in these karamono plays—perhaps because their subject matter is something distant and alien. The general tendency in Nobumitsu's other noh plays does not support a strong political position, however. The question of whether karamono plays have a more explicit political implication can only be answered after a more in-depth reading of other karamono from this period.

Still, it is correct to say that to a certain extent the differences between Nobumitsu's furyū and karamono plays are engendered and supplemented by the use of non-Japanese subject matter. And equally important, we can see Nobumitsu's finesse in noh composition. In the next chapter I will discuss yet another category of Nobumitsu's plays: his mugen dream play. We will see that even though Nobumitsu is better known for his furyū style of most of the plays that I have discussed so far, he is as competent in composing plays that befit the aesthetic preferences of mugen plays.

51. Yokota-Murakami 1997, 136.

Chapter Five

DWELLING IN "MUGEN"

In previous chapters I argued that Nobumitsu's noh plays, while observing the overall structural requirements and conventional practices of noh, demonstrate a considerable amount of deviation from those of the two earlier generations of noh composers. This tendency is easier to identify in plays such as *Funabenkei* and *Momijigari* in which spectacular features or unconventional thematic elements prevail. Other plays such as *Ryōko* and *Kōtei* present the "Chinese" Other that allow for even more flexibility in intertextuality and sources of inspirations. These plays are different from the early Muromachi noh plays created by Zeami and his disciples, in which lyrical elements are emphasized; the main focus of the plays stays within the internal landscape of the protagonists; and the pathos of these plays is conveyed through poetic imagery and literary allusions. The most effective way to convey the intense emotions permeating these plays is through the format of a two-part *mugen* (dream) play—a style that has won high acclaim among modern-day noh scholars and has been established as the representative style of the Zeami aesthetic paradigm.

What about Nobumitsu's mugen noh plays? What special features do they evidence? Are there features that distinguished this group of Nobumitsu plays from those by other noh composers?

Judging from the quantity and quality of Nobumitsu's mugen noh plays, it is safe to argue that this category of plays is the least representative of Nobumitsu's works, and of the late Muromachi period in general. To begin with, there are only four plays that can be identified as mugen noh: the much acclaimed *Yugyō Yanagi* (The Priest and the Willow) and *Kochō* (The Butterfly), whose shite characters, both nonhumans, encounter the waki characters first disguised as humans in the dramatic present, and then with their real identity in the waki's "dreams." *Yoshino Tennin* (The Yoshino deity), which features a heavenly maiden's visit to Mt. Yoshino and her encounter with a local tourist, has a similar structure, albeit shorter. *Kamei* (Kamei the warrior), the last play in the list, is no longer performed. It follows closely the *shura* noh structure in which a warrior reveals to a traveling priest (a waki) details of his final battle and subsequent sufferings. This play, however, was never popular, and has not been performed in a long time.

Yoshino Tennin, Kochō, and *Yugyō Yanagi* are all still performed today. These three plays follow the mugen noh structure and are full of poetic imagery and allusions to classical works in the medieval Japanese literary canon. Nobumitsu demonstrates clearly in these three plays his ability to compose noh plays that fit well in the preferred (modern) aesthetic regime of noh plays and which invoke the mysterious yūgen aesthetics that most define noh plays in its contemporary discourse. *Kochō* and *Yugyō Yanagi*, on close reading, show some interesting features that can be identified with the historical and cultural specifics of the time. Before making a more in-depth analysis of these plays, however, it will be useful to have an overview of what mugen noh plays entailed.

Defining the Mugen Plays

What exactly is mugen noh (夢幻能)? It is translated in various ways, including dream plays, phantasmic plays, or visional plays.[1]

1. For example, Smethurst 1998 and Shimazaki 1976 both describe mugen noh

A closer look at the Chinese characters which make up the term may prove that none of the above translations can fully describe mugen. "*Mu*" means dream while "*gen*," usually used in compound words, refers to illusions or something dreamlike. "*Mu*" and "*gen*" together, then, refers to a dreamlike, illusory state. Often the characters themselves wonder if they are in a dream or in reality (*yume ka utsutsu ka*), suggesting a more ambiguous division between these two states of consciousness in the medieval imagination than in our modern one. I have chosen to use the term "mugen" instead of attempting to provide a translation for it.

Like the use of the category "furyū," "mugen," too, is a product of modern noh scholars. Tashiro detailed the historical development of the term "mugen noh," tracing it back to the November 1905 issue of one of the earliest noh journals, *Nōgaku*. An article by Ikenouchi Nobuyoshi (1858–1934) entitled "Categorization of Noh Plays" (*Nōgaku no funrui*) proposed that noh plays be divided into three categories: *Mugen*, *Genjitsu* (real life), and *Chūritsu* (in between).[2] Following that, in 1926, Sanari Kentarō used this term in his radio lectures on noh, and later on in *Yōkyokudaikan*, an annotated collection of noh texts. It is, however, not until the late 1950s that the concept of mugen noh is discussed in depth by noh scholars Yokomichi Mario and Omote Akira in their commentary in *Yōkyokushū*. In the introductory article to this two-volume anthology, genzai noh (Noh plays that feature living persons in the present time) and mugen noh were compared and identified as possible categories of noh plays.[3] It is from that time on that the term "mugen noh" became popular and eventually an integral part of the modern noh discourse.

---

as "visional." Even though the term "dream" play may be apt in describing the specific characteristic of plays that involve a "dream sequence," these medieval dreams may not necessarily have the same signification as various English terms connote. All three of the modern English terms that are used here either risk ascribing too much of the dream element, or carry a religious undertone.

2. Tashiro 1994, 5–22.

3. It is also in this article that furyū noh was discussed. Yokomichi and Omote 1960–1963, 7–12.

Mugen noh plays are often presented in the following frame-work—a traveler (waki), usually related to some kind of religious institution, visits a place he has never been to before. There the traveler encounters a local person (shite) who reveals to him a past event that has happened there. As the exchange between the two progresses, the local person eventually reveals that she/he is the protagonist of that specific event. Before disappearing, the local person promises to return in her/his real identity. During the *nakairi* (mid-play entrance) another local person (ai-kyōgen), who also lives in the dramatic present, reiterates or elaborates on the event that was described by the first local person, usually in the form of answering further questions from the traveler. At the end of this exchange, the traveler is urged to say a prayer for the unfortunate soul whom he met earlier on. Then the main protagonist (nochi-jite) reappears, this time in a costume befitting his or her identity in the tale told earlier, and performs a dance. The dance can be either a celebration of attaining enlightenment thanks to the traveler's prayer, or an expression of the sinful attachment and the resulting torments the protagonist has been suffering. Act Two of the play takes place in a liminal space assumed to be in the waki character's "dream" (*yume*) in the modern sense, although as I have mentioned, it is dubious as to whether it is really a dream.

Not all mugen noh revolve around a ghost awaiting enlighten-ment. Another important kind of play using the "dream" sequence is the play that has celestial beings first appearing in the disguise of "a person in the vicinity" who meets the waki. In Act Two, the celestial being(s)—often Shinto deities but at times Buddhist representatives—resumes her/his supernatural identity and performs a boisterous and lively song and dance as a gesture to bless the land or sing praise to share the joy and teachings of the religious institution to which they belong. The appearance of the celestial beings in Act Two of the play is often called a "revelation" (*takusen*) or a "miracle" (*kizui*) even though they are categorized under the broad rubric of "dream" play. Nobumitsu's *Yoshino Tennin* (The Yoshino deity) and Konparu Zenpō's *Arashiyama* (Mt. Arashi) are two such examples.

Mugen noh is the most popular form among the various styles of noh plays—most plays by the second generation noh practitioners are mugen noh, represented by some of Zeami's famous plays. Even though Zeami did not coin the term "mugen noh," it is clear that he skillfully deployed the illusionary space between consciousness and dream to exercise his creativity in the aesthetics of yūgen. Most of the plays that are attributed to Zeami underscore the fact that the structure of the two-part dream play, where the shite appears in two different forms of one character, is very much a preferred prototype for the practitioner. Examples are plentiful. Most of the warrior plays attributed to Zeami, for instance, *Atsumori*, *Sanemori*, *Kiyotsune*, and *Tadanori*, featuring the defeated Taira clan warriors, are all classified as mugen noh.[4] Although with some variations in the nature of the encounter or relationship between the shite and the waki in Act One, Act Two of these plays inevitably sees the resumption of the original warrior identity of the protagonists. They then narrate the sorrowful stories of their lives, emphasizing especially the major event that they are so attached to that it impedes their enlightenment.

All these plays share several common features. The protagonists, no longer persons of the present living world, are able to appear before the traveler to present their stories. Because of attachments to specific events in their lives, they are not able to attain enlightenment and gain release from their suffering. The arrival of the traveler—often one associated with some kind of religious institution—gives them an opportunity to seek repose and end the torments. In the case of deity plays the arrival of the traveler forms part of the congratulatory gesture to the land or the deity. This formula allows the play to fully expand on some of the most critical features proposed by Zeami—the use of songs and dance and allusions to the classics, especially when the protagonists narrate the tales of their lives.

---

4. This category of plays is also called *shūra noh* or *shūramono,* referring to tales of the ghosts of dead warriors who were believed to have descended into the *shūra* (or *Ashūra*) realm of existence because of their deed when alive.

Among the various scholarly discussions of mugen noh, the following by Konishi Jun'ichi is the most revealing of how mugen noh is received:

> In the current repertoire, it is the plays of this kind [*fukushiki mugen nō*] that we feel are most typical of nō. In the first part, the waki (usually a traveling priest) enters the stage. He visits a place with historical associations. There he meets a character (the maejite, the principal role, here not in true appearance). At a given point this character exists, returning in its true form (nochijite) to appear to the waki as in a dream. Now the shite role assumes its character as in the past, the actor performs the events of that distant past, disappearing (stage exit) again at dawn. The waki's dream, and the play, are over. The former-part shite (the maejite) is the main character's specter, and the latter (the nochijite) is none other than a vision of the dead spirit of that character, who appears in the waki's dream. *Fukushiki mugen nō (two-part dream pieces) are unique to nō, unparalleled in other theaters of the world.*
>
> Of course, nō is not limited to either two parts or dream pieces. There are also many one-part and many genzaimono (living figure) nō, in which persons yet living (at the time of the action) are the central characters. If one ignores differences in language and music, the genzaimono cannot be said to be unique to nō, for these plays have a form that is present in the theaters of other countries.[5] (Italics mine)

Konishi's second paragraph underscores the reason why many

---

have championed mugen noh as the ultimate representative of the noh theater—the use of "dream" is a unique feature that is not found anywhere else. In addition, with the exception of deity plays, the often melancholic narrative that usually makes up the plot of mugen noh during Zeami's time also contributes to its popularity.

Nobumitsu's *Mugen* Noh Plays

After Zeami and Zenchiku's time, for some reason noh practitioners composed fewer mugen plays, as shown in the repertoire of Nobumitsu and his peers. Among the four plays attributed to Nobumitsu, *Yoshino Tennin* is classified as a female play under the modern Gobandate category. The play, divided into two acts, starts with a person who lives in the capital (Kyoto) embarking on a trip to Mt. Yoshino to admire the cherry blossoms. He runs into an elegant-looking woman in the mountains, who claims that she too visits the mountain because of the cherry blossoms. They praise the beauty of the cherry blossoms, alluding to poetic works from Japanese and Chinese sources. The woman finally discloses that she is actually a celestial being who has come to view the flowers. She also promises to perform an ancient dance for the traveler when the moon is out. Act Two of the play centers on the elegant *chūnomai* dance that the nochi-jite performs.

Unlike *Kochō* and *Yugyō Yanagi*, *Yoshino Tennin* does not involve any dramatic development in its plot, nor does it engage in any kind of multiple chronotope like some of the other Nobumitsu plays I have discussed earlier. Its basic structure and stylistic features are all typical of mugen plays that present encounters between female deities and human beings. In his commentary to the play, Sanari calls it an extremely "lightweight" play, especially when compared to other similar plays that depict spring and cherry blossoms.[6] Another way of looking at this play, however, is that it is yet another indication of Nobumitsu's versatile talent in

---

6. Sanari 1982, vol. 5, 3290.

composition: not only was he good at composing dramatic plays, he was also good at creating lyrical-oriented plays that emphasized poetic imagery.

While *Yoshino Tennin* is a short play that focuses on a brief encounter between a celestial being and a commoner on a spring evening, we see a much more complex use of time and space in *Kochō* and *Yugyō Yanagi*. If time is divided into the past, the present, and the future, then a common feature in these two mugen plays is that the past has ceded its significance to the present or the future.[7] There is a strong tendency for the narratives to be oriented toward the future and to ignore the past. The present becomes the transitory space where the different temporalities (in which the characters dwell) confront and contest against each other, and eventually what is sustained and perpetuated is often the future, while the past becomes at best static, and at worst, obscured.

This kind of temporal framework contrasts with what is found in the earlier mugen noh plays produced by Zeami and his peers. In these earlier plays, the past is the centripetal force toward which the characters and events gravitate. One excellent example is the play *Matsukaze*, in which the ghosts of the two young women will keep appearing on the same seashore, awaiting the next priest to come along to hear their stories. In *Tadanori*, the shite Tadanori appears before a traveling priest (waki) to recount the last battle of the Taira family, as well as the anguish of having his name left off his poem when it was included in an imperial anthology. Just like the desolate sisters at the seashore, the warrior poet Tadanori is trapped forever in the past agony of a defeat in war and the consequent dismissal of his name.

---

7. It is worth noting that out of the 26 extant noh plays attributed to Nobumitsu, only *Yugyō Yanagi, Kochō,* and *Yoshino Tennin* have a distinctive mugen noh structure. Some other two-part Nobumitsu plays in which the nochi-jite reappears in his real identity in Act Two (versus what he "appears" to be, usually as an elderly person or a person living in the vicinity, in Act One) include *Atagokūya* (Priest Kūya at Mt. Atago), *Kōtei, Kusenoto,* and *Momijigari* in the current repertoire and several others in the nonperformed repertoire.

The only Nobumitsu play that sees its protagonist stuck in the vicious cycle of the past is *Kamei*. This play is based on one of the characters in the Soga Brothers tales, and Kamei can be identified as modeled after some of the defeated warriors in earlier plays. It is noteworthy that this is the only play on a defeated warrior that Nobumitsu had composed. Nobumitsu's contemporary, Konparu Zenpō, too, has only one play that features the ghost of a defeated warrior, *Ikuta Atsumori*. It is clear that late Muromachi noh practitioners did not, whether intentionally or not, compose many mugen plays of this kind. In general, there are more plays about living people in the present age than there are mugen plays.

Was It Me or Was It the Butterfly—Multidimensionality in *Kochō*[8]

In *Kochō*—the story of a butterfly and her enlightenment—time is presented in a manner different from the earlier plays. Time is used in a versatile manner: we see the skillful transition of different frames of time from the past to the present. Temporal reference is not stable in the play, given the constant movement that the protagonist engages in as she tells her story to the priest. And as my analysis will reveal, the butterfly's treatment of the past varies greatly from that by protagonists of other mugen noh plays'

Like many two-part dream plays, *Kochō* starts with the short *shidai* section sung by the waki character, a priest, when he first comes on stage.[9] A native of Yoshino, the priest wants to "see the famous old sites in the capital" and embarks on a journey.[10]

The *michiyuki* (traveling song), presented in verse form, foretells the delicate and elaborate confusion of time and space

---

8. I have used my own translation of the text cited in this chapter. See Shimazaki 1976 for a complete translation of this play.

9. A *shidai* is the song the waki or shite, usually the former, sings when he first enters the stage. *Nanori* refers to the self-introduction of the character.

10. Yoshino is situated outside Nara, which was the ancient capital during the eighth century.

that will continue throughout the play:

> On Mount Miyoshi,
> deep snow on the towering peak remains serene.
> deep snow on the towering peak remains serene.
> Spring breezes, late for the blossoming flowers
> blow across the mountain at Kisa, while we cross
> Mikasa Mountain, in the distant haze
> luxuriant with budding nara leaves[11]
> with their broad shade over the avenue leading to
> the flower capital, we have arrived
> the flower capital, we have arrived.[12]

Like most parts of this play—and noh plays in general—this traveling song is full of allusions to existing Chinese and Japanese poems as well as other forms of characteristic wordplay and puns. When the waki priest starts out on his journey, there is still deep snow on the top of Mt. Yoshino. The sight of the snow brings a chill and makes one worry that it will be too cold for the cherry blossoms to bloom in time for spring. Here is the very first hint of a key temporal motif in this play—the uncertainty of time. It is not clear if the flowers are really going to bloom, or if the snow is going to melt, even though it is already spring. The balmy spring breeze that follows them along the road comes from the mountain, where the same chilly snow is also found. Finally when they reach

---

11. "Nara" is a variety of oak tree, also known as the Japanese oak. Here the nara tree puns with the name of the ancient capital Nara whence the priest originates his travel.

12. Noh text: 三吉野の。高嶺の深雪まだ冴えて。高嶺の深雪まだ冴えて。花遅げなる春風の吹きくる象の山越えて。霞むそなたや三笠山茂き梢も楢の葉の。広き御影の道直ぐに。花の都に着きにけり。花の都に着きにけり。Sanari 1982, vol. 2, 1143. The first part of this traveling song borrows heavily from two earlier poems: one attributed to Fujiwara Shunzei in *Shinsenzaishū*, Spring, number 8. 新千載集、春きぬと／みかきが原は／霞めとも／なほ雪さゆる／三吉野の山。The second poem is attributed to Priest Saigyō in *Shinkokinwakashū* (Spring) no. 79. 新古今集、よしの山／桜の枝に／雪散りて／花遅げなる／年にもあるかな。

their destination, the capital, their attention is attracted by the green leaves of the nara tree, which in a wordplay also reminds one of the ancient capital Nara, where they originated. By the end of this short traveling song, we have experienced the oscillating movements in time between spring and winter, and in space, between Kyoto and Nara.

In this introductory section, numerous sets of images are juxtaposed among various distinct seasonal elements, creating a rapid succession of different time frames. Within this rapid shift of temporal framework the tale of a butterfly seeking enlightenment for an unusual reason unfolds gradually. The priest reaches the capital and is walking along Ichijō, or First Avenue. He finds himself looking at an ancient palace where moss has grown on the cypress bark thatched onto the eaves. Growing low on any area that is dark, damp, and undisturbed, moss is a concrete representation of the passage of time, or of something neglected, forgotten. The sight of moss covering what used to be a majestic palace evokes a pathos that only the passage of time could produce—nothing but an empty building is left as a memento of those glorious days. The priest, too, shares these thoughts and begins to wonder if this place has had its share of glory in the past. Upon approaching what looks like a gate, he sees in the palace an extraordinarily beautiful plum tree in bloom.

The priest is so engrossed in admiring the plum blossoms that he is not aware of a village woman approaching him. Suddenly accosted by a female stranger, the priest is taken aback. Rather than answering the woman's question as to who he is, he says to himself:

How very strange! From what seems like a deserted mansion out came a woman, and she is talking to me. Now then, what place is this?[13]

---

139. 不思議やな人ありとも見えぬ屋づまより。女性一人来り給ひ。われに言葉をかけ給ふぞや。さてここをばいづくと申し候ぞ。Sanari 1982, vol. 2, 1144.

A woman emerging into the present space of the priest, from what seems like a residence that belongs to the past, has the priest wondering about her identity, but their exchange moves on to the building. The woman confirms the priest's speculation that this ancient palace has an extraordinary history, and that in spring a plum tree in full bloom will attract the court members to come and admire its beauty. And because it is this *exact* same plum tree that had attracted the attention of one and all a long time ago, the mysterious woman ends her informative tale by urging the priest to examine it closely.

Here we see two sets of chronotopes interacting with each other, resulting in a fluid temporality and a confusing space.[14] The association made between the plum blossoms and the court nobles is such that both would have to share an actual physical space and time frame, just like the woman who is speaking with the priest—both are sharing a common space in a common temporal zone. But the court nobles' enjoyment in the play is an allusion to an early chapter in *The Tale of Genji*, in which the young protagonist Genji performs a butterfly dance.[15] This literary/fictive space, strictly speaking, is a separate dimension from that in which the woman and the priest are engaged. But the woman has clearly illustrated that she once was a participant in the activities of that dimension as well. In other words, the woman is engaging in more complex dimensions of existence

14. "Chronotope" is a literary concept expounded by Bakhtin. I am using this term loosely to indicate the use of time and space, as well as the temporal-spatial relationship shown in the play. See Holoquist 1981, 84–258, on Bakhtin's use of the concept in European novels.

15. The chapter in question is chapter 24, entitled "Butterflies." *The Tale of Genji* (源氏物語 *Genji Monogatari*), considered by some to be the world's first novel, was written by the Heian court lady Murasaki Shikibu (?–1014) around 1008. The 54-chapter narrative details the life and romantic entanglements of a fictive court noble, Hikari Genji. There are three well-known English translations of the work: Waley 1925–1928, Seidensticker 1976, and Tyler 2001. *The Tale of Genji* has a profound presence in the noh repertoire. Plays often allude to the poems in the text, and several noh plays are based on characters in it. See Janet Goff for a book-length study of noh plays based on this novel.

than her counterpart, the waki priest. The question is how complex are these dimensions?

The woman's tale is related to a literary/fictive past (*The Tale of Genji*) which is superimposed on a purportedly present/real time—that of the priest and the woman—as well as a concrete physical plant which was transposed from the world of a fictive (literary) past into another dramatic (fictive) past, which is assumed to be real (present) within this specific narrative space of the play.

The knowledge of the woman and her implied multiple presences in the different temporal and spatial dimensions suggest that she is of no common origin. When the priest asks her name, she offers an answer that introduces other key motifs of the play: the fragrance (scent) and the beauty (sight) of the flower, as well as her nostalgia (emotions) that is related to the flowers. All these elements are presented through the *ageuta* section sung by the chorus. This section centers around an allusion to a poem from the *Shinkokinwakashū*, one that involves several natural objects engaging in exchanges relating to the past:[16]

> I ask the fragrant plum blossoms
> of times long past I ask
> of times long past,
> the spring moon
> does not answer. Quiet tears
> glimmer on my sleeves,
> sweet scents of the passing years, and
> the growing moss on the ancient palace eaves.
> Alas! The name of this self who lingers
> longing for the past is

---

16. Compiled around 1205 and consisting of nearly 2,000 poems, the 20-volume *Shinkokinwakashū* is one of the most important waka poetry anthologies. It had a profound impact on later works, including the noh theater. See Keene 1993, 245–276, for a description of this anthology. Here Nobumitsu has cited the poem in its entirety. Composed by Fujiwara no Ietaka (1158–1237), the poem is found in *Shinkokinwakashū* (Spring) no. 45 が香に／昔をとへば／春の月／こたへぬ影ぞ／袖にうつれる。

like the sea folks of Akashi Bay
whose dwellings are always uncertain.
Uncertain too, is my shameful self.
Uncertain too, is my shameful self.[17]

One general characteristic of noh is its inherent nature as a performance text that emphasizes music and dance, while the style of its lyrics are influenced by *renga* (linked verse), which results in lines that are not grammatical. Rather than conveying concrete information as the spoken lines do, the chanted poetic passages often present sets of images centering on a main theme or a recurrent motif.[18] The recurrent motif in this section is the plum blossom—the key image of the play—although several other images are present too. The images from nature alternate between the past and the present: in the original poem, the poet grows nostalgic about the past when looking at the plum blossom of the present on a moonlit spring night. The past is not retrievable, signified by the silence of both the plum blossom and the moon. But there is still a vaguely tangible connection between the past and the present, represented by the silent yet slowly moving shadow of the flower in the moonlight, and its fragrance. Even though neither the shadow nor the fragrance can claim to possess actual material forms, they can still be detected by human senses of sight and smell.

Fujiwara no Ietaka's poem is cited in its entirety by Nobumitsu in this play—indicating the importance of the poem. Here, the image of a lonesome poet, on a moonlit night, longing for a past that does not return, converges with that of the protagonist in the play. Both the poet and the shite share the same sentiment in their

17. 梅が香に。昔を問とへば春の月。答へぬ影もわが袖に。移る匂ひも年を経る古宮の軒端苔むして。昔恋しきわながをば。何と明石の浦に住む。海士の子なれば宿をだに定めなき身は。恥かしや定めなき身は恥かしや。Sanari 1982, vol. 2, 1146.

18. This is a key feature especially in the Zeami aesthetic paradigm, although wordplay including puns, pivot words, pillow words, etc., are important characteristics in noh plays in general.

yearning for something. In this segment of the play, the identities of these two melancholic persons obsessing over an unreachable goal gradually merges to become one. But it is still not totally clear in the lines yet. We only know that the moving shadow and fragrance bring the shite back to a present that has existed in the past: the ancient palace. Incorporated deeply within this present is the past—which is further emphasized by the growing moss on the eaves of the palace. This interplay of the past and the present finally crystallizes in the claim that it is indeed this *me* who has lingering sentiment for the past.

The next question following this sequence of remembering the past is then, naturally, whose self is it that is deeply attached to the past? Namely, who is the "poet" who has been speaking the lines? The section hints at the unique identity of the poet—someone who is like the sea folk without a permanent home, someone whose identity is unstable. This is also the question that comes to the mind of the priest, and he voices his query. With the waki's question it is clear now that the poet, at this point of the play, refers to the shite. Just like the poet who wants to return to the past but gets no answer from the moon or the plum blossom, the shite who wants to meet the plum blossom on time, too, gets no answer from the moon, the fragrance, or the plum blossom. The shite admits that she indeed is not a human being. She describes herself as one who flits among the plants and one that has the perpetual wish to make the acquaintance of the plum blossom tree. And since her wish cannot be realized due to the timing of the blooming season, she often sheds tears as red as the plum blossoms *every* spring.

> Every spring
> tears red as the blooming blossoms I shed
> It is my destiny—
> A life
> that bears no karmic ties with the plum blossoms.[19]

---

19. 来る春毎に悲しみの。涙の色も。紅の。梅花に縁なきこの身なり。Sanari 1982, vol. 2, 1146–1147.

Here we see the gradual revealing of a prominent motif in many a mugen noh: the suffering of attachment—what is special about this particular attachment is that it is to neither a person nor an event, but a continuing desire to be acquainted with the blossoming plum tree.[20] At this juncture, the chorus sings the following *kuri* lines, reiterating not only the identity of the woman, but also introducing yet another dimension of existence: the dream world.

> Indeed this flirtatious me
> immersed in the colors of the blossoms.
> A transient one who flitters among the flowers
> it is all but a game in a butterfly's dream.[21]

The common space in which the butterfly and the priest interact becomes more complicated every moment. The butterfly flies from one realm to another—under the quiet spring moon, among the various plants, and now into the dream world. With the mention of dream it becomes even clearer that the butterfly is actually occupying multiple dimensions of space and time. The rapid transition from one dimension to another produces a kaleidoscopic effect, and contributes to the confusion of the multiple identities of the butterfly. The *sashi* section of the play describes the life of the butterfly, yet only further confuses the issue:

> In this way comes and goes the spring, summer,
> and fall.
> Born as a butterfly

---

20. It is worth noting that this attachment is different from that of most shite characters whose attachment is either a strong emotion (like jealousy, anger, or love) or a concrete event (like having one's name included in a poetry anthology). But here the butterfly's attachment is to be able to *continue* playing in a plum blossom tree for years to come.

21. 色に染み。花に馴れ行くあだし身は。はかなきものを花に飛ぶ。胡蝶の夢の。戯れなり。 Sanari 1982, vol. 2, 1147. "Iro" suggests a flirtatious nature, although it also refers to the color of the beautiful blossoms.

I am destined to pledge my life to the flowers
Still I lament that I am fated to be apart from the
plum blossoms
I therefore disguised myself and came to you.
Please pray for me so that I will be reborn on the
wonderful lotus petal.[22]

The plum blossoms often bloom very early—in early spring
when there will still be snow on the ground, a time still too cold
for a butterfly to survive. The butterfly gets to flit and flirt with
other flowers, but not the plum blossoms that she longs for most.
Recognizing this as a form of attachment she seeks help from the
priest so that she can be reborn into the Buddhist Pure Land and be
able to realize her wish. It is paradoxical that the butterfly's purpose
in attaining enlightenment is to fulfill a long-term desire—rather
than get rid of it as in most other mugen noh protagonists.

This particular development in the play underscores a new
approach toward enlightenment. In most plays enlightenment
is celebrated as liberation from stubborn attachment to worldly
desires and the sufferings such desires entail, as seen in the many
thanksgiving dances performed by the rejoicing protagonists in
the finales of plays such as *Ukifune* (Ukifune) and *Bashō* (The
banana tree).[23] Another emphasis is on the possibility of all
transient beings attaining enlightenment, such as the iris spirit
in *Kakitsubata* by Zenchiku or the pet chicken in *Hatsuyuki*
by Zenpō. But here in Nobumitsu's *Kochō*, the function of
enlightenment has taken on a new meaning—realization of a
cherished wish. In other words, a return to the attachment that
is the greatest hindrance to enlightenment in the first place. This
treatment of enlightenment is curious, and forms one of the
special features of this play.

---

22. されば春夏秋を経て、草木の花に戯るる。胡蝶と生まれて花にの
み。契りを結ぶ身にしあれども。梅花に縁なき身を嘆き。姿を変えて御
僧に言葉を交はし奉り。Ibid., 1147.

23. *Ukifune* is a play based on one of the later characters in *The Tale of Genji*,
see more details in Goff 1991, 182–192.

After the butterfly makes her request to the priest, the chorus cites two more tales that are related to butterflies from the classical literary tradition. First is the story of the Chinese philosopher Zhuang Zhou or Zhuangzi (Sōshi) who has a dream about a butterfly. In the Chinese classic *Qiwulun*, one of Zhuangzi's famous writings, he describes a dream that he has.[24] Hansen translates it as follows:

> Once Zhuang Zhou dream-regarded [himself] as a butterfly—a fluttering butterfly fulfilling its desires and purposes who did not know Zhou. Suddenly he woke and plainly was Zhuang Zhou. We do not know if Zhou dream-regarded himself as a butterfly or a butterfly dream-regarded himself as Zhuang Zhou ...[25]

The image of a butterfly transforming into a person in Nobumitsu's *Kochō* is similar to that of Zhuang Zhou's story. Kinoshita has correctly pointed out that with Nobumitsu's Chinese learning and his connections with the Gozan Zen prelates, borrowing from the Chinese classics is only to be expected.[26] Here again we can see Nobumitsu's skill in allusive variation—not only has he incorporated a well-known Chinese source into his play, he has also presented a central theme that incorporates this main thread seamlessly. Zhuang Zhou's butterfly dream conveys the famous (and probably eternal) riddle of which subject is dreaming—an ultimate puzzle between the identity of the dreamer and the dreamed. This confusion is preserved in Nobumitsu's presentation of the butterfly, whose identity changes progressively with the unfolding of the play. The use of this popular Chinese tale

---

24. Xie 1988, provides a detailed examination of Zhuangzi's life and work. See pp. 3–4 for his quotation of the Shiji's biography of Zhuangzi and pp. 171–202 for an annotated selection of *Qiwulun* (齐物论 On the equality of things), one of Zhuangzi's writings in which the butterfly anecdote is found.

25. Hansen 1992, 296; see Xie 1988, 200, for the original Chinese text.

26. Kinoshita 1987, 94.

suggests two pertinent features: the confusion between the dream and the real life of Zhuang Zhou (and perhaps the butterfly, and by extension her various metamorphoses), as well as the shift from Japan to China as the play develops.

The second tale alluded to by the chorus moves the butterfly back to Japan, to the fictive world of the shining prince Genji. Chapter twenty-four of *The Tale of Genji* is called "The Butterfly." In this chapter a party in celebration of spring is held at Ichijō Palace, the setting of the present play. During the party the host Murasaki no Ue has four beautiful little children perform a dance in butterfly costumes. Later she writes a poem on the emotion of the butterfly toward the season, and this is cited in its entirety by the shite in the play.[27] Our protagonist, the butterfly, is probably comparing herself to the "silly" butterflies who are able to flit among the flowers even though autumn is approaching, unlike she who is never able to approach her beloved plum blossom. The butterfly protagonist is also remembering this specific event referred to by Murasaki no Ue since it is in exactly this year that the butterfly was able to flit among the plum blossoms because they bloomed unusually late.

Before the end of this act, the shite tells the priest to wait and that she will come to meet him in a dream. With that last statement, she vanishes into the evening sky. Notice that the general direction of the temporal flow in Act One—even though often times it alternates between the past and the present—is forward-oriented: from the past to the present, daytime to night. This style of progress is much clearer in Act Two of the play when the final direction of the temporal progression is toward the

---

27. The poem is: 花園の胡蝶をさへや下草に秋待つ虫は疎く見るらん。Seidensticker 1976 translates the poem as: "Low in your grasses the cricket awaits the autumn/ And views with scorn these silly butterflies" (Book 1, 423). Tyler 2001 translates it as "Will you look askance, O pine cricket in the grass, longing for autumn, even at these butterflies from my own flower garden?" (Book 1, 445). Goff 1991 and Shimazaki 1976 provide more details on the *Genji* chapter, which in brief demonstrates the subtle rivalry among Prince Genji's many lovers, although I think that the shite does not use the poem in this sense.

future—now the butterfly will be able to enjoy herself among the plum blossoms.[28]

The butterfly is not attached to a past that keeps returning to haunt her or obstructs her path of salvation, which distinguishes her from most protagonists in noh plays that involve a mugen sequence. Her attachment is to a blossoming plum tree in nature whose biological time progresses in a cyclical manner. In other words, even though the butterfly in Act One describes events in the past, it only serves to highlight her ultimate wish for the future—acquaintance with the plum blossoms. This wish can only be realized after she attains salvation. The butterfly first describes to the priest events of the past, only to highlight the tree, and this past is quickly discarded because it is no longer of any relevance. As soon as one understands that it is a blossoming plum tree that is the butterfly's concern, the past loses its significance in the butterfly's endeavor. It becomes only one of the temporal realms she happens to be engaged in. This transition from one time frame to another is uncommon in mugen noh plays, in which the protagonists are most often perpetually engaged in one specific moment (period) of time in the past, be it a period of romantic encounter such as *Matsukaze* (Matsukaze) or of nostalgic prosperity *Ikuta Atsumori* (Astumori at Ikuta). The entirety of these past segments make up the tale of these protagonists, and there is no connection to the future—only a point at which enlightenment is attained.

The story of the butterfly is reiterated by the ai-kyōgen—a villager,[29] but his explanation, while informative, also creates more confusion. He explains that the ancient palace where the priest met the young woman was the old mansion of one of Genji's wives, where Genji often came to party with other court nobles. The butterfly came in the summer, but was saddened because it was unable to see the plum tree blossom in the early spring.

---

28. I have discussed the pattern of temporal flow elsewhere. See Lim 2005, 33–51.

29. I use Sanari Kentarō's kyōgen text. See Sanari 1982, vol. 2, 1148–1150.

One year the tree bloomed very late and the butterfly was able to flitter among the blossoms with joy. But after that the plum tree never bloomed late again, and the butterfly grew more and more despondent. Upon hearing the priest's account of his meeting with the woman who claimed to be the butterfly, the villager confirms that the butterfly must have turned into human form to communicate with the priest.

The villager's tale of the butterfly triggers more questions—from what perspective, one wonders, is he speaking? His detailed account of the history of the butterfly suggests that he too, has participated in the multilayered chronotope. The butterfly has engaged in a progressive temporal sequence, although each spring when the plum tree blooms, the butterfly is not around. To say that the butterfly is not available in early spring either means that the butterfly is not yet born in the early spring or that it is still too cold for the butterfly to be active. The implication is that it is a real world where insects live at the mercy of Mother Nature, following biological time. But the villager's explanation also implies that precisely because of this real-world description, the butterfly grows to be melancholy—a statement only possible in a metaphorical sense. Or, to view it from another perspective, a statement that brings the whole account into a fictive world, a realm different from everyday life. The fact that the spirit of the grieving butterfly has taken a human form only reinforces the feeling of a metaphorical world.

There is the biological/natural time frame of both the butterfly and the plum blossoms that prohibits a second encounter; there is the fictional time frame in which Genji, Lady Murasaki, and his court nobles resided and competed and there is the atemporal/literary time frame in which the butterfly dwells and experiences the melancholy of failing to enjoy the blossoms. The multiple dimensions of chronotope involve all the characters in this play, creating a mysterious mazelike framework for the unfolding of the story. At this point the audience (and the readers) are totally lost, but this contributes to the mysterious and surprising atmosphere.

In Act Two, yet another chronotope is introduced when the enlightened butterfly appears to thank the priest. This time it is the realm of existence that is interpreted via the Buddhist concept of sentient and nonsentient beings.[30] The nochi-jite, the butterfly, even though theoretically a nonsentient being, has attained salvation as a result of the priest's prayers. The significance of this transformation, for the butterfly, is that she is no longer constrained by the law of nature, and is now able to flit among the plum blossoms to her heart's content. Here two temporalities can be detected. First is the physical garden, in the present, where the encounters of the butterfly and the plum blossoms, and the priest and the villager, take place. This is all within the present. Second is the other realm that the butterfly has gained successful entrance to—the realm of enlightenment, yet again a new chronotope (or nonchronotope?) different from the dream world or the natural/material world.

The transformation and constant movement of the butterfly from one realm to another is disconcerting. Even the priest, who has played an important role in the butterfly's transformation, becomes confused at this juncture. His question indicates his perplexity:

> The dawning moon is shining not just on the flowers. I see one who is as beautiful as a butterfly. Are you not the person whom I encountered before?[31]

And the butterfly answers with a very simple interrogative statement, "why is it that you called me person?" (*hito to wa ikade*).[32]

---

30. In the different schools of Buddhism in medieval Japan, whether all beings are able to attain enlightenment is often a topic of debate. Shively presents a detailed description and analysis of noh plays with plants (and other nonsentient creatures such as a butterfly and a snow spirit) as their protagonists. Among other things, Shively argues that Muromachi period Buddhism had accepted the doctrine that all beings are capable of attaining enlightenment.

31. 有明の月も照り添ふ花の上に。さも美しき胡蝶の姿の。現れ給ふはありつる人か。Sanari 1982, vol. 2, 1151.

32. Ibid.

The confusion of subjectivity creates a somewhat humorous effect. The priest describes the appearance of the nochi-jite—the human form of the spirit of the butterfly—as "beautiful as a butterfly" (when she *is* actually a butterfly), and juxtaposes the image with that of the woman he had met moments ago. The gentle rebuke from the butterfly in objecting to his calling her a "person" reflects a paradoxical attitude toward her own identity; that even though she is now (in Act Two) still in human form, she identifies herself as only a butterfly (as she later does in this conversation). It is, however, as a human that she could first talk to the priest and then attain salvation. The butterfly's constant declaration that she is nonhuman can be understood as a rejection of human identity. This is also reminiscent of Zhuang Zhou's riddle of who is who in his tale of the butterfly dream. One wonders whether a dichotomy of human being versus nonhuman being is suggested here, like the comment made by the elderly woodcutter in *Ryōko*, although the issue is not pursued any further in this play. The butterfly dances the finale of the play with lines of praise from the chorus:

> Spring, summer, and autumn,
> I flit among the flowers one and all.
> Laden with frost, the white chrysanthemum,
> around its branch I dance round and round
> like the turning of the little Wheel of Law
> rolling on to enlightenment.
> In this spring night
> the butterfly becomes the Bodhisattva of song and
> dance.
> Into the dawning cloud
> with great elegance
> Into the dawning cloud
> with great elegance
> she disappears into the colorful morning mist.[33]

33.春夏秋の花も尽きて。霜を帯ひたる。白菊の。花折り残す。枝を廻り。廻り廻るや小車の。法に引かれて仏果に至る。胡蝶も歌舞の菩薩の

Finally, the butterfly has transcended her biological constraints. While flying among the flowers, the butterfly has led the readers/audience into the world of the Buddhist Law. The transition from the natural world into the enlightened world is clear, but the mention of salvation brings forth the ultimate confusion; has the butterfly attained salvation, and does that mean becoming the Bodhisattva of dance and song? Or, perhaps, the Bodhisattva of song and dance has transformed herself into the spirit of a butterfly to propagate the teaching of Buddhism?

Many different levels of signification take place in this way, and have prompted scholars to come up with various interpretations. Kinoshita Fumitaka thoroughly traces the Chinese sources that Nobumitsu used in the play, concluding that the play is a showcase of Nobumitsu's profound mastery of Chinese literary traditions.[34]

Janet Goff, on the other hand, highlights Genji's presence in the play, and discusses it as an attempted spin-off of the great ancient work.[35] These two arguments, although claiming two very different sources of influence, are equally justified. This is because however short and simple the play may seem to be on the surface, it is rich in subtext and is replete with dramatic and literary features.

Shimazaki contends that in some plays the shite character, even though appearing to be seeking enlightenment, is in fact already an enlightened being. The main purpose of their appearance is a musical presentation of a narrative. In the case of *Kochō*,

> ... even a story as such hardly exists, except faint allusions to a series of events in *Genji Monogatari*. Two poems composed on the occasion are quoted unspecifically, interwoven in songs. The total effect is that of a visionary world of pure lyricism and exquisite beauty.[36]

舞の。姿を残すや春の夜の。明け行く雲に。羽根うち交はし。明け行く雲に。羽根うち交はし。霞に 紛れて。失せにけり。Sanari 1982, vol. 2, 1152.

34. Kinoshita 1987, 89–98.

35. Goff 1991, 42.

36. Shimazaki 1976, 113.

Shimazaki's comment that this is a play of lyric beauty underscores one important characteristic of *Kochō*. However, it may trivialize the story into simply a showcase of literary aesthetics and thus ignore the other important features such as the complex multidimensionality engaged in the progress of the narrative, as well as the presentation of a Buddhist worldview.

As Shively pointed out, a confirmation of the possibility of enlightenment for plants and insects was the more dominant Buddhist discourse in the late Muromachi period.[37] We see here the spirit of the butterfly attaining enlightenment and presenting a beautiful thanksgiving dance.

Kinoshita explains the use of the image of Bodhisattva of song and dance here with reference to two other plays: *Kakitsubata* and *Asagao*.[38] In *Kakitsubata*, the Bodhisattva of song and dance is identified with the Heian poet Ariwara no Narihira (825–880). In *Asagao* (which is no longer performed), the shite who is the spirit of the morning glory plant (*asagao*) also assumes the identity of the Bodhisattva of song and dance, which is interpreted by Kinoshita as a direct influence from *Kakitsubata*. There are many other noh plays that either employ the images of this particular Bodhisattva, or mention him/her in passing. The Bodhisattva of Song and Dance refers to two of the thirty-seven Bodhisattvas in the Diamond realm Mandala of the Shingon sect. They are in charge of music and dance in the Pure Land, and one of their earliest associations in noh plays could well be with Ariwara no Narihira and Izumi Shikibu.

Another explanation of the Bodhisattva of Song and Dance, according to various Buddhist dictionaries, is "a beautiful dance." Many shite characters who attain enlightenment in Act Two of the plays are transformed into this Bodhisattva and perform a dance to celebrate their salvation. Whichever way the name is defined, the musical and celebratory nature that is inherent in

---

37. Shively 1957, 135–161.
38. Kinoshita 1987, 96. See Itō 1983, Book 1, 258–266, 422–424, for both the play and a short commentary. Also Brazell 1988, 63–80, for an annotated translation of *Kakitsubata* by Susan Klein.

this Bodhisattva is one of the reasons why these figures appear in noh plays, especially what is known as "kabunō" (song and dance plays) so regularly. This, however, does not mean that we can simply conclude that the use of this particular Bodhisattva is a technical device in a music-oriented noh play. Religious and sociocultural discourse can be discerned here. The active use of a Buddhist image is an indication of the prevalence of Buddhism in medieval life. Also, situating a Bodhisattva in the heart of performance is an attempt to associate the genre with a more elevated and respected social institution.[39]

Kochō has been in the active repertoire since its earliest performance recorded in 1545 (14th year of Tenmon), although this is not likely to be its debut date since Nobumitsu died in 1516 and his last dated play was Yugyō Yanagi.[40] Among Nobumitsu's plays, Kochō and Yugyō Yanagi most demonstrate a structure similar to the mugen plays. Categorized under the third group— women plays—Kochō stands out in the repertoire of Nobumitsu's works for its profuse use of literary images and poetic techniques as Shimazaki suggests. Sanari comments that the gorgeous yet short-lived butterfly is very appropriate subject matter for noh plays intending to present the essence of splendor (karei) and tranquility (kanjaku), and therefore this is an extraordinary play.[41] Kinoshita claims that the subject matter of the play reflects the world of Chinese textual scholarship (kanseki kyōju) in Nobumitsu's time.[42] Both comments are a positive evaluation of the literary nature of the play. This skillful manipulation of literary sources in turn becomes the foundation of yet another appealing element of the play: its unusual chronotopes. It is within the

---

39. Association with established institutions seems to be one of the conventional ways to ascribe legitimacy to oneself. Noel Pinnington similarly describes the relationship between an art form and Buddhism as "... identification of Buddhism with a particular art, even metaphorically, enabled that art to cross the border from profane to sacred ... " See Pinnington 2006, 31.

40. See Appendix 1 for a list of plays attributed to Nobumitsu.

41. Sanari 1982, vol. 2, 1142.

42. Kinoshita 1987, 89.

poetic lines and imageries that the butterfly emerges and transits from one realm to another, contributing greatly to the pleasure of the play.

Despite Myself I Overstayed—*Yugyō Yanagi*

Yugyō Yanagi is believed to be Nobumitsu's last play, composed about two years before his death. Performance records indicate that debut of the play was at a subscription noh performance near Kyoto, and Nobumitsu played the shite role. *Yugyō Yanagi* has since been a popular piece for the Kanze school. A two-part dream play (*fukushi mugen nō*) about the encounter between the spirit of an aged willow tree and a traveling priest of the Jishū sect, it has occupied a special position in Nobumitsu's repertoire for several reasons: the subdued elegance portrayed by a withered willow tree, its almost perfect mugen noh structure, and the consistent reference and allusion to both the Japanese and Chinese classics. Omote Akira points out that both *Kochō* and *Yugyō Yanagi* reflect Nobumitsu's changing style in composition, from visually oriented to one that gradually inclined toward yūgen as the noh practitioner aged.[43]

Perhaps what is even more appealing to contemporary noh scholars about this play is its similarity to Zeami's *Saigyō Zakura* (Saigyō's cherry blossom trees).[44] A very popular noh play, *Saigyō Zakura* has been included in many anthologies beginning with *Utaishō* in the Tokugawa period and on into modern anthologies. As the title suggests, Zeami's piece has the spirit of the cherry blossoms as its protagonist, although both plays rely heavily on the poems by the poet/priest Saigyō (1118–1190) as the point of departure for their plot. Strictly speaking, there is not a strong plot in either play—a characteristic of the mugen noh plays in general. In *Saigyō Zakura* the waki character is the priest Saigyō himself. Upset by the streams of visitors from the capital viewing the cherry

43. Omote 1986, 266–267.
44. See Tyler 1992, 215–224, for a translation of the play.

blossoms in his yard, he blames the cherry tree for disrupting his peace. The spirit of the cherry tree (shite) appears and confronts him in "person" and then dances to a poetic enumeration of the various kinds of cherry blossoms (*sakura-zukushi*).

Yugyō Yanagi is the Nobumitsu play that follows most closely the aesthetic principles highly valued in modern-day noh discourse. The regular, almost inevitable, reference to Zeami's *Saigyō Zakura* whenever this play is mentioned provides some clues to the appraisal and reception of this play. Omote suggests that it was a trend during Nobumitsu's time for practitioners to imitate others' plays, and the similarities between the two plays can only be accounted for by this trend toward imitation: that *Yugyō Yanagi* is influenced by *Saigyō Zakura*. That said, Omote described the play as Nobumitsu's most sophisticated piece, one that embodies profound yūgen aesthetics and marks the creative high point of his development from the earlier spectacular-style plays.[45] Nishino, in his prefatory comments to the play in *Yōkyoku Hyakuban*, also calls the readers' attention to *Saigyō Zakura*. Nishino calls the play an elegant piece that illustrates Nobumitsu's Chinese learning while presenting a list of itemized comparisons between the two. As Nishino notes, contrasts of imagery and content between the two plays are easily identifiable: the capital versus the provinces, spring versus autumn, old cherry tree versus old willow tree, attachment to the spring versus nostalgia for the past, and Saigyō versus a Yugyō priest.[46]

Indeed we can see many parallels between *Saigyō Zakura* and *Yugyō Yanagi*. Both plays use poems by Priest Saigyō from the imperial anthology *Shinkokinwakashū*. The protagonists are both spirits of plants who appear as old men instead of the more common young woman. Structurally speaking, too, the spirits of both protagonists first disguise themselves in human form to interact with the waki characters. In Act Two of both plays the protagonists present long lists of famous items: cherry blossom spots within and around the capital area in Zeami's play, while Nobumitsu's play presents famous willow tree–related tales from Chinese and Japanese sources. These parallels provide the audience, both medieval and modern, with sufficient references to fully appreciate the plays.

In *Yugyō Yanagi*, one important motif is the *michi*. Michi is an important concept in premodern Japanese literary tradition, encompassing a multitude of meanings, ranging from the most common understanding of "road," to that of "path for the acquisition of excellence in an artistic genre," to a Buddhist metaphor for the "path to enlightenment."[47] The very title of the play, *Yugyō Yanagi*, indicates the significance of this recurrent motif, which plays an important organizing role, especially in Act One. The waki, a *yugyō hijiri*, or an itinerant priest, is the first hint at this motif. The term *"yugyō"* in the play refers to the itinerant priests of the Jishū sect in medieval Japan, and is defined as "traveling for [religious] acts."[48] Founded by the Buddhist monk Ippen (ca. 1239–1289), this particular Buddhist sect advocated the continuous evocation of *Amida Butsu* (Amida Buddha) to achieve enlightenment. Ippen and his followers, known as *yugyō hijiri* (itinerant holy men/priests), traveled all over Japan to distribute talismans with Amida Buddha's name on them.[49] Together with their *nenbutsu odori*, a dance accompanied by ritual chanting of the name of Amida, the Jishū sect became one of the most popular Buddhist sects in the medieval period. The motif of *michi* should be especially important in plays that involved the itinerant Jishū priests because they were supposed to be constantly on the road to distribute prayer cards. In another noh play, *Seiganji* (The Seigan

---

47. Noel Pinnington presents a detailed description of the use of the concept of michi in noh. See Pinnington 2006,

48. Shively 1957, 151.

49. Thornton 1999 translates "Yugyō Hijiri" and "Yugyō Shōnin," respectively, as "itinerant holy men" and "itinerant saint." On the other hand, Janine Beichman 1986, in her translation of *Yugyō Yanagi*, uses "wandering saint" for "Yugyō Shōnin" and calls the Yugyō Hijiri in the play "priest" (Keene, 1970, 221). I have decided to use "priest" to describe these religious practitioners, following Beichman's translation.

Temple), the waki character Priest Ippen is understood to have distributed 600,000 talismans as he traveled through Japan. In *Yugyō Yanagi* too, the waki, a Jishū monk, is on his way to distribute talismans when he encounters the shite.

Other than *Seiganji*, the Jishū itinerant priests also appear in other noh plays such as *Sanemori* (Sanemori). In the latter the famous Heike warrior appears before an itinerant priest to relate his final battle and its tragic outcome. In *Seiganji* the shite character is the famous Heian female poet Izumi Shikibu. Her spirit engages in a lively exchange on the principals of the Jishū sect with yet another itinerant priest.[50] The two plays adopt different approaches in presenting the *yugyō hijiri* while unfolding his narrative, although neither one develops the motif of pathway/traveling as extensively as *Yugyō Yanagi*.

The key image of *Yugyō Yanagi* is an aged willow tree situated on a quiet pathway along a stream. The drama of the play unfolds when the shite, an old man (who turns out to be the spirit of the old willow tree) suggests to the waki—an itinerant preist of the Jishū sect who is visiting the Shirakawa Barrier (*Shirakawa no Seki*)—that he should use another less-known trail for his excursion around the area. The waki, like the waki in most mugen plays, is on a journey without specific routes. When he is faced with several directions to choose from, he meets the shite who instructs him to use an ancient pathway instead of the "broadest path," which is the easiest way. The fact that an unknown old man appears to point the priest to a more difficult and unknown road suggests the somewhat limited knowledge of the priest in terms of knowing his way around this place. Or perhaps the old man is more enlightened than the priest? Perhaps the spirit of a willow tree is only constrained by its physical body before it can *fully* achieve enlightenment, although it might already be enlightened. Or has the willow tree been waiting all this time for a traveling priest to come along so that he can instruct the priest on the proper

---

50. Foard 1988 touches briefly on the popularity of the Jishū sect in the medieval period. See especially p. 440.

way of traveling, and by implication, the proper way of attaining enlightenment?

Examined from the temporal perspective, this road motif also has a linear structure that extends from the past to the present. The shite, the spirit of the willow tree, mentions the earlier visits of other traveling priests to this location. And finally, Saigyō the poet, even though he is neither a *yugyō hijiri* nor a character in the play, nevertheless functions as a metaphor for traveling, as he is the one whose work serves as the foundational imagery of the play. One of the first things the willow tree offers the traveling priest at the very beginning of the play is his guidance to the road the earlier traveling priests have used, using the Saigyō poem as yet another landmark:

> Alongside the road where the clear brook flows
> I thought of taking a quick break under the willow shade,
> but despite myself I overstayed.[51]

The narrative of the play continues to unfold along this motif of the pathway. The priest is surprised to find that there is an ancient trail that those preceding him have taken, and needs no persuasion to embark on this recommended road. The old man at this point introduces the famous ancient willow tree, and hints at his own purpose in guiding the priest—a request for prayer to help the willow tree achieve enlightenment and attain Buddhahood. The description of the willow tree, spoken by the waki, presents time in a concrete and poetic manner:

> Indeed along the bank where the river has ceased flowing stands the remains of a withered willow tree.
> Buried among crawling vines and deepening moss,

---

51. Sanari 1984, vol. 5, 3197. This poem by Saigyo is cited in its entirety from *Shinkokinwakashū* no. 262 (Summer). 道のべに／清水流るる／柳かげ／しばしとてこそ／立ちとまりつれ。

> the aging willow tree can hardly be seen. What a
> sight of the passing years of stars and frosts.[52]

The age of the celebrated willow tree is shown by its description as entangled with creepers and covered with moss. As in *Kochō*, moss is used to indicate the passage of time. The presence of the moss is further enhanced by the vines, which also grow slowly and often on surfaces off the ground, in other words surfaces that have stayed still for a long time. The use of these two images, together with the dried-up riverbank, are powerful and convincing, invoking the quiet progression of time. In terms of the interaction between time and space, *Yugyō Yanagi* has a more stable frame of reference than *Kochō*.

The representations of the past and the future are distinctively defined against each other, and not only is there no confusion of the temporal realm as in *Kochō*, but the transition from one temporality to another is very clear. The past has an intricate role to play here: even though the willow spirit relies on the past, such as an ancient path earlier priests had treaded on or a poem from generations ago, it is not where the spirit dwells nor where his attachment is. After recounting these past events, no further allusions are made to them as the play unfolds. The significance of the past here is not so much the occurrence of a particular event, but a means by which the future can be reached.

Instead of a strong attachment to the past that hinders his enlightenment, the willow spirit does not suffer from any this-worldly attachment. Paradoxically, what is stopping him from gaining enlightenment is precisely his desire to gain enlightenment. The focus of the aged willow tree's quest, then, lies on a future that will allow him to attain Buddhahood, which he ultimately manages to do, becoming the Bodhisattva of Song and Dance.

---

52. げに川岸も水絶えて。川そひ柳朽ち残る。老木はそれとも見えわかず。蔦葛のみ這いかかり。青苔梢を埋む有様。誠に星霜年ふりたり。Sanari 1984, vol. 5, 3196.

After requesting the priest to pray for his enlightenment, the old man with messy gray hair disappears behind the tree and reappears later in Act Two donning a black hat and a hunting cloak. Like the beginning of the same section in *Kochō*, the waki priest is surprised to find a different-looking old man wearing a court hat (*eboshi*) approaching him, and the enlightened spirit of the willow tree has to explain that he is the same old man who has attained enlightenment. The first emphasis in Act Two, then, is a tribute to the power of prayer, which has allowed the willow tree to attain enlightenment and become the Bodhisattva of Song and Dance, like the butterfly in *Kochō*. The significance of the Bodhisattva of Song and Dance here is very different from *Kochō*, since it does not suggest further confusions of the chronotope but, rather, serves as the final confirmation that the willow tree has attained enlightenment. It is therefore a unifying motif. The figure of the Bodhisattva also facilitates the performance of dance and song since it incorporates both musical elements and the celebration of salvation.

The second emphasis of Act Two, a presentation of the list of willow trees, is more on showcasing the composer's knowledge of the literary renditions of the willow trees in both Japanese and Chinese than on providing a libretto to choreograph the shite's dance. The reference made is a perfect example of one special noh feature: allusions to various literary sources to create a flowing list of imagery of one specific item, here the willow tree. This is premised on a vaguely detectable connection between each allusion, often accomplished with wordplay or puns. It starts with a reference to a Chinese poem in *Santaishi* right at the beginning of Act Two, when the enlightened spirit of the willow tree returns to meet the Yugyō priest. In their subsequent exchanges they start with praises for Buddhism, which has enabled the willow tree's enlightenment. The imagery of their topics of exchange develops from the Buddhist Law to the construction of the first boat in Chinese legend, which then relates back to the leaves of the willow tree. A new thread starts with the Chinese Imperial Palace, which leads to Buddhist temples in both China and

Japan, interspersed with imagery of beautiful willow and cherry blossom trees.[53] After the singing and performance of the list, this section ends with the willow tree spirit thanking the priest again and disappearing.

To summarize, one can argue that before the mid-play entrance of the shite the poem by Saigyō presented by the chorus in the earlier part of the play punctuates the flow of the play with the image of a willow tree that has prolonged the stay of an accidental traveler. The willow tree poem forms the bridge between the two acts of the play: now the michi motif converges with that of the willow tree and, subsequently, with Buddhist teaching. In the final line of the play, after praising the Buddhist teachings, the enlightened spirit of the willow tree who has become the Bodhisattva of Song and Dance, vanishes. All that is left behind is the old mound and the withered willow tree. All is quiet now because the past is deserted and crystallized into what is remaining on the stage, while the spirit moves on to the enlightened land.

Situating Mugen Noh in Nobumitsu's Repertoire

As Konishi has pointed out in no uncertain terms, mugen noh plays occupy a unique position in the noh repertoire. The liminal space in which the narratives unfold has attracted not only Japanese audiences since the medieval period, but has also enchanted writers and dramatists of other times and cultures. William Butler Yeats' (1865–1939) At the Hawk's Well is an exemplary work inspired by mugen noh.[54] The perennial realm of dreams or

---

53. For a translation of this section, see Keene 1970, 230–233.

54. William Butler Yeats (1865–1939) developed an interest in Japanese noh theater under the influence of Ezra Pound (1885–1972). At the Hawk's Well is set in the "Irish Heroic Age" and is narrated by three musicians and two characters who wear masks. The structure is based loosely on a noh play, where the musicians and the characters speak in lyrical lines. See Qamber 1974, 121–130, for the text of the play.

one's unconscious allows the characters to delve into their deepest thoughts and explore their most intense emotions. In plays like this, time is usually crystallized into solid intervals wherein the narrative unfolds. And within these consolidated time frames, the emotions that inform the narratives (loss, desire, anguish, etc.) usually stem from events that happened in specific locations. In other words, in most mugen noh plays the past plays an important role in constructing the temporal frame of the narratives.

In the late Muromachi period this approach to time changes, and was manifested in the number of mugen noh plays created. As mentioned earlier, relative to the total number of noh plays produced during this period, the number of mugen noh plays is small. Those that are still performed today number less than half of those performed in earlier times. Critics and historians have explained this trend as a change in audience preference in the face of a more chaotic political climate. This generalization, although not incorrect, ignores other factors, including a more expanded approach to play creation during this time. Nobumitsu's mugen noh plays provide an excellent illustration of this point. The emphasis on temporal frame has shifted from the past to the future, while the concentration of intensely sad emotions give way to the more lighthearted and cheery mood in which the late Muromachi protagonists tell their stories.

Part Three

肃不覺起舞你言中系之後

滥觞于佛世者是于作先弦

名宗松法号本雅　乾予永記

其藝聚起与家譜之聚出者故

耶書如专係以銘之曰

衣冠巖宗　鬚鬢蟠然

出入把肩　低郢幸莚

以役納諫　梨有優海

身在今世　志存昔賢

松有太雅　蕙膠續絃

歲五十三　齡兩八寸

夫是之謂　觀世延年

Chapter Six

(DE-)CONSTRUCTING FURYŪ

The Age of Furyū Noh

Noh scholar Ishii Tomoko whose 1998 book *Furyū Nō no Jidai: Konparu Zenpō to Sono Shūhen* (translated by the author as "Komparu Zempo and the Age of Furyu [Spectacle] Nō Performance") is on Konparu Zenpō—Konparu Zenchiku's grandson and Nobumitsu's contemporary.[1] Ishii's title is representative of a common attitude among contemporary Japanese scholars that the late Muromachi period is indeed the period of furyū noh.[2] In her book, Ishii posits Konparu Zenpō as

1. Some scholars have written articles related to plays produced in this period. Yamanaka 1998 has some articles on noh performance in the late Muromachi period. Several other Japanese noh scholars such as Oda 1985, Nishino 1975, Eguchi 2007, 25–48, and Ikai 2007, 1–24, have all written articles on late Muromachi plays. This list is not exhaustive, although it is clear that relative to discussions of plays attributed to Zeami and his peers, there have been less attention paid to the late Muromachi period works.

2. See, for example, Yokomichi et al. 1987, 258, and Nihon Geinōshi Kenkyūkai, ed., *Nihon Geinōshi 4,* 223, where reference was made to Nobumitsu. Ueki et al. 1965 also cite the prolific production of furyū noh by Nobumitsu and his contemporaries. Yamanaka 1998, 168, describes Nagatoshi's works as furyū noh. During the special exhibit "*Sengoku Jidai no Nō*" (Noh during the Warring Period), organized by the National Noh Theater in Tokyo in 1999, an article introducing the

one of the representative noh practitioners of this period. She cites cultural, societal, and political elements that informed Zenpō's noh repertoire and provides detailed readings of some of his plays.

Although Ishii has presented insightful readings of Zenpō's plays, one disappointment with the book is that it does not elaborate on the meaning of "furyū noh." There are traces of Ishii's attempts to illustrate what she envisions to be the features of furyū, but these often stop short of a description of what is spectacular and what seems to be an unusual or innovative style of presentation relative to other noh plays. In terms of content, she identifies a more complex incorporation of various events, such as prayer and battles, especially in plays like *Yakamochi* that have a religious theme.[3] Visual elements are doubtlessly a crucial feature in any performance genre, although how their presence alone in the plays could be used to define an "era" (*jidai*) remains unanswered.

The assumption that the term "furyū" needs no elaboration underscores the unquestioned acceptance among researchers on the nature of late Muromachi noh. While the ready welcome of the term is itself illustrative of present-day noh discourse—a need or preference to ascribe categories in the repertoire—questions of what defines an age that is represented by a subcategory in a performance genre need to be examined in the light of its specific historical and cultural contexts. In this chapter, I examine the discursive construct of furyū and its implications for modern noh discourse, especially in terms of how it is used to define a noh play. Before that, however, it will be useful to examine the usage of furyū in a broader paradigm.

period in question emphasizes the furyū style of noh during this period (*Sengoku Jidai no Nō*, 25).
    3. Ishii 1998, 56.

The Meanings of Furyū

Tracing its original and multiple meanings in the Chinese literary tradition, Philip Harries asserts that "furyū in the sense of gallantry is particularly common in the poetry and prose of the Six Dynasties and Tang periods ..."[4] Within the Japanese context, the term has had various meanings since the Nara period. Citing examples from *Manyōshū*, the earliest poetry anthology in Japan, Harries also identifies the term to mean "cultured," "exceptional refinement," and "dalliance." By the end of the Heian period, the term encompassed not only refinement, courtliness and artistic accomplishment, but also intricacy and ingenuity,[5] ornateness and lavishness of decoration, especially with regard to furnishings, painting, personal adornment, and dress. Since its earliest introduction to Japan, furyū has always had the connotation of some form of visual extravaganza—a reminder of the performativity and the theatrical. Harries also emphasizes the compatibility of furyū with dance, which Moriya Takeshi, a cultural historian and anthropologist, has taken up in his writing.[6]

Moriya presents a more detailed description of the use of furyū within the context of cultural and performance history in Japan. He identifies three areas: artifacts, events, and performance.[7] Like Harries, Moriya examines the use of the term since the Heian period, when conspicuous artifacts were produced and exhibited. These furyū items ranged from small objects such as hair combs to larger constructions such as carts. Not only were these handicraft items literally "extraordinary," they were also often extremely costly to make. Furyū is used as well to describe a state of things or participants in events, which were either excessively beautiful, or digressing from the usual

---

4. Harries 1984, 138.

5. Ibid., 143.

6. Ibid., 142.

7. Moriya 1985, 60. Nose 1972, 398–399, also similarly describes the meaning of the term.

conventions in an extravagant manner. Moriya cites as an example the dressing of some participants in the *Gion Matsuri* (The Gion festival), where he uses words such as "lavishness" and "exotic" to describe these festive possessions and their participants.[8]

The third usage that Moriya identifies is related to both performances and rituals that incorporate a strong component of our modern concept of "performance." The earliest example that Moriya found was a kind of group dance that was recorded as early as the beginning of the twelfth century. He highlights the nature of this event as one that was rowdy and often frenzied and out of control—in other words, a *transgression* of conventional behavior patterns. And this often led to interference from the authorities; sometimes the events were banned because they were disruptive to public order. Here Moriya emphasizes again the "extraordinary" nature of performance that was associated with the concept of furyū. One key feature of these rituals and performances was their defiance of the conventional standard of behavior.[9]

Moriya's descriptions hint at the ambiguous nature of the term furyū, which, like many terms in aesthetics, is complex and resistant to a single definition or interpretation. What can be identified as the common feature among these different forms is an element of eccentricity—a *deviation* from the conventional norm in an extravagant manner.

In the realm of premodern Buddhist practices, the term furyū is often found used in relation to "*ennen*" (延年) and "*nenbutsu*" (念仏). *Ennen* refers to the general category of entertainment performed after Buddhist sermons in temples like the Tōdaiji in Nara between the Heian and the end of Muromachi periods, while *Ennen no furyū* refers specifically to one of the performance genres in *Ennen*. *Nenbutsu furyū* describes another religion-related dance performance, one that was popularized by the Jishū sect founder monk, Ippen (1239–1289).[10] The Japanese anthropologist Gorai

8. Moriya 1985.
9. Moriya 1985.
10. Ippen advocated calling the Amida's name to attain enlightenment. He often figures in noh plays and other artistic genres. See Chapter 5 for a more

Shigeru has provided a succinct definition of these activities that were broadly categorized under furyū. He describes them as the transformation of religious incantations and rituals into performance through the use of masquerade and costumes, as well as the transformation of religious chants into entertainment by their incorporation into popular secular songs.[11]

Yokomichi Mario's Definition

Judging from its uses in literary, cultural, and performance studies, it is clear that furyū is a versatile aesthetic idea that shares the age-old connotation of something lavishly visual, nonconforming, and at times popular in orientation. The choice of furyū to describe the late Muromachi plays reaffirms these largely performance-centered features. But does furyū noh, a category proposed in modern times to describe noh plays with a spectacular style of presentation, share a similar connotation of "transgression" when used to describe a theatrical genre from the premodern period? The answer to this question may lie in the first in-depth discussion of the term, in the early 1960s. Yokomichi Mario, a prominent Japanese noh scholar, proposed the term in the commentary to the two-volume noh anthology, *Yōkyokushū*, in the *Nihon Koten Bungaku Taikei* series published by Iwanami Shoten.[12] In this anthology, the editors Yokomichi Mario and Omote Akira present a comprehensive introduction to noh, including its structure, stage, and the different kinds of plays.[13] In the section on the categorization of plays, Yokomichi

---

detailed description of him. For more details on *furyū odori* and *Ennen* see Nihon Geinōshi Kenkyūkai, ed., *Nihon Geinōshi 4*, 49–76, and Suwa and Sugai 1998.

11. Gorai 1998, 200.

12. A similar discussion on the various categories of noh plays can be found in a later book, Yokomichi 1986. The discussion of furyū noh is also included as an appendix to one of the chapters, 55–58.

13. Although the other editor of this series is Omote Akira, it is clear from other sources that Yokomichi is the main contributor to this commentary. *Nihon Koten Bungaku Taikei* 41 (1960): 6–12.

sets out to classify existing noh plays so as to highlight their
different characteristics.

This was, however, not the first modern scholarly attempt to
categorize noh plays. An earlier example appears in Sanari Kentarō's
(1890–1966) multivolume anthology *Yōkyoku Taikan*, originally
published in 1930–1931. In volume one, Sanari evaluates the ways
to classify noh plays according to their dramatic structure and
characterization, where, for instance, plays that have the protagonist
(shite) appearing in the dream of the waki are called mugen plays.
Plays in which the shite and waki characters are related, such as a
general and his follower, are called "geki-teki mugen noh" (劇的夢
幻能 dramatic dream plays). For plays that do not involve a dream
sequence but have a more complicated role-character structure,
Sanari chose to use the term "geki nō" (劇能) or "dramatic noh,"
which corresponds to contemporary usages in modern Western
theatrical terminology.[14] At the end of volume one, Sanari casually
comments that plays with a complex cast do not necessarily have a
higher artistic value, or "*geijutsuteki kachi*." In other words, "drama"
and "artistic value" are seen as two distinctive categories.[15]

I believe that Yokomichi initially shared Sanari's intention of
classifying noh plays on the basis of *artistic assessment*. Yokomichi
came up with several categories, including geki nō and furyū nō.
Unlike Sanari, Yokomichi uses the term geki to describe "the art
of depicting human beings: their words and acts." By implication,
Yokomichi then argues that Zeami's plays, other than the first category deity plays, are all geki or "dramatic" plays, as they all focus on the
actions and feelings of human beings.[16] With this definition in mind,

---

14. By "modern theatrical terminology" I refer to the contemporary Western-
based definition of "drama." For instance, Patrice Pavis defines the "dramatic" as
"a principle of construction of text and performance which accounts for the *tension* in the scenes and episodes of the *fabula* toward a dénouement (catastrophe
or comic resolution) and suggests that the spectator is captivated by the action"
(Pavis 1998, 112, italics in the original). The usage by Sanari 1984 of "dramatic" is
probably the most common one in present-day theatrical terminology.

15. Yōkyoku and Sanari 1982, vol. 1, 56–61.

16. ある「人間」を描くのに、その人間自身の言葉と行動とをもって
する芸術が「劇」である、という定義も可能だから、その意味で、世阿

noh plays composed by practitioners such as Nobumitsu and his contemporaries are compared with Zeami's "dramatic" plays as follows:

> Certainly not all mugen plays are like Zeami's dra-
> matic plays. As mentioned earlier, different kinds
> of mugen plays were composed for the various
> noh themes. There are mugen plays that focused
> solely on dance such as *Shōjō* (The Drunken
> Apes).And there are the likes of *Ryōko* (Dragon
> versus Tiger) or *Tsuchigumo* (The Spider), which
> aim at attracting attention with interesting visual
> effects by having characters in gorgeous outfits
> performing a variety of movements on the stage.
> In other words, the spectacular and showy aspects
> of the noh theater. From the old times in Japan,
> these kinds of spectacular and showy things have
> been called "furyū," so perhaps we can, for the
> time being, call this kind of noh "furyū noh." So
> other than the "Dream play/Present play" divi-
> sion, we can also examine plays along the lines of
> "Furyū noh/Dramatic noh."[17]

弥はたしかに「人間」を描いている。世阿弥の能は脇能を除けばみな「
劇」で、たとえば鬼さえも「人間」なのである。Itō 1960, 11. In the same
commentary in *Yōkyokushū*, Yokomichi 1986 also divides the plays into different
categories. The categories of mugen noh and genzai noh are introduced. Mugen
noh refers to noh plays in which the main character (shite), usually a dead person,
returns to the living world to tell her/his story to someone, usually a traveling monk
(waki). In the first part of the play the shite character is disguised as a living person to get acquainted with the waki character before disappearing. In the second
part she/he returns at a later time of the day, often in attire that befits her/his real
identity. The shite character (known as nochi-jite, or second shite) tells the waki
character an event that happened a long time ago, and often asks the waki character
to pray for her/his enlightenment. This interaction happens in a liminal temporal
realm, which the waki is not sure is a dream or reality. In contrast to the two-act
mugen play is the structurally less complex "present" play—one that takes place
in the dramatic present and usually involves only living people. Yokomichi and
Omote 1960–1963, 1960, 10.

17. Yokomichi 1986, 11; Yokomichi and Omote 1960–1963.

With their emphasis on plot and character, the late Muromachi practitioners moved noh composition in a direction very different from that advocated by the second generation noh practitioners—Zeami and his disciples. That the name "furyū noh" has secured for itself a firm footing in contemporary noh discourse is demonstrated by the inevitable reference to it whenever the subject of late Muromachi noh plays emerges. The popularity of the term shows that audience and researchers alike have long noticed the somewhat different nature of more well-known plays composed by Zeami's and Nobumitsu's generations. To articulate these differences is an important strategy in highlighting the *representative* characteristics of plays produced during these two generations of noh practitioners.

Yokomichi sets up a comparative framework wherein the furyū noh plays, represented by the works of Nobumitsu and his contemporaries, are situated on one end of the spectrum, and the geki noh, those composed by Zeami, on the other. This comparison, upon closer scrutiny, is clearly inappropriate. "Furyū" is used to describe the visually oriented, flamboyant style of presentation as attributed to the late Muromachi noh plays. Yokomichi used the term to describe "spectacular and showy"—the performance aspects of the late Muromachi productions, in other words, the *style* of the plays. On the other hand, the "art of depicting human emotions" in Yokomichi's argument ostensibly refers to the techniques (such as literary allusions) in presenting the narratives, though within the contrastive framework he proposed it is clear that emphasis is placed on the *content* of the play.

In his ensuing commentary, Yokomichi illustrates his argument by comparing two plays, Zeami's *Kiyotsune* and Nobumitsu's *Funabenkei*. By this comparison he makes clear his contention that furyū noh is spectacular yet lacking in depth. These two plays, *Kiyotsune* and *Funabenkei*, share some similarities in that both are based on stories from the Genpei War, a famous war between the Minamoto and Taira families in the twelfth century in which the once powerful Taira family was eventually defeated. Kiyotsune and Benkei, the warriors named in the titles, were involved in the decade-long warfare between the two clans. Their life adventures, however, were very different. Kiyotsune was a Taira general who took his own life in the face of inevitable defeat; Benkei was famous for his bravery and loyalty toward his master, the Minamoto warrior Yoshitsune.[18]

In the one-part dream play *Kiyotsune*, Kiyotsune's wife (tsure) is outraged when she hears that her husband (shite) has committed suicide. She feels betrayed because Kiyotsune had promised her that they would die together. Kiyotsune's ghost then appears in his wife's dream to explain to her the reasons for his suicide. A significant part of the play is Kiyotsune's narration of the psychological turmoil that eventually leads to his tragic end. Kiyotsune's confession to his wife is presented in elegant poetic language with regular allusions to works from poetry and anthologies and replete with wordplay and puns. The necessary decision of a tragic end for the courtier warrior is presented to us in a moving manner. After his lengthy explanation of his complex internal struggle, Kiyotsune's anguished ghost attains enlightenment.[19]

Funabenkei, a two-part play, showcases a relatively more complicated narrative with more characters. It tells of the Heike hero Yoshitsune's (kokata) attempt to escape persecution from his brother, Yoritomo. In Act One, he sends away his favorite consort, Shizuka (shite), in order to cross the sea. In Act Two, the nochi-jite plays the role of the Taira warrior Taira no Tomomori. His anguished ghost surfaces from the water to seek revenge on Yoshitsune. Luckily, Yoshitsune's loyal attendant Benkei (waki) defeats the ghost and saves the day.[20]

---

18. The Genpei War was not only an important war in Japanese history, it has also inspired many creative works in various genres, ranging from *monogatari* (tales) to noh. Zeami based his *Kiyotsune* on *The Tale of Heike*, while Nobumitsu based his tale on *Gikeiki*, an eight-volume war tale that was written at the beginning of the Muromachi period, another medieval war tale with Yoshitsune as its protagonist.

19. See Nippon Gakujutsu Shinkokai 1985 and Shimazaki 1976 for translations of this play.

20. This play has been translated many times. For instance, see Tyler 1992,

With these synopses in mind, let us return to Yokomichi's comparison:

> Incidentally, we would like to ask what kind of content they [the plays] present. In the case of *Kiyotsune*, Kiyotsune the aristocrat was doubtful of the nature of the war while anticipating the inevitable fate of his clan. But being a nobleman of the Heike clan, he was not able to leave the battlefield. The only option he had was suicide, even though he was well aware of his promise to his wife that they would die together. The play fully depicts the psychological dilemma of Kiyotsune, as well as vividly presenting the almost obstinate love of the wife and the sincere rejection of this very love on the part of the husband. As such, this play, as a "dramatic play" (geki noh), has all the elements that will fully capture the hearts of the audience.
>
> When we come to *Funabenkei*, there is somehow no depiction of the fates of Yoshitsune, Shizuka, and Tomomori, despite the fact that these people were buffeted by fate and were excellent material for a "dramatic play." The brilliant contrast of Shizuka's elegant dance with Tomomori's vindictive dance, the distinctive switch from the scene at the harbor to the sea, and the new technique of using the accompaniment of the orchestra (*hayashi*) and the ai-kyōgen's movements to describe the tempest are all very sufficient to show the interesting features of furyū noh. But to watch the play as a "dramatic noh" would have been extremely boring, even to present-day audiences.[21]

83–95, and Yasuda 1989, 66–88.
21. Yokomichi 1960, 41, 12; Yokomichi and Omote 1960–1963.

After implying that furyū-style noh plays are externally attractive but have no real substance, Yokomichi proceeds to offer excuses for the late Muromachi noh practitioners as to why they composed the way they did, as well as to reveal his hidden worries:

> Nobumitsu and noh artists of his time devoted their energy fully to furyū noh for various reasons. It is conceivable that they composed in response to their roles as troupe leaders at a tender age, the unstable social conditions followed by the weakening of the bakufu government, and the frequent occurrence of warfare. However, what is most frequently performed on the stage today is still furyū noh, such as *Hagoromo* (The Feather dress), *Funabenkei* (Benkei on board), and *Momijigari* (The Autumn excursion), even when the performers think that these plays are relatively less interesting to perform. Mugen plays in the category of dramatic plays, such as *Kiyotsune* and *Izutsu* (The well cradle), have much more performance value. This should be the important focus of attention when one thinks about the nature of noh and its future.[22]

In this concluding comment we see that Yokomichi is anxious that an "inferior" category of noh plays that are "less interesting" and have less "performance value" are actually more popular among audiences. Although convincing at first glance, a closer examination of Yokomichi's assertion indicates a "performativity" that is at best ambiguous—what he describes as "to fully capture the heart of the audience." The meaning of the "performance value" that obviously defines the desirability of the plays cannot be understood without thinking about the "nature" of noh. In turn, when one begins to contemplate the nature of noh, a seemingly

---

22. Ibid.

innocent issue, one will soon realize that it is more complex than it may seem at first glance. It is here that the use of furyū as a category is so important. This "other," obviously less desirable category provides a convenient agency that constitutes what is seen as the "non-nature" of noh. It is not uncommon to hear comments that late Muromachi noh plays are better affiliated with kabuki than with noh. Again, the same mechanism is at play—that furyū noh is really not noh, but something else. It is also noteworthy that here again is manifested the assumption that anyone will understand intuitively the real nature of noh.

A closer look at one of the plays in question, *Funabenkei*, will provide concrete examples of the specific features of furyū noh plays and better insight into the construction of modern-day noh discourse.

Funabenkei as an Illustration of Furyū Noh

Funabenkei begins with Benkei, the waki, explaining the purpose of his trip. He and his master, Minamoto no Yoshitsune (kokata), have to leave the capital to escape persecution by Yoshitsune's elder brother Yoritomo. Yoshitsune has brought along his favorite consort, Shizuka Gozen (shite). Benkei suggests to Yoshitsune that Shizuka Gozen be left behind before they cross the Daimotsu no Ura (Bay of Daimotsu). Shizuka, though resenting the decision, has no choice but to consent. She performs a departure dance to songs at the *kuse* section of the play, comparing Benkei's fate to that of a Chinese minister and substantiates it with consecutive poetic imagery immersed in wordplay and puns:[23]

> Just like Hanrei who left the
> moonlit capital in twilight, sailing toward the
> waters of the western sea

---

23. The minister in question is Hanrei. After helping the King of Yue to successfully restore his power, Hanrei wisely retired from politics.

you depart, bearing the undeserved blame.
If your grievances reach Yoritomo, someday his
brotherly love,
like fronds of the green willows yielding to the
breeze,
will finally change his mind.
The karmic link of brothers will not decay so
easily.[24]

After the dance, Shizuka leaves the party and exits the stage.
Benkei then starts a discussion on their setting out with the
boatman, the ai-kyōgen. Their lighthearted exchange injects a
note of relief after the sad departure dance performed by Shizuka
Gozen. Then the boatman brings out a prop boat, which Benkei,
Yoshitsune, and their entourage board. They set out on what
seems like a pleasant day for crossing the bay. Suddenly, the
fine, sunny day turns into a frightening tempest—ominous dark
clouds foretell the arrival of an unexpected foe. Together with
the rapid beating of the stick drum and the shrill sounds of the
flute, the *onryō* (vindictive spirit) of the Taira general (nochi-
jite) Tomomori appears from the sea. He charges at Yoshitsune's
company on the sea in his military general's outfit and a demon
mask, while recalling the shameful defeat of their family by
the Minamoto clan. Tomomori and Benkei, Yoshitsune's loyal
retainer, engage in a fight accompanied by descriptive comments
from the chorus. Rather than literary allusions, the *nori* section
describes the actual movement of the people engaged in the
fighting:

---

24. かかる、例も有明の、月の都をふり捨てて、西海の波濤に赴き、
御身の咎のなきよしを、歎き、給はば頼朝も、終には靡く青柳の、枝
を連ぬる御契り、などかは朽ちし果つべき。The poetic imagery in this
short section includes the moonlit capital (*tsuki no miyako*), the green willows that flutter in the wind (*nabiku aoyanagi*), the fronds of the willows
(*aoyanagi no eda*), and finally, the karmic link that was foregrounded by
the image of the willows, which is also used to illustrate how Yoritomo will
change his mind.

I will drown Yoshitsune, he says.
Riding on the wild evening waves
he adjusts his halberd, and swirls it around him,
stirring up more raging waters.
The vicious wind bellows, blinding the eyes of one
and all.
Their hearts quiver,
their senses numbed.[25]

These comments are presented in short and crisp phrases, and often with words that produce a percussive effect. The use of shorter phrases that directly depict the actual battle forms a sharp contrast with the lyrics to which Shizuka dances. Shizuka's lines use literary imagery to evoke a melancholic sentiment, while Tomomori's lines heighten the intense rage in his vendetta. The quick, successive comments delivered by the chorus enhance the tension of the battle and resonate with the faster and more varied movements of Tomomori. The play ends when the ghost of Tomomori grudgingly retreats, realizing that he is not able to defeat Benkei.

In this play, the shite plays two different characters: the forlorn lover Shizuka Gozen and the vengeful ghost of the Taira warrior. The transition from the first shite, Shizuka, to the second shite, Tomomori, is flawless. For those who understand the structure of the noh play and the different roles of the shite, the exit of Shizuka is essential to the continuation of the play. However, to unfamiliar eyes, Shizuka's exit will be perceived as simply a natural development of the plot. It marks the end of Shizuka's relationship with the fugitive party, something that may as well happen since the party is heading toward a great danger that is considered unsuit-

---

25.又義経をも、海に沈めと、夕浪に浮かべる、長刀取直し、巴波の紋、あたりを払ひ、潮を蹴立て、悪風を吹かけ、眼もくらみ、心も乱れて、前後を忘ずる、ばかりなり。Nishino, 1998, 352.

able for a woman like Shizuka. Before she bids goodbye, Shizuka performs an elegant female-style dance that conveys her grief in departing from Yoshitsune, leaving the stage in a pensive mood. But the atmosphere changes dramatically as soon as Tomomori appears. Tomomori's battle dance expresses an explosive hatred (especially with the accompaniment of the stick drum) toward Yoshitsune, who a short while ago has just seen a dance of love and devotion from Shizuka. Dance is an important component of the noh theater. The two dances performed here are important not only because they are the embodiment of two contrasting sentiments, but also because they distinguish this play from many others in which the shite role performs only one character and is the sole focus of the play.

This, however, is not the case in *Funabenkei*. Benkei, the waki character whom the play is named after, has many important roles. He is instrumental in Shizuka's departure, and later on it is mainly his faith, bravery, and martial powers that defeat Tomomori. When he informs Shizuka of Yoshitsune's intention to leave her behind, he engages in a direct confrontation with Shizuka as she questions the credibility of the message. Other role types, like many other plays composed by Nobumitsu and his peers, are also actively engaged. Yoshitsune is performed by a child role (kokata) who has very few lines, though he is by no means insignificant in terms of the plot. The role of the ai-kyōgen also differs from most of the other ai-kyōgen who appear simply to reiterate the plot—sometimes in an exchange with the waki, sometimes presenting a monologue. Here he is the fisherman who ferries the company across Daimotsu Bay, with a prop that looks like a boat. He participates actively in the development of the play and brings a temporary emotional reprieve with his lighthearted exchanges with Benkei after Shizuka's reluctant departure.

The audience is therefore being taken through contrasting moods by the different tempos that mark each new development of the play. When the play begins, the dilemma confronted by the fugitive group produces a grave atmosphere, which culminates in Shizuka's farewell dance. The witty exchanges between Benkei and the boatman while they prepare to cross the river are more lighthearted, but are followed by a mood turned swiftly somber. These developments in the plot are also accentuated by the use of the stick drum and the flute, especially in the final section. The appearance of the Taira warrior apparition is heralded by an ominous change of weather, demonstrated by the hurried lines from the chorus and the beating of the stick drum.

These characteristics all share two common denominators: the visual and the aural, which are two dominant characteristics often found in plays by the third-generation noh practitioners, and identified as furyū in modern noh discourse. In addition, the use of poetic language is not prioritized in plays from this generation. Many plays in today's active repertoire, mainly composed by the second generation practitioners, have fewer characters and a more shite-focused plot, like *Kiyotsune*—the play Yokomichi argued exemplified "performance value." Even though Yokomichi did not clearly explain how the act of depicting human beings' words and action is conveyed in a noh play, by contrasting this mode of presentation with that of the "spectacular" performances, one can deduct that he was probably referring to the lyricism and poetic language, as *Kiyotsune* demonstrates. I believe this lyricism constitutes part of Yokomichi's "performance value" agenda, however contradictory it may sound. The claim that a play such as *Funabenkei*, which is more spectacle-oriented, does not depict "the fate of Yoshitsune, Shizuka, and Tomomori" can only be true if such depiction *excludes* stage presentation, or is restricted to only the written lines.[26] The strong emotions of each character are conveyed through their dances as much as the librettos. In other words, the prioritizing of written text over performance plays a role in defining the nature of noh plays. But such prioritizing cannot be understood unless one examines the role of Zeami and his treatises, which I will discuss in the following.

---

26. Yokomichi and Omote 1960–1963, vol. 2, 12.

Assessing Furyū Noh within the Zeami Paradigm

Zeami's efforts in developing the musical (*kabu*), rather than the monomane, elements of the noh theater, as well as his prioritizing of the literary classics, have contributed significantly to the development of the genre's special features.[27] As I have discussed in Chapter Five, mugen noh is highly valued by scholars, and they are believed to have best illustrated Zeami's aesthetic principal.

The aesthetics behind these plays can be discerned in Zeami's several treatises, composed in different stages of his career, that expound both the theoretical and performance aspects of the genre.[28] In his corpus of treatises, Zeami developed a body of intricate and semiphilosophical theories centering around aesthetic concepts such as "*hana*" (flower) and yūgen. Yūgen, originally a term in poetic criticism, was also a stylistic preference of the Yamato-area sarugaku noh troupes. Zeami uses this term extensively in his treatises to describe the profound and mysterious beauty that defines a good noh play—one that the connoisseur appraises and approves.[29] In the treatise *Nōsakusho* (On Noh

---

27. Zeami addresses the issues of monomane in chapter two of his first treatise, *Fushikaden—dai-ni, monomane jōjō* (Omote and Katō 1974, 20–27); see Rimer and Yamazaki 1984, 10–17 for a translation; Hare 2011, 31–37), indicating that monomane was still an important concern in the earlier part of his career. In fact, monomane was a higher priority of the Yamato troupes to which Zeami's Kanze (initially called Yūzaki) troupe belonged. But we can already see Zeami's preference at this stage for presenting something more elegant and beautiful through the use of poetic, rather than "realistic," language—he argues that laborers and rustics should not be too imitated, unless they "have traditionally been found congenial as poetic subjects" (Rimer and Yamazaki 1984, 10). Also see earlier chapters in this book for a discussion of monomane.

28. A good reference to Zeami's works is Quinn's 2005 book *Developing Zeami*. In it Quinn presents an in-depth analysis of Zeami's treatises, positioning her discussion within a framework of stages of development in Zeami's career, together with translation of pertinent sections of the treatises. Also in Hare's 2011 work, an annotated translation of most of Zeami's written work on performance can be found. Hare prefaced each translations with commentary specific to Zeami's work. The introduction, appendixes and glossary also provide readers with information on Zeami's work.

29. See Brown's discussion of the different kinds of patronage during Zeami's

composition), Zeami lists various factors to achieve this ultimate stage of beauty: one of which is to base the play on the appropriate "source material," or *honzetsu tadashi*.[30] This includes the choice of the main character and/or the setting in which the play is going to unfold. Zeami identifies various examples, all of which point toward a body of literary works that was held up as representative of the aesthetic preference of the ruling class at that time.[31]

In addition to theories on aesthetics, Zeami meticulously discusses performance techniques, in both concrete and abstract terms, at times with illustrations. Among other things, he structures role types into three basic modes: the warrior, the female, and the old man.[32] Combining the appropriate source material and character type will achieve the most desirable effect. Here we see Zeami's genius and sense of balance when it comes to theater:

---

time in Brown 2001, 10–15, and Hoff 1992, especially 135–137, for an elaboration on Zeami's perception of good plays and good critics.

30. *Honzetsu*, like other terms found in Zeami's treatises, has been translated in various ways. For instance, Quinn (2005, 138) translates it as "foundation story." *Honzetsu tadashi* appears in various places in Zeami's treatises. Rimer and Yamazaki 1984, 21, translate it as "authentic source" while Hare 2008, 40, translates it as "faithful to their sources." In "Daisan Mondō Jōjō" in *Fushikaden*, Zeami explains that the most superior play is one with appropriate source material that is performed with style. Later, when discussing noh composition, Zeami lists an appropriate source as the first important element to a successful noh performance (*Fushikaden*, 48). Also see Mitake 2001, 87–98, for more discussion on the use of honzetsu in Zeami's noh plays.

31. This ruling class refers mainly to the military class, although it is difficult, if not impossible, to ignore the influence of the courtiers in Kyoto, whose cultural practices were admired by the military leaders. Goff 1992, Chapter 2, and particularly 36–41, presents a detailed discussion of the nature of this aesthetic preference, manifested especially in the close relationship between the poet Nijō Yoshimoto (1320–1388) and Zeami. Other scholars too, explore this sentiment of an admiration and longing for past Heian glory during especially the first half of the Muromachi period. See Imatani and Yamamura 1992, Murai 2001, 22–23, and *Nihon Geinōshi* 1993, 157–168.

32. See *Fushikaden* in Omote and Katō 1974, 124–132, 136–139, for an analysis of the three styles. Also see Rimer and Yamazaki 1984, 151–155; Hare 2011, 135–149, for a translation of this section of his treatise; and Hare 1986, chapters 3, 4, and 5, on an elaboration of these different modes.

he substantiates his abstract theoretical teachings with actual performance instruction, thus constructing a complete scheme of practical training backed up with philosophical and intellectual, albeit at times abstract, reasoning. A combination of these aesthetic preferences results in the kind of noh play that Zeami champions—one with regular reference to the literary classics, both in terms of subject matter and literary style. His emphasis on the musical aspects of the theater—dance and singing—also figures significantly in his treatises. In terms of characterization, the focus is often centered solely on the shite character, who performs all the major dances and whose psychological landscape becomes the best place to exhibit the practitioner's literary talents.[33]

Present-day noh discourse is constructed upon this corpus of comprehensive, philosophical, and literary-oriented aesthetic theories advocated by Zeami, who is the only noh practitioner to devise a systematic body of theories and practical advice on performance. Throughout his long career, Zeami writes treatises that advocate his aesthetical preference—one that emphasizes on poetic presentation of songs and dance—in the noh theater. His writings include literally every aspect on noh, ranging from training methods to commentaries on other related theatrical forms of his time and the skill of other performers; not to mention the incorporation of critical terminology such as hana and yūgen, which eventually became indispensable key words in modern-day noh discourse. Regular references are also made to plays mentioned in these treatises.

Many historical documents have reaffirmed Zeami's position as one of the best noh practitioners, if not *the* best.[34] Noh documents compiled in the Edo period attributed a large number of noh plays to Zeami, though some have been proven to be false attributions

---

33. This prompted scholars to name the approach *shite-ichinin-shūgi*, or "shite-focus performance." See Chapter 4 for a more detailed discussion of the term.
34. I believe that other factors also contribute to Zeami's uncontested position. For instance, the strong position the Kanze family occupied within the world of noh theater throughout the premodern period would have contributed to Zeami's elevated position.

in later studies. Another important testament to Zeami's fame as a noh practitioner is the immense popularity of *Hachijō Kadensho* (Treatise on the Transmission of the Flower in Eight Chapters), an Edo-period noh treatise by unknown author(s). This book was apocryphally attributed to Zeami and was a bestseller during the Edo period.[35] Even though his treatises were inaccessible to the public until around 1908, when Yoshida Tōgō (1864–1918) discovered a set of Zeami's noh treatises in a used bookstore, the popularity of many of his noh plays contributes to his prominence.[36]

In the literary and critical history of noh, the subsequent publication of these treatises marked the beginning of modern scholarly noh discourse. Since then modern scholars have been able to construct a more systematic trajectory in the research of Zeami's aesthetic ideals, which marks the beginning of the *Nōgaku* period identified by Omote as discussed in the Introduction of this book. Starting from the early twentieth century, almost every year in Japan, study groups, academic associations, and journals specifically devoted to Zeami have been formed. In the West, too, the study of Zeami, both his theoretical writings and plays, has always been an important theme in the study of noh theater. The new research agenda made possible by the discovery and distribution of these treatises has further affirmed Zeami's canonical position.

Zeami's approach toward noh established a strong preference for the literary elements of the genre, thereby weakening the importance of other theatricalities of the texts. This preference has made it easy for noh plays to be transformed from performance or theatrical texts to literary texts.[37] I refer to this process as the

---

35. See Rath 1999 for a detailed introduction to the text.

36. This event, as well as a reading of the texts, was serialized in several volumes of the noh journal *Nōgaku*, beginning with its September issue in 1908 (Meiji 41). Using the pen name Yoshida Rakujō, Yoshida Tōgō discussed in great detail the content of these newly found documents. See *Nōgaku* 6, no. 9 (September): 17–28; no. 10 (October): 4–19; no. 11 (November): 7–17; and no. 12 (December): 5–16.

37. By literary texts I mean not so much the librettos, but texts that can be consumed independently without the need to incorporate or consider any form

"textualization" of the noh theater. This textualization process can be detected, arguably, from the time of *Utaishō*.[38] The commentary in *Utaishō* on the *utaibon*, or noh texts that amateur noh performers learned to chant from, marks the first step toward establishing noh as a literary genre as much as a performance genre. Providing commentary on a text assumes an inherent value in that text that needs to be deciphered. Whatever the original intention of the commentary might have been, it nudged the genre in a more literature-oriented direction, achieving what is called the effect of "literary respectability."[39]

The fact that more commentaries were compiled after *Utaishō* demonstrates that noh can be appreciated in two different ways: as a written text and as an actual performance. The scope of noh theater therefore crossed over to be included in the paradigm of literary texts. Fans of the noh theater now had, from the Tokugawa period onward, more choices in the consumption of noh than other theatrical genres. For instance, despite its close affinity to noh on stage, kyōgen did not enjoy the same literary prestige. *Tenshō Kyōgenbon* (A Book on Kyōgen from the Tenshō Period), written around 1578 (Tenshō 6) and the only surviving book on Muromachi period kyōgen, records only play synopses. Neither did the other two theatrical genres, kabuki and bunraku (puppet theater), produce annotated commentaries (*chūshakusho*) to

---

of theatrical elements. Students who read Japanese literature in places outside of Japan where it is hard to gain access to an actual noh performance, for instance, could read noh plays as poetic articulation of a narrative.

38. *Utaishō* is a commentary on lines from the noh anthology *Yōkyoku Hyakuban*. This very first noh annotation and commentary was compiled under the command of the General Toyotomi Hidetsugu (1568–1595) in the fourth year of Bunroku (1595). See *Nihon Shomin Bunkashiryō Shūsei*, vol. 3, 319–656.

39. Shakespearean scholar Lukas Erne argues that the writing of theatrical texts is an attempt for the author to "raise the literary respectability of playtexts" (*Shakespeare as Literary Dramatist* [Cambridge, New York: Cambridge University Press, 2003], 220). The compilation of commentaries is different from transfering a dramatic text from its oral form onto paper, but the end result is not unsimilar. Writing and commentaries both accord a literary value to the text, enabling a performance text to be consumed as a literary text.

accompany the play texts that were being published.[40] Various reasons explain this phenomenon. Commoners, especially the merchants, were the major patrons of the kabuki and bunraku theater. The aesthetic preferences of this audience differed greatly from that of the Muromachi military leaders, inevitably compelling a different trajectory of development. There was also no need for the practitioners of kabuki or bunraku theater to resort to any cultural reference to enhance the status of the genre as a matter of survival. While a sense of nostalgia for the glorious Heian court culture still lingered in the Muromachi period, such sentiment had mostly disappeared during the chaotic years of civil war. Unlike the early Muromachi period, the intended Tokugawa theater audience—the commoners—did not identify themselves with the classical canon. It therefore did not encourage the need for receiving kabuki and bunraku as anything other than a *performance* genre. Present-day kabuki, bunraku, and kyōgen remain very much theatrical genres whose literary value is not the most important consideration in terms of appreciation of the texts. Noh, on the other hand, is often identified as the representative classical theater with a compatible literary status of Japan.

The Nature of Noh and the Value of Furyū Noh in Contemporary Noh Discourse

It is clear that Zeami's works (both plays and treatises) dominate as the ultimate standard against which the noh theater is measured in present-day noh discourse—plays that do not conform to the aesthetic standard of the Zeami paradigm do not qualify as good noh plays. The question remains, however, whether such a comparison is appropriate or if it makes sense in terms of providing an acces-

---

40. Even though entire kabuki plays started to be written down at the end of the seventeenth century, they were not read as literary texts. See Inoura Yoshinobu and Toshio Kawatake, *The Traditional Theater of Japan* (New York, Tokyo: Weatherhill, 1981) and Ortolani 1990, Chapter VII, for a brief history of the kabuki theater.

sible and useful framework with which to study noh plays from the late Muromachi period.

Zeami's emphasis on the presence of a body of classic literature as the foundation of noh plays is seen in his treatises on noh composition. We therefore see that, in addition to the necessary performance elements such as dance and music, a strong effort is being put into the librettos, that is the literary aspect of the plays. It is little wonder, then, that noh is often referred to as *shigeki*, or poetic (lyrical) drama. The term *shigeki* is a translation of the Western term described by Patrice Pavis in the following manner:

> Action in lyrical drama was limited in scope, and plot had no function other than to handle moments of lyrical stasis. The lyrical and the dramatic came together in a destructuring of the tragic or dramatic form. Music was only an external component added to the text; the text "musicalizes" itself in a series of motifs, words and poems that are valuable in themselves rather than in relation to a clearly defined dramatic structure.[41]

Although Pavis is referring to a specific theatrical genre from nineteenth-century Europe, the emphasis on the independent nature of elements such as poetry is intriguingly similar to that of Zeami's noh plays. Even though music in Zeami's noh has a much more important role than in the poetic drama discussed above, we can see the destructuring relationship between lyric and drama as presented in Pavis' argument. Zeami's poetic drama, like its counterpart in the West, shares a strong resemblance to poetry, except that this poetry can be, and often has been, performed. When written down, the literary features of these plays are not

---

41. Pavis, *Dictionary of the Theatre: Terms, Concepts, and Analysis* (Toronto: University of Toronto Press, Canada 1991), 112.

lost because they are words that can be retained on the pages and not performance that is restricted by temporal and spatial constraints.

Many late Muromachi noh plays, however, do not prioritize literary characteristics; we see a different approach in noh composition by the late Muromachi noh practitioners. A talented and prolific noh practitioner like Nobumitsu was able to create plays like *Funabenkei,* which balances lyricism and theatricality, while his peers and disciples such as Zenpō and Nagatoshi did not really prioritize lyricism in their works, even though it does not mean that these plays are beyond recognition as noh plays. With its specific role-character structure and the use of the chorus, noh has a distinctive presentational style which late Muromachi noh practitioners adhered to. Their plays, however, do not qualify as lyrical drama, or the ideal form of noh, because of their emphasis on the theatricality rather than the literary. This also explains why furyū-style plays are often compared to kabuki plays, whose emphasis on the visual and dramatic aspects of the stage is in stark contrast to Zeami's contemplative no plays. The emphasis on theatricality in the furyū-style plays is promptly acknowledged in modern noh discourse, though it is precisely this emphasis that condemns them to an inferior category within the genre.

In this concluding chapter I discuss the discourse on noh in present-day scholarship and how this discourse has inherently excluded furyū-style plays. This oversight needs reconsideration. As I have shown in Part Two, Nobumitsu's plays show intrinsic artistic value as a theatrical form that survives time. Because noh plays also acquired a second identity—literature—with Zeami's lyrical drama plays that can be read as enchanting literature in the conventional sense, furyū-style plays that remained focused on performance are considered inferior. And the small number of extant plays by his peers as we can see in the present day active repertoire too, demonstrate theatrical and literary features that merit more serious scholarly attention.

Nobumitsu, the Late Muromachi Noh, and Modern Noh Discourse

This book starts out with a set of questions related to the late Muromachi period noh theater: who is Nobumitsu? Why are plays created in this period often called "furyū plays"? Why are they seldom discussed in modern noh scholarship? And finally, where do Nobumitsu and the late Muromachi period noh stand in modern noh discourse?

The key to these questions lies in one representative noh practitioner from that period—Kanze Kojirō Nobumitsu, the son of On'ami and grandnephew of Zeami. As evident from his biography and plays, Nobumitsu inherited aspects of the theatrical aesthetics—monomane and yūgen—from his two renowned predecessors. Many of Nobumitsu's plays, such as those discussed in Chapters Three and Four, feature more than one main character and emphasize the visual and aural aspects of presentation. These performance elements facilitate the use of monomane and the actual enactment of a more complex narrative on stage. His discussion with the Gozan Zen prelate Keijō Shūrin on performance in the *Kanze Kojirō Portrait Inscription* also subtly reaffirms the importance of monomane in performance, as alluded to in an episode in the Buddhist sutra *Kengūkyō*. On the other hand, plays discussed in Chapter Five demonstrate another set of performance features in Nobumitsu's plays—an emphasis on lyricism and poetic imagery. These two elements are often associated today with the "typical" noh structure and content—the yūgen play which was highly esteemed by Zeami.

But most characteristic of his plays is undoubtedly the artistic creativity that the noh practitioner Nobumitsu displays. That Nobumitsu himself is a talented noh composer who was able to introduce new performance techniques and allude to familiar sources to create innovative plays is evident in the plays that I have analyzed. Among the extant twenty-five noh plays attributed to Nobumitsu, more than half are still performed today. This is second only to Zeami. The range of plays in Nobumistu's repertoire is impressive: battles between the living and the supernatural, adventures of mythological characters, "Chinese" subject matter, and tales of the enlightenment of nonsentient beings, just to name a few. Some of these plays exhibit features that are not often used, while some stick closer to the conventional style of composition. All of them demonstrate Nobumitsu's skill in noh composition and performance as well as his knowledge of the literary canon of his time.

There is, of course, more than one factor that underpins Nobumitsu's versatile repertoire. First and foremost is his artistic talent. Influences from earlier plays can also be detected. And yet another important factor is the evolution of the genre itself. By Nobumitsu's time, noh was established as a form of officially sanctioned performance, accepted especially by the cultural elite and the military leaders who were its most powerful patrons. After the two earlier generations of noh practitioners' experimentations and productions of plays, the noh theater had established a firm infrastructure as manifested in written texts (versus oral transmission), structural components (role types and chorus), and a score of treatises thanks to Zeami and his disciples. The late Muromachi period, when Nobumitsu started to compose, is when noh had fully established itself as an art form rather than merely being one of the many plebian performance genres which had burgeoned since the Heian period. Many of these earlier genres, including sarugaku's earliest competitor, dengaku, did not further develop as a theatrical form. Sarugaku, on the other hand, blossomed into one of the many cultural forms that late Muromachi period cultural elites embraced.

As I have shown in this study, Nobumitsu (and his peers) and the theatrical genre that they represented were part of the cultural elite. The joint effort in the creation of a portrait inscription with Keijō is one example, his friendship with Sanjō Nishi Sanetaka is another. This status of noh as a cultural form allowed Nobumitsu more power in terms of negotiating his audience's preferences and creating plays—we therefore see a different kind of play that does not seem to be adhering to any one specific aesthetic category.

Much more than any of his predecessors, Nobumitsu was able to practice more initiative and innovation in noh composition without needing to pay special consideration to the preferences of any particular group of patrons. Audience preference is never unimportant, but compared to Zeami's time when sarugaku was challenged by, among other things, its social origin, Nobumitsu needed no overt persuasion to convince his audience that noh was an established art form with its own distinct identity. Instead, his interactions with his audience/patrons lay in the transmission of knowledge in noh ranging from composition to mask appreciation to performance techniques—an interaction mode shared by other noh practitioners from the late Muromachi period.

Since Nobumitsu's time the noh theater has been confronted with various challenges and changes: ranging from its institution-alization in the Tokugawa period to financial crisis in the early Meiji period. Today, noh is one of the intangible cultural heritages of Japan. Many scholars and artists, both from Japan and other parts of the world, are interested in the genre in many different ways. Scholars present their findings on noh, ranging from his-torical accounts to examinations of individual practitioners to aes-thetic theories pertaining to the genre. This body of scholarly work includes those that brand the late Muromchi noh as furyū nō. The effort to identify the late Muromachi noh plays has, whether in-tended or not, also distinguished them from their predecessors. A close scrutiny of this usage indicates unfavorable nuances—that furyū noh, because of its prioritization of theatricality and there-fore often a weaker or lack of emphasis on lyricism, is at best an inferior form of noh. I have shown in this book that this impres-sion is very much misconstrued.

Late Muromachi noh plays, including those created by Nobumitsu and his peers as well as those by amateur composers, still adhered to the basic structure of noh even though the general emphasis of these plays is more on theatricality than lyricism. However, because noh has acquired a second identity in modern times—as literature—especially with the higher number of lyrical noh plays by Zeami and his peers, furyū-style plays that remained focused on performance are considered less noh-like. It is hard to argue against the importance of Zeami's systematic aesthetic paradigm—which prioritizes elegant lyricism and treats mimicry as secondary—in defining noh. It is, however, also equally important to acknowledge that the noh theater can and should be expressed and experienced in more than one dimension. Plays by Nobumitsu and his peers are by no means limited to simply the style of boisterous modern plays that are bereft of poetic language. Close readings of these plays show that the third generation of noh practitioners and their theater has entered a new stage—one that has incorporated not only features of the genre from the earlier generations, but also one that has gradually expanded beyond familiar bounderies to create new plays.

The institutionalization of the noh theater in the Tokugawa period saw another trend in the development of noh—one that, as Ikenouchi Nobuyoshi argued in *Nōgaku Seisuiki*, became stagnate in terms of composition of new plays.[42] By this stage noh practitioners focused more of their energy on refining their skill than on exploring new possibilities in play composition. The institutionalization of noh as the official ritual of the shogunate had a great impact on the social and cultural milieu in which noh practitioners composed and performed. The noh that we see today is closest to what noh was like in the latter half of the Tokugawa period, although if the institutionalization of noh had not taken place, we might today be watching something very different.

---

42. Ikenouch 1992, 411. Also see Looser 2008 for an analysis of the process of the institutionalization of noh.

BIBLIOGRAPHY

Sources in English

Akamatsu Toshihide and Philip Yampolsky. "Muromachi Zen and the Gozan System." In John Whitney Hall and Toyoda Takeshi, eds., *Japan in the Muromachi Age.* Berkeley, Los Angeles, London: University of Berkeley Press, 1977: 313–329.

Atkins, Paul S. *Revealed Identity: The Noh Plays of Komparu Zenchiku.* Ann Arbor: Center for Japanese Studies, University of Michigan, 2006.

Aston, W.G., trans. *Nihongi: Chronicles of Japan from the Earliest Times to A.D. 697.* Tokyo: Charles Tuttle Co., 1972.

Beichman, Janine. "Drifting Fires: An American Nō." *Asian Theatre Journal* 3.2 (1986): 233–260.

Berry, Mary Elizabeth. *The Culture of Civil War in Kyoto.* Berkeley, Los Angeles, London: University of California Press, 1994.

Bethe, Monica, and Karen Brazell. *Nō as Performance: An Analysis of the Kuse Scene of Yamamba.* Ithaca, NY: China-Japan Program, Cornell University, 1978.

Brazell, Karen, ed. *Traditional Japanese Theater—An Anthology of Plays.* New York: Columbia University Press, 1998.

Brevoort, Deborah. "Blue Moon Over Memphis—A Noh Drama about Elvis Presley." Kagaya Shinko tr. *Journal of the Noh Research Archives* 15 (2004): 86–172. Musashino University Nō Research Center. Tokyo, Japan.

Brown, Steven T. *Theatricalities of Power: The Cultural Politics of Noh.* Stanford: Stanford University Press, 2001.

Collcutt, Martin. *Five Mountains: The Rinzai Zen Monastic Institution in Medieval Japan.* Cambridge, MA: Harvard University Council of East Asian Studies, 1981.

de Bary, William Theodore, and Irene Bloom, *Sources of Chinese Tradition,* 2nd ed. vol. 1. New York: Columbia University Press, 1999.

185

De Poorter, Erika. *Zeami's Talks on Sarugaku: An Annotated Translation of the Sarugaku Dangi, with an Introduction on Zeami Motokiyo.* Monographs of the Netherlands Association for Japanese Studies. Amsterdam: J.C. Gieben, 1986.

Dobbins, James C., trans. Ōsumi Kazuo. "Buddhism in the Kamakura Period." Adapted and expanded. In Kozo Yamamura, ed., *The Cambridge History of Japan, Vol. 3: Medieval Japan,* 544–582. Cambridge: Cambridge University Press, 1990.

Elam, Keir. *The Semiotics of Theatre and Drama.* New York: Methuen, 1980.

Erne, Lukas. *Shakespeare as Literary Dramatist.* New York: Cambridge University Press, 2003.

Ernst, Earle. *Three Japanese Plays from the Traditional Theatre.* New York, Toronto: Oxford University Press, 1959.

Foard, James H. "Seiganji: The Buddhist Orientation of a Noh Play." *Monumenta Nipponica* 35, 4 (Winter 1980): 437–456.

Fontein, Jan, and Money L. Hickman. *Zen Painting and Calligraphy: An exhibition of works of art lent by temples, private collectors, and public and private museums in Japan, organized in collaboration with the Agency for Cultural Affairs of the Japanese government.* Boston: Boston Museum of Fine Arts, 1970. Date of exhibition: Nov. 5–Dec. 20, 1970.

Goff, Janet. *Noh Drama and The Tale of Genji—The Art of Allusion in Fifteen Classical Plays.* Princeton: Princeton University Press, 1991.

Graham, Masako Nakagawa. *The Yang Kuei-Fei Legend in Japanese Litearature.* Lewiston, NY: The Edwin Mellen Press, 1998.

Hall, John Whitney, and Toyoda Takeshi, eds. *Japan in the Muromachi Age.* Berkeley, Los Angeles: University of California Press, 1977.

Hansen, Chad. *A Daoist Theory of Chinese Thought: A Philosophical Interpretation.* New York: Oxford University Press, 1992.

Hare, Thomas Blenman. *Zeami's Style—The Noh Plays of Zeami Motokiyo.* Stanford: Stanford University Press, 1986.

Hare, Tom, trans. *Zeami: Performance Notes.* New York: Columbia University Press, 2008.

Harries, Philip. "Furyū, a Concept of Elegance in Pre-modern Literature." In Gordon Daniels, ed., *Europe Interprets Japan,* 137–144. Tenterden, Kent, UK: Paul Norbury Publications, 1984.

Hickman, Money L., et al. *Japan's Golden Age: Momoyama.* New Haven: Yale University Press, 1996.

Hisamatsu, Senichi. *The Vocabulary of Japanese Literary Aesthetics.* Tokyo: Centre for East Asian Cultural Studies, 1963. Second printing 1978.

Hoff, Frank. "Seeing and Being Seen: The Mirror of Performance." In James Sanford, William LaFleur and Masatoshi Nagatomi, eds., *Flowing Traces: Buddhism in the Literary and Visual Arts of Japan,* 131–148. Princeton: Princeton University Press, 1992.

Holquist, Michael, ed. *The Dialogic Imagination by M.M. Bakhtin: Four Essays.* Caryl Emerson and Michael Holquist, trans. Austin: University of Texas Press, 1981.

Imatani Akira and Kozo Yamamura. "Not for Lack of Will or Wile: Yoshimitsu's Failure to Supplant the Imperial Lineage." *Journal of Japanese Studies* 18.1 (Winter 1992): 45–78.

Inoura Yoshinobu and Toshio Kawatake. *The Traditional Theater of Japan.* New York, Tokyo: Weatherhill, 1981.

Keene, Donald, trans. *Essay in Idleness: The Tsurezeregusa of Kenko.* New York: Columbia University Press, 1967.

————, trans. Mishima Yukio. *Five Modern Nō Plays.* Tokyo: Charles Tuttle Co., 1967.

————, ed. *20 Plays of the Nō Theatre.* New York: Columbia University Press, 1970.

————. *Yoshimasa and the Silver Pavilion: The Creation of the Soul of Japan.* New York: Columbia University Press, 2003.

Klein, Susan Blakeley. "Woman as Serpent: The Demonic Feminine in the Noh Play Dōjōji." In Jane Marie Law, ed., *Religious Reflections on the Human Body,* 100–116. Bloomington and Indianapolis: Indiana University Press, 1995.

Konishi, Jun'ichi. *A History of Japanese Literature, Volume Three: The High Middle Ages.* Aileen Gatten and Mark Harbison, trans. Earl Miner, ed. Princeton: Princeton University Press, 1991.

Kroll, Paul W. "Po Chu-I's "Song of Lasting Regret": A New Translation. *T'ang Studies* 8–9 (1991): 97–104.

Konparu, Kunio. *The Noh Theater: Principles and Perspectives.* New York, Tokyo, Kyoto: Weatherhill/Tankosha, 1983.

Lim, Beng Choo. "Performing *Furyū Nō*: The Theatre of Konparu Zenpō." *Asian Theatre Journal* (Spring 2005): 33–51.

————. "The Nobumitsu Portrait Inscription: An Annotated Translation." *Monumenta Nipponica* 55.4 (Winter 2000): 567–577.

————. "They Came to Party—An Examination of the Social Status of the Medieval Noh Theater." *Japan Forum* (Spring 2004): 111–133.

Looser, Thomas D. *Visioning Eternity: Aesthetics, Politics and History in the Early Modern Noh Theater.* Ithaca, NY: Cornell University East Asia Program, 2008.

Mair, Victor H. *Wandering on the Way: Early Taoist Tales and Parables of Chuang Tzu.* Honolulu: University of Hawai'i Press, 1994.

Matisoff, Susan, and Yamazaki Masakazu, trans. "The Aesthetics of Transformation: Zeami's Dramatic Theories." *Journal of Japanese Studies* 7.2 (Summer 1981): 215–257.

McCullough, Helen, trans. *The Tale of Heike.* Stanford: Stanford University Press, 1988.

Moriguchi Yasuhiko and David Jenkins, trans. Kamo-no-Chomei. *Hojoki: Visions of a Torn World.* Berkeley: Stone Bridge Press, 1996.

Nippon Gakujutsu Shinkokai. *The Noh Drama: Ten plays from the Japanese*, selected and translated by the Special Nō Committee, Japanese Classics Translation Committee. Tokyo: Tuttle, 1985.

Ortolani, Benito. *The Japanese Theatre: from Shamanistic Ritual to Contemporary Pluralism.* Revised edition. Princeton: Princeton University Press, 1990.

Pavis, Patrice, ed. *Dictionary of the Theatre: Terms, Concepts, and Analysis,* Toronto: University of Toronto Press, 1998.

Philippi, Donald, trans. and ed. *Kojiki.* Tokyo: University of Tokyo Press, 1968.

Phillips, Quitman E. *The Practices of Painting in Japan, 1475–1500.* Stanford: Stanford University Press, 2000.

Pinnington, Noel John. "Models of the Way in the Theory of Noh." *Japan Review* 18 (2006): 29–55.

————. *Traces in the Way: Michi and the Writings of Konparu Zenchiku.* Ithaca, NY: Cornell University East Asia Program, 2006.

Qamber, Akhtar. *Yeats and the Noh.* New York, Tokyo: Weatherhill, 1974.

Quinn, Shelley Fenno. *Developing Zeami: The Noh Actor's Attunement in Practice.* Honolulu: University of Hawai'i Press, 2005.

Rath, Eric C. "Challenging the Old Men: A Brief History of Women in Noh Theater." In Steven Brown and Sara Jansen, eds., *Women & Performance: A Journal of Feminist Theory Performing Japanese Woman,* 23 (2001): 97–112. New York University, Women and Performance Project, 2001.

————. "Legends, Secrets, and Authority: *Hachijō Kadensho* and Early Modern Noh." *Monumenta Nipponica* 54.2 (Summer 1999): 169–194.

————. *The Ethos of Noh Actors and Their Art*. Harvard University Asia Center for the Harvard-Yenching Institute, 2004.

Raz, Jacob. "The Actor and His Audience—Zeami's Views on the Audience of the Noh." *Monumenta Nipponica* 31.3 (Autumn 1976): 251–274.

————. *Audience and Actors: A Study of Their Interaction in the Japanese Traditional Theatre*. Leiden: E.J. Brill, 1983.

Rimer, J. Thomas, and Yamazaki Masakazu, trans. *On the Art of the Nō Drama: The Major Treatises of Zeami*. Princeton: Princeton University Press, 1984.

Sanford, James H., William R. LaFleur, and Nagatomi Masatoshi. *Flowing Traces: Buddhism in the Literary and Visual Arts of Japan*. Princeton: Princeton University Press, 1992.

Seidensticker, Edward G., trans. Murasaki Shikibu. *The Tale of Genji*. London: Secker and Warburg, 1976.

Shimazaki, Chifumi. *The Noh: Volume III, Woman Noh*. Book 1. Tokyo: Hinoki Shoten, 1976.

Shively, Donald. "Buddhahood for the Nonsentient: A Theme in No Plays." *Harvard Journal of Asiatic Studies* 22.1/2 (June 1957): 135–161.

Smethurst, Mae J. *Dramatic Representations of Filial Piety: Five Noh in Translation*. Ithaca, NY: Cornell University East Asia Program, 1998.

Terasaki, Etsuko. *Figures of Desire: Wordplay, Spirit Possession, Fantasy, Madness and Mourning in Japanese Noh Plays*. Ann Arbor: Center for Japanese Studies, The University of Michigan, 2002.

Thornhill III, Arthur. *Six Circles, One Dewdrop: The Religio-aesthetic World of Komparu Zenchiku*. Princeton: Princeton University Press, 1993.

Thornton, S.A. *Charisma and Community Formation in Medieval Japan—The Case of the Yugyo-ha* (1300–1700). Ithaca, NY: Cornell University East Asia Program, 1999.

Tyler, Royall, trans. *Japanese Nō Drama*. London and New York: Penguin Books, 1992.

————, trans. Murasaki Shikibu. *The Tale of Genji*. New York: Viking, 2001.

Waley, Arthur, trans. Murasaki Shikibu. *The Tale of Genji*. London: George Allen & Unwin Ltd, 1925–1928.

————. *The Nō Plays of Japan*. New York: Grove Press, 1920.

Wilkinson, Endymion. *Chinese History: A Manual*. Revised and enlarged ed. Harvard University Asia Center for the Harvard-Yenching Institute, 2000.

Yasuda, Kenneth. *Masterworks of the No Theater*. Bloomington: Indiana University Press, 1989.

Yokota-Murakami, Gerry. *The Formation of the Canon of Nō: The Literary Tradition of Divine Authority*. Osaka: Osaka University Press, 1997.

Sources in Japanese
(All publishers, unless otherwise stated, are in Tokyo)

Amano Fumio. *Nō ni tsukareta kenryokusha: Hideyoshi nōgaku aikōki*. Kodansha Senshomechie, 1997.

————."Goyō yakusha Zōami wo torimaku kenkyū—futatsu no "Zōami Gazōsan" kara—." *Tessen* 482 (April 2000): 4–5.

Arai Hakuseki. *Arai Hakuseki zenshū* vol. 6. Naigai Insatsu Kabushiki Kaisha, 1907.

Dōmoto Masaki. *Zeami*. Geki Shobō, 1986.

Eguchi Fumie. "Muromachi kōki no nō to nōmen—nōsakusha betsuni mieru nōmen yōhō no hensen." *Nōgaku kenkyū* 32 (2007): 25–48.

Geinōshi Kenkyūkai, ed. *Nihon geinōshi 3: Chūsei*. Hōsei Daigaku, 1993.

————, ed. *Nihon geinōsh 4: Chūsei—kinsei*. Hōsei Daigaku, 1985.

————, ed. *Nihon shomin bunka shiryō shūsei*. vol. 3: Nō. Sanichi Shobō, 1978.

Gorai Shigeru. *Odori Nenbutsu*. Heibonsha, 1998.

Gōtō Hajime. *Nō no keisei to Zeami*. Kikuragesha, 1966.

Haga Kōshirō. *Sanjōnishi Sanetaka*. Yoshikawa Kōbunkan, 1960.

Haga Yaichi and Sasaki Nobutsuna, eds. *Yōkyoku sōsho: kōchū*, 3 vols. Kyoto: Rinzen Shoten, reprint, 1987.

Hayashiya Tatsusaburō, ed. *Kotai chūsei geijutsuron: Gei no shisō, michi no shisō 2*. Iwanami Shoten, 1995.

Ienaga Saburō. *Sarugaku nō no shisōshiteki kōsatsu*. Hōsei Daigaku, 1980.

Ikai Takamitsu. "Naginata wo motsu Tomomori no seiritsu—*Ikarikazuki, Funabenkei* wo meguru shiron." *Nōgaku kenkyū* 32 (2007): 1–24.

Ikenouchi Nobuyoshi. *Nōgaku seisuiki.* Sōgensha, 1992.

Ishii Tomoko. *Furyū nō no jidai: Konparu Zenpō to sono shūhen.* Tokyō Daigaku Shuppankai, 1998.

———. "Yōkyoku chūshaku to geinōshi kenkyū—kaishakushi toshite no nō katatsuke." *Geinōshi kenkyū* 108 (January 1990): 1–9.

Itō Masayoshi, ed. *Yōkyokushū,* 3 vols. Shinchōsha, 1983–1988.

Kanako Naoki, "Chōryō." *Kokuritsu Nōgakudō* 97 (September 1991): 20–21.

Kawaguchi Hisao, trans. and annotated. Fujiwara Akihira. *Shin sarugakuki.* Tōyō Bunkō 424, Heibonsha, 1983.

Kinoshita Fumitaka. "Yōkyoku *Kochō* no kōsō." *Chūsei Bungaku* 32 (1987): 89–98. Chūsei Bungakukai.

Kobayashi Shizuo. *Yōkyoku sakusha no kenkyū.* Nōgaku Shorin, 1942.

Kokuritsu Nōgakudō. "*Sengoku jidai no nō—Kokuritsu Nōgakudō '99 tokubetsu tenji*" (Special Exhibit at the National Nō Theatre '99). 1999.

Komatsu Matsuhiko. "Nō no naka no Ikai (6): Togakushisan—Momijigari." *Kanze* (January 2004): 58–63.

Kōsai Tsutomu. *Seishi sankyū.* Wanya Shoten, 1979.

Kubota Jun, ed. *Shinkokinwakashū.* 2 vols. Shinchō Nihon Koten Shūsei, Shinchōsha, 1979.

Matsuoka Shinpei. *Chūsei genō wo yomu.* Iwanami Seminā Bukkusu 83. Iwanami Shoten, 2002.

Mitake Akiko. *Kabunō no kakuritsu to tenkai.* Perikansha, 2001.

Morisue Yoshiaki. "Nō no hogosha." *Nōgaku zensho* 2 (1981): 198–234. Tōkyō Sōgensha.

Moriya Takeshi. "Mitsu no furyū." *Geinōshi kenkyū* 91 (October 1985): 60–63.

Murai Yasuhiko. "Chūsei ni okeru ōchōshōkei." *Kokuritsu Nōgakudō* 213 (May 2001): 22–23.

Nakamura Itaru. "Nō to Nenbutsu Kidoku—*Sanemori, Seiganji, Yugyō Yanagi* wo chūshin ni—." *Muromachi nōgakuron.* Wanya Shoten, 1994.

Nihon Geinōshi Kenkyūkai, ed. *Nihon geinōshi 3, Chūsei.* Hōsei Daigaku, 1983.

———, ed. *Nihon geinōshi 4, Chūsei-kinsei.* Hōsei Daigaku, 1985.

Nishino Haruo. "Nobumitsu no nō, jō." *Geinōshi kenkyū* 48 (January 1975): 33–47.

————. "Nobumitsu no nō, ge." *Geinōshi kenkyū* 51 (October 1975): 41–52.

————, ed. *Yōkyoku hyakuban*. Iwanami Shoten, 1998.

Nishino Haruo and Hata Hisashi, eds. *Nō Kyōgen jiten (shintei zōho)*. Heibonsha, 1999.

Nishio Minoru and Tanaka Makoto, eds. *Yōkyoku Kyōgen: Zōho Kokugo Kokubungaku Kenkyūshi Taisei 8*, Sanseidō, 1977.

Nishise Hideki. "Muromachi kōki no yōkyoku sakusha to sono shūhen—Konparu Zenpō no jidai to sakuhin." *Geinōshi kenkyū* 95 (October 1986): 15–30.

Nogami Toyoichirō. *Nō: Kenkyū to hakken*. Iwanami Shoten, 1948.

Nose Asaji. *Nōgaku Genryūkō*. Iwanami Shoten, 1972.

Oda Sachiko. "Nō no butai sōchi—tuskurimono no rekishiteki kōsatsu, jo" *Nōgaku kenkyū* 11 (1985):107–142.

————. "Sakuhin Kenkyū: Rashōmon." *Kanze* (April 1996): 26–33.

————. "Sakuhin Kenkyū: Ryōko." *Kanze* (June 1985): 20–49.

Omote Akira. "Kanze Kojirō Nobumitsu no seinen saiken, jo." *Kanze* 7 (1999): 34–39.

————. "Kanze Kojirō Nobumitsu no seinen saiken, ge." *Kanze* 8 (1999): 48–53.

————. *Nōgaku Shinkō II*. Wanya Shoten, 1986.

————. "Nō no henbō—enmoku no hensen tōshite—." *Chūsei Bungaku* 35 (1990): 33–50.

————. *Yamato sarugakushi sankyū*. Iwanami Shoten, 2005.

———— et al. "Edo shoki nōbangumi shichishū, sono ichi." *Nōgaku kenkyū* 18, 19, 24. Hōsei Daigaku, 1999.

———— et al. "Edo shoki nōbangumi shichishū, sono ni" *Nōgaku kenkyū* 19. Hōsei Daigaku, 1999.

———— et al. "Edo shoki nōbangumi shichishū, sono san." *Nōgaku kenkyū* 24. Hōsei Daigaku, 1999.

————. "Kanze ryū shi sankyū (sono jūni), Zeami shukke chokugo no Kanze za, Ōei sanjūyonen ennō kiroku o megutte," *Kanze* (June 2000): 27–32.

Omote Akira and Amino Fumio, eds. *Iwanami kōza: Nō, kyōgen I: Nōgaku no rekishi*. Iwanami Shoten, 1987.

Omote Akira and Itō Masayoshi, eds. *Konparu kodensho shūsei.* Wanya Shoten, 1969.

Omote Akira and Katō Shūichi, eds. *Zeami Zenchiku.* Nihon Shisōtaikei 24. Iwanami Shoten, 1974.

Omote Akira and Takemoto Mikio, eds. *Iwanami Kōza: Nō kyogen II: Nōgaku no densho to geiron.* Iwanami Shoten, 1988.

Ōsone Shōsuke and Horiuchi Hideaki, eds. *Wakan rōeishū.* Shinchōsha, 1983.

Ōwa Iwao. *Hadashi no kenkyū.* Yamato Shobō, 1993.

Sakurai Eiji. *Muromachibito no seishin.* Kodansha, 2001.

Sanari Kentarō, ed. *Yōkyoku Taikan.* 8 vols. Meiji Shoin, 1982.

Sanjō Kintada, *Gogumaiki. Dainihon kokiroku,* vol. 2. Iwanami Shoten, 1984.

Shirakawa Shizuka. "Ryōko no seikai." *Kanze* 6 (1985): 23–32.

Suwa Haruo and Sugai Yukio, eds. *Kōza Nihon no engeki 3: Chūsei no engeki.* Benseisha, 1998.

Taguchi Kazuo. *Nō kyōgen kenkyū—chūsei bungei ronkō.* Miyai Shoten, 1997.

Takahashi Ryūzō, ed. Sanjō Nishi Sanetaka. *Sanetaka Kōki.* Zoku Gunshoruijū Kanseikai, Taiyōsha, 1958–1963.

Takemoto Mikio. "Zeami bannenki no nō to nō sakusha." *Nō to kyōgen* 1 (2003): 123–127.

Tamamura Takeji, ed. *Gozan bungaku shinshū.* 8 vols. Daigaku Shuppankai, 1967.

Tanaka Makoto, ed. *Mikan yōkyokushū.* Koten Bunko, 1963–1980.

———, ed. *Shizayakusha mokuroku. Nōgaku shiryō* vol. 6. Wanya Shoten, 1955.

Tashiro Keiichirō. *Mugen nō.* Asahi Sensho 500. Asahi Shinbunsha, 1994.

Ueki Yukinobu, Kitagawa Tadahiko, and Nakamura Yasuo. "Momoyama jidai no butai geinō—nō no ryūdō to kotei." *Geinōshi Kenkyū* 8 (January 1965): 28–42.

Uemura Kankō. *Gosan bungaku zenshū.* 7 vols. Kyoto: Shinbunkaku, 1992.

Uno Shun'ichi and Tanaka Migaku, eds. *Tsunogawa nihonshi jiten (shinhen).* Asao Naohiro, Tsunogawa Shoten, 1997.

Yamanaka Reiko. *Nō no enshutsu: sono keisei to henyō.* Chūsei Bungaku Kenkyū Sōsho 6, Wakakusa Shoten, 1998.

Yashima Sachiko. "'Ōei sanjūyonen ennō kiroku' ni tsuite." *Kanze* 67 (August 2000): 50–56.

Yokomichi Mario, Nishino Haruo and Haneda Hisashi eds. *Iwanami kōza: Nō, kyōgen III: Nō no Sakusha to Sakuhin*, Iwanami Shoten, 1987.

————. *Nōgeki no kenkyū*, Iwanami Shoten, 1986.

————, ed. *Iwanami kōza: Nō kyogen bekkan: Nōgaku zusetsu*, Iwanami Shoten, 1992.

Yokomichi Mario and Omote Akira, eds. *Yōkyokushū*. 2 vols. Nihon Koten Bungaku Taikei 40, 41, Iwanami Shoten, 1960–1963.

Sources in Chinese

Qiu Xieyou. *Xinyi Tangshi Sanbaishou*. Revised ed. Taibei: Sanmin Shuju, 1999.

Xie Xianghao. *Zhuangzi Daodu*. Sichuan: Bashu Shushe, 1988.

Zhang Zhongyu. *Bai Juyi "Changhenge" yanjiu*. Beijing: Zhonghua Shuju, 2005.

Appendices

Appendix 1 Works Attributed to Nobumitsu

a. Plays in the active repertoire (genkōkyoku)

Appendix 1
WORKS ATTRIBUTED TO NOBUMITSU

A. List of Noh Plays

Often a play has more than one name. Listed here are primary names, with secondary names and the first known performance date of the plays in parentheses. Kanji, if known, are listed after each romanized name. Plays that are no longer performed are identified with an asterisk, while plays that are not extant are marked with a question mark. See section C Summary of Plays for a synopsis of each play.

There are various historical documents that compiled the lists of plays by the composers, and information from these different texts is sometimes different.[1] I base my list on *Nōhon Sakusha Chūmon* (能本作者注文 An index of noh composers), a text that identifies noh composers with their works. In a concluding sentence this text attributes thirty-two plays to Nobumitsu although the list has only thirty-one titles. It is believed that Nagatoshi, Nobumitsu's eldest son, was consulted in the compilation of the book by the Shinto priest Yoshida Kenshō. The final version of the book was finished around 1524 (Daiei 4). Another important historical text is *Shiza yakusha mokuroku* (四座役者目録 An account of the performers of the four troupes). Authored by two different Kanze performers, the two-volume work introduces noh and kyogen actors in the late Muromachi and Tokugawa periods.[2]

---

1. A transcript of these historical texts can be found in Nishio Minoru and Tanaka Makoto, eds. *Yōkyoku Kyōgen: Zōho Kokugo Kokubungaku Kenkyūshi Taisei 8*, Tokyo: Sanseidō, 1977.

2. Tanaka Makoto, ed. *Shizayakusha mokuroku*. In *Nōgaku shiryō* vol. 6. Tokyo: Wanya Shoten, 1955. The editor Tanaka Makoto, an important noh scholar, has provided many insightful comments on the historical development and the nature of this text in the Afterword of the book.

a. Plays still performed

Atagokūya (Atago) 愛宕空也 （愛宕）
Chōryō 張良
Funabenkei 船弁慶
Kochō 胡蝶
Kōtei (Myō-ō-kyō) 皇帝 （明王鏡）
Kusenoto 九世戸
Momijigari (Koremochi) 紅葉狩 （惟茂）
Orochi 大蛇
Rashōmon (Tsuna) 羅生門 （綱）
Ryōko 龍虎
Tamanoi 玉井
Yoshino Tennin 吉野天人
Yugyōyanagi 遊行柳

b. Plays that are no longer performed

Fuji 富士
Futarimiko 二人神子
Haen 巴園
Hikami 氷上
Hoshi (Kōso, Kan no Kōso) (1452) 星 （高祖, 漢の高祖）
Idaten 韋駄天
Kamei 亀井
Kibune 貴船
Mitsusue 満季
Murayama 村山
Taisei Taishi 太施太子
Tomotada 知忠

c. Plays no longer extant

Jō no Tarō 城の太郎
Kōbōjo けうぼう女
Miidera Zenji 三井寺前師 （禅師）
Morinaga 盛長
Rōtosha 労度差
Yasusada 保貞

B. Treatises

Only two treatises are attributed to Nobumitsu.

Kanze Kōjirō Gonnogami Densho *(The teaching of Kanze Kojirō Gonnogami, 1492)*. This text, untranscribed, can be found in the collection of the Kanze Shinkurō family. See *Nō Kyūgen II*, 1988 (Omote and Amino 1988).

Koezukaukoto *(On chanting, 1511)*. This text is discussed in *Nōgakushi Shinkō* (Omote 1986).

C. Summary of Plays

I have divided these plays into two types: those that are still being performed (*genkōkyoku* 現行曲) and those that are not (*bangaikyoku* 番外曲). In the following synopses, English translations of the titles are mostly mine. I indicate an existing English translation title whenever there is one.

The *gobandate* (五番だて) system is used to describe the plays. This system of categorization was established in the Edo period and is commonly used today to categorize noh plays. The five categories have a fixed order, although sometimes the categories have more than one name. I list all the names that are commonly in use today:

First:	Deity plays 神能	*wakinō* 脇能
Second:	Warrior plays 男	*shuramono* 修羅もの
Third:	Woman plays 女	*katsuramono* 鬘もの
Fourth:	Miscellaneous plays 雑	*zatsunō* 雑能
Fifth:	Demon plays 鬼	*kirinō* きり能

Not every anthology or critic agrees on how each play should be categorized, so I include the more common categorizations that I have found.

Plays are described as One-Act or Two-Act depending on whether there is a *nakairi* (mid-play entrance)—where the shite character leaves the stage temporarily to prepare for his/her next entrance.

The ai-kyōgen texts are based on Sanari Kentarō's *Yōkyoku Taikan* (Sanari 1982). Synopses of the plays are derived from various noh anthologies and my personal observations from live performances and video recordings.

a. Plays in the active repertoire (genkōkyoku)

Atagokūya (Atago) 愛宕空也 （愛宕）
Priest Kūya at Atago

Category	Demon play
Setting	Kyoto, Mt. Atago
Characters	*Shite* old man
	Nochi-jite Dragon King
	Waki Priest Kūya
Props	A paper scroll
Structure	Two-Act

Synopsis

The waki, a traveling priest called Kūya, visits Mt. Atago. While he is preaching, an old man appears and asks Priest Kūya for the Shari—relic of the Buddha—to help cure his three sufferings. The old man reveals that he is the Dragon King who lives in Mt Atago. The Dragon King informs Priest Kūya that the Buddhist Shari is hidden in the scroll of Buddhist scripture. They find the Shari in the scroll and the grateful Dragon King grants Priest Kūya a wish. The priest asks that water be brought to this mountain so that residents of the mountain do not have to travel far for fresh water. After the kyōgen interlude, the Dragon King keeps his promise by breaking up a big boulder, whereby water gushes out. The Dragon King then disappears into the faraway valley. ❁

Chōryō 張良
General Chōryō

Category	Demon play, Miscellaneous play
Setting	Kahi, a province in Kan (Han) China
Characters	*Shite* Old man
	Nochi-jite Kōsekikō
	Waki Chōryō
	Kyōgen Chōryō's subordinate
	Tsure Kannon (Goddess of Mercy)
Props	Two platforms representing a bridge
Structure	Two-Act

Synopsis

Chōryō, while on his way to meet a mysterious old man whom he encountered in a dream, tells the story of how in his dream he helped put on the old man's shoe as the latter demands. After Chōryō has respectfully done so, the old man arranges for a meeting and promises that he will then hand over a secret treatise of military training to Chōryō. Upon arrival, Chōryō finds that the old man is already there. After being chided for his tardiness, Chōryō is told to go back and meet the old man again in five days' time.

The kyōgen, one of Chōryō's subordinates, enters and retells the story. He introduces the old man as Kōsekikō, who wants to help the Kan emperor, Kōso, win his battle by giving Chōryō, who is the Kan emperor's minister, a secret military treatise.

In Act Two, Chōryō appears with more elaborate costumes and carries a sword. Kōsekikō, too, dons a more formal outfit and carries with him a scroll. Chōryō's final test is to retrieve the old man's shoes from the river where a giant dragonlike creature awaits him. Chōryō bravely pulls out his sword and the creature submits. Upon receiving his shoes, Kōsekikō hands Chōryō the secret treatise and explains that the creature in the river is actually Kannon, who was testing Chōryō's sincerity and will become his Guardian Deity from now. With that final disclosure, Kōsekikō returns to the high mountains and turns into a large, yellow boulder. ❀

Funabenkei 船弁慶
Benkei on Board

Category	Demon play, Miscellaneous play
Setting	The Daimotsu shore
Characters	*Shite* Shizuka
	Nochi-jite Ghost of Taira no Tomomori
	Waki Musashibō Benkei
	Kokata Minamoto no Yoshitsune
	Kyōgen Boatman
Props	A boat
Structure	Two-Act

Synopsis

Minamoto no Yoshitsune and his followers are waiting for a ship at the shore of Daimotsu. Before they depart, Benkei advises Yoshitsune to leave his consort Shizuka behind because it is inconvenient to bring along a woman. Yoshitsune obliges. Shizuka bids farewell by presenting Yoshitsune with an elegant dance. After Shizuka leaves, Benkei has an exchange with the boatman, the kyōgen, about the weather and their crossing. When the party is in the middle of the river, the weather suddenly changes and the ghost of Taira no Tomomori appears. He has come to avenge his family's defeat and attempts to drown Yoshitsune. Benkei battles the ghost with sword and also chants his rosary. Tomomori leaves without getting his revenge. ❈

Kochō 胡蝶
The Butterfly

Category	Woman play
Setting	Kyoto, the Grand Palace at First Avenue
Characters	*Shite* woman
	Nochi-jite spirit of a butterfly
	Waki traveling priest
	Kyōgen villager
	Tsure traveling priests accompanying the waki
Props	A small stand on which a plum blossom is placed
Structure	Two-Act

Synopsis

A traveling priest from Mt. Yoshino visits Kyoto, the capital. At an ancient palace he spots extremely beautiful plum blossoms. While he is admiring the beautiful blossoms, a woman approaches him and describes to him events in the past that took place at the palace. She then reveals that she is the spirit of a butterfly who wants to attain enlightenment so that she can flit freely among the plum blossoms.

A villager, the ai-kyōgen, appears and reaffirms the woman's identity, the glorious past history of the palace, and the extraordinary beauty of the plum blossoms.

In Act Two the butterfly attains enlightenment thanks to the prayer of the priest. She performs a dance to celebrate her new identity and changes into the Bodhisattva of Song and Dance before disappearing. ❀

Kōtei (Myō-ō-kyō) 皇帝 (明王鏡)
The Emperor, The Mirror of Myōō

Category	Demon play
Setting	The Palace of Kan Emperor Gensō, in the springtime
Characters	*Shite* old man
	Nochi-jite spirit of Shōki
	Waki Emperor Gensō
	Tsure court ministers
	Tsure illness demon
	Kokata Yōkihi
	Kyōgen court official
Props	A larger platform representing the palace, on which a smaller platform is placed to represent Yōkihi's sickbed
Structure	Two-Act

Synopsis

The court official announces that Yōkihi, Emperor Gensō's favorite consort, has suddenly fallen ill. (Yōkihi sits behind a veiled platform, which is revealed when Emperor Gensō sits down.) While the emperor is lamenting over Yōkihi's sufferings, an old man suddenly appears from nowhere. He claims himself to be Shōki who has come to repay the past kindness that he received from one of Gensō's ancestors. He then gives the emperor a magic mirror with which to capture the demon who is causing Yōkihi's illness. Gensō sees the illness demon with the help of the mirror, although he fails to kill it.

In Act Two the old man arrives at the palace in his official outfit on a horse. He successfully slaughters the illness demon, and Yōkihi recovers immediately. Before disappearing, Shōki asks to become the Guardian Deity of both the emperor and Yōkihi. ✿

Kusenotō 九世戸
The Kuse Gate

Category	Deity play
Setting	Tanga
Characters	*Shite* — old fisherman
	Nochi-jite — Dragon King
	Waki — Minister
	Shite-zure — younger fisherman
	Waki-zure — followers of the Minister
	Nochi-zure — female deity
	Kyōgen — the Guardian Deity at the Kuse Gate
Props	A stand in which a pine tree is placed; also two hand props that represent heavenly torches used by the deities in Act Two
Structure	Two-Act

Synopsis

The Minister is on his way to pay homage to Kusenotō, a sacred spot in the land of Tango. There he meets two fishermen who tell him about the legend of the place.

The Heavenly Grandson Hohonomi no Mikoto has invited the Monjū Buddha from India to descend here, which is also where the Monjū Buddha returned to after visiting the Dragon Palace. The three sing praises to the deities and their blessings to the land. When the minister asks the old fisherman his name, the fisherman answers that he is the deity serving Monjū Buddha and promises to return later with the heavenly lantern.

The Guardian Deity of the gate of Kusenotō appears and introduces the place again. After his monologue, a female deity and the Dragon King appear, each holding a heavenly lantern. They perform a dance and then disappear into the sea. ❀

Momijigari (Koremochi) 紅葉狩　惟茂
Autumn Excursion

Category	Demon play	
Setting	Shinano	
Characters	*Shite*	noble woman
	Nochi-jite	demon
	Waki	Taira no Koremochi
	Tsure	Koremochi's followers
	Tsure	noble woman's attendants
	Kyōgen	the Hachiman Deity
Props	A platform on which a veiled structure stands and from which the demon later appears	
Structure	Two-Act	

Synopsis

A noble woman enters with her attendants to admire the gorgeous autumn colors. While they are settling in to view the maple leaves, Koremochi enters with his entourage. The noble woman invites Koremochi to join their party. After some hesitation Koremochi joins the party and eventually gets very drunk. As night approaches the noble woman and her attendants disappear.

The Hachiman Deity enters with a sword. He is here to alert Koremochi of impending danger. The Hachiman Deity also reveals that Koremochi's real intention in coming to the mountain is to exorcise a demon and the demon has disguised itself as a beautiful woman in order to kill Koremochi! The deity finds Koremochi, warns him, and gives him the sword he has brought.

Koremochi wakes up the moment the demon reappears in its fearsome true form. They fight and Koremochi finally kills the demon. ❁

Orochi 大蛇
The Eight-headed Serpent

Category	Demon, Miscellaneous
Setting	Land of Izumo of ancient time
Characters	*Shite* old man Tenazuchi
	Nochi-jite the eight-headed serpent
	Waki Susanoō no Mikoto
	Tsure old woman Ashinazuchi
	Tsure two porters who carry Princess Kushiinada onto the stage in Act Two
	Kokata Princess Kushiinada
	Kyōgen a tree spirit
Props	Two platforms: the shite, tsure, and kokata sit on one behind a closed veil; the smaller one is where the serpent sits
Structure	Two Act

Synopsis

Susanoō no Mikoto comes to the land of Izumo. He encounters an old couple who are crying with their daughter. They tell him that in the past, an eight-headed serpent has come to devour their daughters, one every year. Now they have only one daughter left and the serpent is coming soon. Susanoō offers to kill the serpent if they will let him marry the daughter. The couple agrees, and Susanoō gets to work: he turns the princess into a comb and constructs eight big vessels filled with poisonous wine.

The tree spirit appears to retell the story, while all the characters exit the stage to get ready for the serpent. After the tree spirit's monologue, Susanoō returns. The serpent appears, drinks the poisonous wine and gets drunk. Susanoō kills the serpent and finds in its tail a sword called the Murakumo no Ken. ❀

Rashōmon (Tsuna) 羅生門 (綱)
The Rashōmon Gate, General Tsuna

Category	Demon play
Setting	Act One: Kyoto, Minamoto no Raikō's residence
	Act Two: Kyoto, Gate of Rashōmon
Characters	*Shite* none
	Nochi-jite a demon hiding at the Gate of Rashōmon
	Waki Watanabe no Tsuna
	Tsure Minamoto no Raikō
	Tsure other warriors
	Kyōgen Tsuna's retainer
Props	A small platform on which is placed a veiled stand where the demon hides
Structure	Two Act

Synopsis

Minamoto no Raikō, at a banquet with his retainers, asks if there have been any interesting stories lately. One of his retainers replies that the Rashōmon Gate is haunted. Tsuna refutes the story and volunteers to investigate the place. Tsuna's retainer enters and recounts the happenings while Tsuna exits to get ready.

In Act Two, Tsuna enters with a sword and a whip to indicate that he is riding on a horse. He ventures through the rainy night and gets to the Rashōmon Gate. After placing a placard on the altar of the gate as proof of his visit, he turns to leave. At that juncture the demon, who has been hiding on the gate, pulls him from behind. Tsuna realizes that this is the demon and quickly breaks loose, which infuriates the demon. They have a fierce battle, and Tsuna cuts off one of the demon's arms. The demon rises to the sky and escapes, leaving behind a threat that he will return to take revenge someday. ✸

Ryōko 龍虎
The Dragon and the Tiger

Category	Miscellaneous play
Setting	China
Characters	*Shite* woodcutter
	Nochi-jite a tiger
	Waki a priest
	Tsure another woodcutter
	Tsure a dragon
	Kyōgen a local deity
Props	A platform decorated with bamboo and plants
Structure	Two Act

Synopsis

A traveling Japanese monk comes to China to further pursue Buddhist studies. He runs into a woodcutter and starts a discussion on the different approaches to enlightenment. While the woodcutter is reproaching the monk for traveling so far to seek enlightenment when he could have done it at home, the monk becomes distracted and abruptly changes the topic. He notices changing color at one corner of the horizon and asks the woodcutter for an explanation. The woodcutter explains that the unusual look is due to the constant battles between a tiger and a dragon. He then gives the priest directions on how to get closer, after which they all leave the stage. The local deity appears and explains the story again.

In Act Two, the traveling priest comes to a bamboo grove. In no time, the tiger emerges from a cave in the bush and the dragon descends from the sky. They start fighting and the dragon is defeated and retreats to the bamboo grove. ✿

Tamanoi 玉井
The Jeweled Well

Category	Deity play	
Setting	Dragon Palace	
Characters	*Shite*	Princess Toyotama
	Nochi-jite	Dragon King
	Waki	Hohodemi no Mikoto
	Tsure	Princess Tamayori
	Nochi-zure	Princess Toyotama
	Kyōgen	fumi-clam and other sea creatures
Props	Two stands: one with a small tree, the other with a square frame to represent a well
Structure	Two Act	

Synopsis

Hohodemi no Mikoto tells the audience that he has lost his brother's fishing hook and has come to the Dragon Palace to look for it. He is hiding behind the jeweled well when the Dragon King's daughters discover him and take him back to the palace.

Hohodemi no Mikoto marries Princess Toyotama and spends three years at the Dragon Palace. Act One ends with the announcement of their decision to return to the land. The kyōgen, a clam, retells the story.

In Act Two, Princess Toyotama is played by the nochi-tsure, whereas the nochi-jite takes up the role of the Dragon King. The Dragon King gives Hohodemi no Mikoto presents and performs a dance for him as a farewell gesture. After the dance, the couple leaves on the back of a crocodile. ❁

Yoshino Tennin 吉野天人
The Deity at Yoshino

Category	Woman play
Setting	Springtime at Mt. Yoshino in Yamato
Characters	*Shite* woman
	Nochi-jite female deity
	Waki visitor from the capital
	Waki-zure two other visitors from the capital
	Kyōgen deity at Mt. Yoshino
Props	A small platform on which stand some cherry blossoms
Structure	Two Act

Synopsis

The waki and his friends visit Mt. Yoshino from the capital to view a certain kind of cherry blossom called the *chimoto no sakura*, which was transplanted from Kyoto to Mt. Yoshino. At the mountain they encounter a woman who shares the same interest in the flowers. Before she disappears she tells them that she is a deity who is attracted by the flowers. She advises the visitors to stay till dark, when she will come to perform the ancient *Gosechi no mai* dance for them.

Then the kyōgen, a local deity of Mt. Yoshino, appears and reiterates the events. When he has finished, music and fragrances descend from heaven to announce the arrival of the deity. After she performs the dance, she rides on a cloud and disappears. ❂

Yugyōyanagi 遊行柳
The Priest and the Willow

Category	Demon play
Setting	The lad of Iwayo, at Shirakawa
Characters	*Shite* old man
	Nochi-jite spirit of the willow tree
	Waki traveling monk
	Kyōgen villager
Props	One big platform used as the old tomb
	from which the spirit emerges
	in Act Two
Structure	Two Act

Synopsis

The traveling priest comes to the gate of Shirakawa and runs into an old man who offers to show him a path that was traveled by the holy priests of old. He also tells the priest that there is a famous willow tree along the roadside. Under the tree the two talk about Saigyō, whose poem about the tree has made it famous. After the old man suddenly disappears, the priest has an exchange with the local villager and again hears about Saigyō and his poem about the tree.

In Act Two, the old man reappears from the old tomb and identifies himself as the spirit of the willow tree. He thanks the priest for his prayer and disappears. ❁

b. Plays that are no longer performed (bangaikyoku)

As plays, these works have not been performed for a long time. Features such as props and character-role relationships become more arbitrary. Besides references to existing sources, these features presented below are mainly deductions from the play texts. Again, as we are not sure if these plays were still performed during the Tokugawa period when the *Gobandate* system was established, they are not categorized like plays that are still performed. Therefore, categories are not included in this section.

My main source of information here is the voluminous series *Mikan Yōkyokushū* and *Bangai Yōkyoku Zoku*, edited and compiled by Tanaka Makoto. Another anthology I use is the three-volume *Yōkyoku Sōsho*, edited by Haga Yaichi and Sasaki Nobutsuna.

Futarimiko 二人神子
The Two Female Shamans

Setting	Not clear	
Characters	*Shite*	Matsuwaka's mother
	Waki	Utsumi no Nanigashi
		(Mr. Somebody from Utsumi)
	Tsure	Matsuwaka's wet nurse
	Kokata	Matsuwaka

Synopsis

Matsuwaka's mother wants to avenge the murder of her husband. She discusses this with her son and his wet nurse, and they come up with an excellent way to approach Utsumi no Nanigashi, their enemy. When Nanigashi returns from a pilgrimage, he runs into three *shirabyōshi* dancers who are actually Matsuwaka and his company in disguise. They perform the story of a famous Chinese assassin and successfully surround Nanigashi without his realizing it. When he understands what is happening, it is too late—Matsuwaka and his mother enjoy the sweet taste of victory. ❀

Haen 巴園
The Ha Garden

Setting	China, Han dynasty	
Characters	*Shite*	an elderly gardener
	Waki	a minister
	Tsure	the gardener's wife
	Tsure/kokata	a little citrus deity
	Tsure/kokata	another little citrus deity
Props	A small platform representing the peach from which the citrus deities appear; a walking stick belonging to the old gardener	

Synopsis

The minister of Emperor Kan receives the imperial order to visit Ha-en, an orchard where it is said that some miraculous fruit was found. Upon meeting the gardener and his wife, the minister is shown a citrus tree that bears fruit with extraordinary fragrance and attracts beautiful birds. The minister is told of the story of the legendary Chinese figure Seiōbo (Xiwangmu, Heavenly Mother of the West), who is often associated with another miraculous fruit, the peaches.

As the minister is about to take his leave, a voice from the citrus fruit invites him to stay until dark. The gardener and his wife entertain the minister with wine while awaiting the arrival of the citrus deities. When the deities finally appear, they perform a dance with the gardener and his wife. In the finale, the gardener throws his walking stick into the air and it turns into a dragon. Together with the two deities, they all rise into the sky. ✸

Hikami 氷上
River Hikami

Setting	Shiga at Mutsu, present-day Aomori and Iwate prefectures
Characters	*Shite* an old fisherman
	Nochi-jite Dragon King
	Waki Fujiwara no Kagemi
	Tsure Minister of Emperor Shōmu (701–756)

Synopsis

Emperor Shōmu's minister is on his way to Shiga in search of gold for the construction of a Buddha statue. The minister was sent by the Emperor because the Emperor received a divine oracle from the Jizō deity at Mt. Kinbu instructing him to seek help from the miraculous Kannon at Shiga. Upon arrival at Shiga, the minister runs into an old fisherman, who shows him the holy temple where the Kannon is and is asked to wait for a while.

Fujiwara no Kagemi, the waki, enters. He is an official in the province of Michinoku and is on his way to the capital to report on the sighting of a round golden object that floats on the Hikami River. Upon hearing this, the minister hands Kagemi an arrow with which to pluck the gold out of the river. The fisherman also tells them that he will disclose to them the location of the gold.

In Act Two, Fujiwara no Kagemi comes to the bank of the River Hikami. Not only is the gold there, but he also finds the Dragon King guarding it. Kagemi explains to the Dragon King why he needs the gold, and the Dragon King reverentially hands it to him. Kagemi then returns to the capital while the Dragon King returns to the Dragon Palace. ❁

Hoshi (Kōso, Kan no Kōso)
星 (高祖, 漢の高祖)
The Star, Kōso, Kōso of the Han Dynasty

Setting	Han dynasty, China	
Characters	*Shite*	Kōu
	Waki	Kanshin, Kōu's general
	Tsure/kokata	deity in charge of war
	Tsure	Kanshin's fellow officer

Synopsis

Kanshin, Kōu's general, attempts to usurp the Qin emperor's capital several times but has not been successful. When he is discussing the matter with Kishin, his colleague, a deity descends from heaven and instructs Kanshin to tell Kōu to pray to the deity in charge of war.

In Act Two, Kōu follows the instructions and the deity of war descends to help him fight his battle. At the end of the battle, Kōu demands that the deity become his guardian deity. ❀

Idaten 韋駄天
The Deity Idaten

Setting	China	
Characters	*Shite*	Idaten
	Waki	Setsu-ritsushi

Synopsis

During the Budhist monk Setsu-ritsushi's morning sermon, a man always brings him food. Ritsushi tells the audience that today he will ask the man for his name. When the man arrives they sing praises to Buddhist teachings, and the man reveals that he is Idaten, the Prince of the Northern Heaven. Idaten is famous for protecting the Buddha's relic (*shari*) from being stolen by a demon. Hearing who he is, Setsu-ritsushi wants Idaten to tell him how he warded away the demon. Not only does Idaten tell the story and show Setsu-ritsushi the *shari*, but he actually presents it to Setsu-ritsushi for his temple. After they both sing praises of Buddhist teachings, Idaten returns to his abode in the Northern heaven. ❂

Kamei 亀井
Kamei

Setting: Otsushū
Characters: *Shite*   villager
              Nochi-jite   spirit of Kamei
              Waki   a priest from Kishū

Synopsis

The priest from Kishū was asked to visit Otsushū by the mother of the Kamei brothers, who were killed in the Bunji war (1189). Upon arrival, the priest runs into a villager. As their conversation unfolds, the priest realizes that the villager seems to have witnessed the last battle of the brothers. Upon questioning, the villager admits that he is the ghost of Kamei, the younger of the two brothers who were killed. Kamei laments the ephemeral nature of life and wants the priest to bring a message to his mother.

In Act Two, the ghost of Kamei reappears in his warrior attire. In order for the priest to recount to Kamei's mother what happened in this battle, Kamei performs the last battle scene, with the accompaniment of the chorus. Kamei's spirit disappears after a long and elaborate account of the final battle, leaving behind only the breeze in the pines. ✿

Kibune 貴船
At the Kibune Shrine

Setting	Kibune Shrine	
Characters	*Shite*	Izumi Shikibu
	Waki	priest at the Kibune shrine
	Tsure	Izumi Shikibu's attendants
	Tsure	Fujiwara no Yasumasa

Synopsis

The waki announces that he had heard the night before about a pilgrimage party visiting his shrine. The pilgrim is Izumi Shikibu, who is offering a scroll of one hundred poems to the temple. Shikibu meets the priest and they discuss the functions of waka, citing regularly from the preface of *Kōkinshū* by Ki no Tsurayuki. Shikibu also performs a dance for the deity. Just then her estranged husband walks by the shrine. They clear up their misunderstanding and return home together. ❂

Murayama 村山
Murayama

Setting   Sanuki, in present-day Kagawa
                 Prefecture
Characters   *Shite:* Murayama no Nanigashi
                 (Mr. Murayama Somebody)
                 Waki   Nagao
                 Tsure   Kōzuke's wife
                 Kyōgen attendants
                 Kokata Matsuwaka

Synopsis

Murayama's master, Kōzuke, has gone to the capital to settle a court case. Kōzuke's wife is telling Murayama her worries for her husband, when an attendant brings the news that Kōzuke was killed by a man named Nagao who is on his way to hunt down Kōzuke's family. Although Murayama wants them to escape, Kōsuke's wife and child, Matsuwaka, both want to stay and avenge their loved one's death. When Nagao arrives he is met with the fierce resistance of the family despite the fact that Nagao is very strong. Finally, Nagao is so deeply moved by the courage of the family that he decides not to persecute them further by making a vow to the Hachiman deity. ❁

Taisei Taishi 太施太子
Prince Taisei

Setting	Tenchiku, Haranai	
Characters	*Shite*	Taishakuten
	Waki	Minister from the country Haranai
	Tsure	other ministers
	Tsure	Dragon Princess

Synopsis

Prince Taisei's minister is on his way to set up a notice board inviting people to the palace to receive treasure that Prince Taisei is distributing. The minister explains that because of Prince Taisei's sincerity in wanting to help the poor, the deity Bonten granted his wish by giving him the Wish-fulfilling Gem from the Dragon Palace. At the Palace, instead of asking for valuables, a woman requests to take a closer look at the precious Wish-fulfilling Gem. She takes a close look and snatches it, to everyone's surprise. The woman then escapes but announces that she is none other than the Dragon Princess.

In Act Two, Taisei Taishi demands that feverish prayers be offered to Taishakuten so that he will help to retrieve the gem. Answering the Prince's request, Taishakuten brings along a heavenly army and attacks the Dragon Palace. The heavenly army eventually forces the Dragon Princess to surrender the gem, and Taishakuten and his entourage return to their heavenly abodes. ✿

Tomotada 知忠
Tomotada

Setting	Hōshōji Temple, near Kyoto	
Characters	*Shite*	Hyōhe Tamenori
	Waki	Gotō Hyōe Minamoto
	Kokata	Tomotada

Synopsis

Hyōhe Tamenori is on his way to the capital to meet up with Kagekiyo, who has promised to assist Tamenori's lord Tomotada in a coup to restore the Taira family. But upon arriving at the meeting place, Tamenori receives a letter from Kagekiyo saying that their plot has been discovered and that the Minamoto family is on their way to attack them. Realizing that they will soon be destroyed, Tamenori decides to fight the final battle. Gotō Hyōe Minamoto, the enemy, tries to launch a surprise attach but is confronted by strong resistance. However, in view of the huge number of enemies, Tamenori advises the young Tomotada to commit suicide, which the latter calmly does. Tamenori wraps the body of his lord in a piece of cloth and fights his way out of the capital. ❂

Appendix 2
A CHRONOLOGY OF NOBUMITSU'S LIFE

1398   Kanze Motoshige (later changes name to On'ami) is born.

1413   Inuō Dōami dies.

1427   Kanze Jurō, Kanze Saburō and other Kanze troupe members perform at Kōfukuji.

1430   Motoshige becomes the Gakutō (music supervisor) of Seiryōgu (Seiryō Shrine) at Daigoji (Daigo Temple) under the auspices of Ashikaga Yoshinori.

1432   Motomasa, Zeami's son and official leader (*Tayū*) of the Kanze troupe, dies.

1433   Motoshige becomes Kanze Tayū, with Yoshinori's support.

1434   Zeami exiled to Satō Island.

1435   Nobumitsu is born.

1436   Fatalities occur when audience starts a fight at the female sarugaku kanjin nōh performance at Katsurakawara.

        Ashikaga Yoshimasa is born.

1437   On'ami offends Yoshinori but is pardoned quickly under the mediation of Akamatsu Mitsusuke, another military general.

1443   Zeami dies.

1449   Yoshimasa becomes shogun. Nobumitsu's performance in front of the emperor takes place around this time.

1450   The Kanze troupe loses Yoshinori's support and starts kanjin sarugaku noh. The income from this performance goes to the troupe instead of to public welfare, as the term kanjin originally meant.

1452	Motoshige performs *Kan no Kōsō* (*Hoshi*) at a *takigi-sarugaku* performance in front of a shrine.
1457	Motoshige retires as troupe leader, and changes his name to On'ami. His son, Masamori, becomes *Tayū* of the Kanze troupe.
1461	Masamori performs at the residence of Yoshinori and is rewarded 100 strings of *mon* (coin).
1464	A three-day kanjin noh performance is held at the Tadasugawara River bank. Both On'ami and Masamori perform.
	Kongo waki actor Torakiku is ordered by Ashikaga Yoshinori to join the Kanze troupe.
1465	Zenchiku and On'ami perform, together with other troupes, for Yoshimasa at Nara.
	On'ami, Masamori, and Nobumitsu perform at the retired emperor's palace, the first large-scale performance that has detailed documentation of Nobumitsu's participation.
1467	The *Ōnin* War begins.
	On'ami dies.
1468	Poet Shinkei (1406–1475) writes *Hitorigoto*, praising On'ami's performing skill.
1470	Masamori dies suddenly after a performance.
1472	Nobumitsu assumes the *Gakutō* (Music Supervisor) position during a sarugaku noh performance at the Imperial Palace.
1474	The four Yamato troupes (Kanze, Konparu, Hoshō, and Kongō) boycott takigi noh performance at Kōfukuji (Kōfuku Temple) because the temple did not pay them promptly. The conflict is resolved quickly.
1475	Nobumitsu, still known as "On'ami's youngest son," performs at Kōfukuji.
1478	Nobumitsu and Masamori's son, Yukishige, the official troupe leader, put on a three-day kanjin noh performance for the reconstruction of Seiganji. This is the first large-

scale noh performance after the Ōnin War. Ashikaga Yoshihisa and his mother, Hino Tomoko, are present.

1480	Konparu Zenpō becomes Konparu *Tayū*.
1481	Nobumitsu and Yukishige perform noh at the military quarter.
1483	Two Konparu waki performers, Hikichi Genshirō and Morikiku Yashichirō, are ordered by Yoshihisa to join the Kanze troupe.
1484	Yukishige accepted military general Hatakeyama's invitation and performs kanjin noh at Nanao.
1487	Nobumitsu remarries.
1488	Nagatoshi is born.
1493	The Kanze and Konparu troupes perform together at Yushoken, a military quarter, and are rewarded handsomely.
1497	Nobumitsu writes *Kanze Kojirō Gonnogami Densho*.
1499	Nobumitsu performs with Yukishige at Daijōin.
1500	Yukishige, the official Kanze *Tayū*, dies. He was succeeded by his young son, Motohiro.
1509	Nobumitsu visits Sanetaka at Sanetaka's residence. In his diary, Sanetaka records an exchange on Nobumitsu's age.
1511	Nobumitsu writes *Koetsukaugoto* and a kusemai dance, *Toraokuri*.
1514	Kanze *Tayū* Motohiro performs kajin noh at Shinkurotani, and Nobumitsu plays the shite role in his latest play, *Yugyō Yanagi* (The Priest and the Willow).
1516	Nobumitsu dies. He is said to be buried at Shōkokuji, Kyoto.

Appendix 3
GENERATIONS OF
KANZE TROUPE LEADERS

Generation	Name	Dates
First	Kan'ami 観阿弥	1333–1384
Second	Zeami 世阿弥	1363–1443
Third	Motomasa 元雅	?–1432
Fourth	On'ami 音阿弥	1398–1467
Fifth	Masamori 政盛	?–1470
Sixth	Yukishige 之重	?–1500
Seventh	Motohiro 元広	?–1522
Eighth	Mototada 元忠	1509–1583

Appendix 4
GLOSSARY OF THE MAJOR ROLE TYPES

ai-kyōgen   Sometimes known as *ai*. The performer who plays the role of (usually) a local resident who reiterates the events that have transpired so far during the mid-play entrance (*nakairi*) of the shite characters.

kokata   A child performer who, other than the role of children, sometimes plays the role of deities or a person with important social position. For instance Yoshitsune in *Funabenkei*.

shite   The main character who is similar to the "protagonist" in a modern Western drama. Sometimes in a two-part noh play the shite actor performs two different characters in Act One and Act Two, as was the case in many of Nobumitsu's plays. In two-act plays the shite who performs in Act One is also called *mae-jite,* and in Act Two, *nochi-jite.*

tsure   Characters who accompany the shite, such as the entourage of the beautiful woman in *Momijigari*. Koremochi's followers are *waki-zure.*

waki   The character who assumes the role of the interlocutor with the shite, for instance, a traveling priest or a minister. This role is often seen as secondary and therefore less important in a noh play. However, in many of the late Muromachi plays the waki has important dramatic presence.

Appendix 5
SUCCESSIVE GENERATIONS OF
MUROMACHI SHOGUN

Generation	Name		Dates	Reign dates
1	Ashikaga Takauji	足利尊氏	1305–1358	1338–1358
2	Ashikaga Yoshiakira	足利義詮	1330–1367	1358–1367
3	Ashikaga Yoshimitsu	足利義満	1358–1408	1368-1394
4	Ashikaga Yoshimochi	足利義持	1386–1428	1394–1423
5	Ashikaga Yoshikazu	足利義量	1407–1425	1423–1425
6	Ashikaga Yoshinori	足利義教	1394–1441	1429–1441
7	Ashikaga Yoshikatsu	足利義勝	1434–1443	1442–1443
8	Ashikaga Yoshimasa	足利義政	1436–1490	1449–1473
9	Ashikaga Yoshihisa	足利義尚	1465–1489	1473–1489
10	Ashikaga Yoshitane	足利義植	1466–1523	1490–1493 1508–1521
11	Ashikaga Yoshizumi	足利義澄	1480–1511	1494–1508
12	Ashikaga Yoshiharu	足利義晴	1511–1550	1521–1546
13	Ashikaga Yoshiteru	足利義輝	1536–1565	1546–1565
14	Ashikaga Yoshihide	足利義栄	1538–1568	1568–1568
15	Ashikaga Yoshiaki	足利義昭	1537–1597	1568–1573

INDEX

CORNELL EAST ASIA SERIES

CORNELL
East Asia Series

eap.einaudi.cornell.edu/publications